NEW ESSAYS ON ADAM SMITH'S MORAL PHILOSOPHY

edited by

Wade L. Robison
and
David B. Suits

RIT PRESS
ROCHESTER, NEW YORK
2012

New Essays on Adam Smith's Moral Philosophy
Edited by Wade L. Robison and David B. Suits

Copyright © 2012 Rochester Institute of Technology and individual contributors.
All rights reserved. No part of this book may be reproduced in any form or by any mechanical or electronic means without written permission of the publisher and/or individual contributors, except in the case of brief quotations embodied in critical articles and reviews.

Published and distributed by
RIT Press
90 Lomb Memorial Drive
Rochester, New York 14623-5604
http://carypress.rit.edu

Inquiries about the content of this publication may be directed to the editors in care of
Department of Philosophy
College of Liberal Arts
Rochester Institute of Technology
92 Lomb Memorial Drive
Rochester, New York 14623

Printed in the U.S.
ISBN 978-1-933360-63-8

Cover image: Etching based on an enamel paste medallion by James Tassie, 1787.
Cover text: Adam Smith, *The Theory of Moral Sentiments*, Part I, Section I, Chap. I, paragraph 1.

   Library of Congress Cataloging-in-Publication Data

New essays on Adam Smith's moral philosophy / edited by Wade L. Robison & David B. Suits.
    p. cm.
  Includes index.
  ISBN 978-1-933360-63-8 (alk. paper)
  1. Smith, Adam, 1723-1790. Theory of moral sentiments.
  2. Ethics—Early works to 1800. I. Robison, Wade L. II. Suits, David B.
  BJ1012.N483 2012
  170.92—dc23

2012010579

NEW ESSAYS ON ADAM SMITH'S MORAL PHILOSOPHY

NEW ESSAYS ON ADAM SMITH'S MORAL PHILOSOPHY

1 INTRODUCTION

13 SMITH ON TASTE AND CRITICISM: TEXTS AND CONTEXTS
    Peter Jones

35 *THEORY OF MORAL SENTIMENTS* 1759 VS. *THEORY OF MORAL SENTIMENTS* 1790: A CHANGE OF MIND OR A CHANGE IN CONSTRAINT
    Maria Pia Paganelli

45 THE "ADAM SMITH PROBLEM" AND ADAM SMITH'S UTOPIA
    Doğan Göçmen

71 MODERN NATURAL LAW MEETS THE MARKET: THE CASE OF ADAM SMITH
    Amit Ron

95 REVISITING SENTIMENTALISM: A SMITHIAN NORMATIVE MORAL THEORY
    Monica Gerreck

115 *THE THEORY OF MORAL SENTIMENTS* AND SMITH'S ACCOUNT OF SYMPATHY
    Tony Pitson

137 "THE MOST CRUEL MISFORTUNE": SUFFERING INNOCENCE IN THE THEORY OF MORAL SENTIMENTS
    Vincent Bissonette

151 TAMING RESENTMENT
    Michael S. Pritchard

173 SKEPTICISM AND IMAGINATION: SMITH'S RESPONSE TO HUME'S *DIALOGUES*
    Ryan Patrick Hanley

195 HUME'S DEATH AND SMITH'S PHILOSOPHY
    Chad Flanders

211 "A DELICATE AND AN ACCURATE PENCIL":
ADAM SMITH, DESCRIPTION, AND PHILOSOPHY AS MORAL PEDAGOGY
Colin Heydt

229 INDEX

245 CONTRIBUTORS

INTRODUCTION

Wade L. Robison and David B. Suits

Adam Smith's *The Theory of Moral Sentiments (TMS)*[1] was published in 1759, and although it was not the instant success of *The Wealth of Nations (WN)*, it was well received. Hume wrote that "the Public seem disposed to applaud it extremely". Yet those familiar only with *WN* would no doubt be surprised by some of Smith's sentiments regarding the moral sentiments.

Those of our contemporaries who collect all manner of apps for their cellphones should recognize themselves in Smith's remarks about how individuals collect

> trinkets of frivolous utility. What pleases these lovers of toys is not so much the utility, as the aptness of the machines which are fitted to promote it. All their pockets are stuffed with little conveniencies. They contrive new pockets, unknown in the clothes of other people, in order to carry a greater number. They walk about loaded with a multitude of baubles, [...] some of which may sometimes be of some little use, but all of which might at all times be very well spared, and of which the whole utility is certainly not worth the fatigue of bearing the burden. [*TMS*, 180]

As Smith says, the motive for such behavior is the "aptness of the machines" for their ends, and this motive works its magic on us as well. We imagine ourselves apt for greater things and so strive to improve ourselves and bring ourselves to public notice to ensure our "wealth and greatness", only to discover, "in the last dregs of life", that they "are mere trinkets of frivolous utility, no more adapted for procuring ease of body or tranquillity of mind than the tweezer-cases of the lover of toys" (*TMS*, 181).

The Wealth of Nations is a sustained argument for the efficiency of what we know as the free enterprise system, but though Smith there claims that the quality of life of even the poorest will approach that of an African king with his retinue of servants, his view in *TMS* is that wealth provides us with "more means of happiness", but not happiness itself. In short, the argument of *WN* leaves us with at least two unanswered moral questions:

---

1   Bibliographic information for all references can be found in the Select Bibliography at the end of this essay.

1

What is it to live a moral life?
Is justice served, or best served, by the free enterprise system?

To realize that *WN* leaves both questions unanswered would no doubt surprise those who think God's invisible hand guides the free enterprise system to distribute wealth in exactly the right and just way.[2] *TMS* is a helpful antidote to such shallow thinking, and although the collection of essays in this volume will not address every issue of import in *TMS* or provide definitive answers to the two questions left by *WN*, they will give us a better understanding of the complexities and subtleties of Smith's thoughts about matters of morality and about his relations with his friend David Hume, from whom he drew much of his moral theory, with disagreements, of course.

We begin with an introductory chapter by Peter Jones, setting Smith's stage, as it were, the context within which he was writing. In "Smith on Taste and Criticism: Texts and Contexts" Jones argues that context matters if we are to understand a writer. Consider an economic example. In a village or even a town as large as Edinburgh at the time, a butcher who puts his thumb on the scales is not going to have an easy time of it. Word will get around, and the local grapevine will throttle his business even as those who continue to frequent his shop check whether his thumb is on the scales whenever he weighs their meat. Trust matters in towns and villages, and the means for punishing cheating are readily available: customers go elsewhere. How different is modern commerce! If you purchase a faulty toaster, then those of us about to purchase a toaster are clueless that we should not consider the model that you bought. Unlike yesterday's butcher, today's manufacturer does not have to be concerned about the village grapevine. Readers' comments on such internet retailers as Amazon are beginning to work the way grapevines used to work, but this is only a recent phenomenon and even at its best does not replace the village grapevine. So context matters even for what might be thought to be the general truths of capitalism.

But we cannot fully comprehend how different Smith's world was from ours without considering other aspects of eighteenth century life in such a town as Edinburgh. Jones asks whether we can enter into Smith's context. Meanings work in contexts, and eighteenth century thinkers addressed the issues of their day in their own language. Smith's sensory life was different from ours in many ways. Scotland is far north, dark in the winter; light was from flickering candles. Edinburgh was a walled city without sewage; the diet consisted of little meat or fruit, no cheese or fresh water fish; most business was conducted in taverns; there was no concept of tourism; no art hung in galleries.

---

2 "They say the invisible hand of the free market is really God at work", says sociologist Paul Froese, co-author of the Baylor Religion Survey (quoted in Grossman, "Baylor Religion Survey").

No music was heard in concert halls as we are used to. Most of the musical works of the time (many operas, for example) were not preserved, so that when Smith writes about music, he is thinking of works now unknown to us, performed in ways other than what we are used to. Performances were filled with improvisation, for example, which involved a skill of changing with context.

"Only by the exercise of sympathy in determining the contexts can the character, identity, meaning, and quality of conversation be sensed; only then can the implications and benefits of improvisation be grasped; only then can the propriety of judgment and behavior be assessed." As Jones concludes, "the moral domain is a theatre of conversations in which the context contributes as much to the performance as the mood, the skills, and the journeys of the audience".

We move from an introduction about Smith's times to an issue that confronts any scholar of Smith, what is called the Adam Smith Problem. The problem has been "solved" in a variety of ways, and Maria Pia Paganelli states the problem and summarizes the solutions well in her paper, "*Theory of Moral Sentiments* 1759 vs. *Theory of Moral Sentiments* 1790: A Change of Mind or a Change in Constraint?" The problem concerns the consistency or lack of consistency between *TMS* and *WN*, and, as we might imagine, it has been argued among scholars both that the books are consistent with each other and that they are inconsistent with each other. It has been argued that they are not just consistent, but that *WN* is "like a long footnote to" *TMS*. It has been argued that they are consistent, the main concern of *WN* being natural liberty, while *TMS* is "an additional source of support". Finally, in agreement with some others, Paganelli argues that to come to the true view, we must first examine the sixth edition of *TMS* (the final revision Smith made after publishing *WN*) and compare it to the first edition of 1759.

She picks a single issue to follow through *WN* and the two editions of *TMS*: the approbation gained from having material possessions. When we conduct ourselves appropriately, we gain approbation. This gives us incentive to act morally. But the desire to gain approval can also motivate us to accumulate visible wealth. "What Smith is telling us, then, is that we are willing to gamble moral approbation for wealth approbation", Paganelli argues. "This is not surprising given that material possessions are easier to recognize, and therefore approve, than moral (mis)behaviors."

It has been claimed that Smith changes his mind about this matter in the 1790 edition, but that is incorrect, Paganelli says. Smith realized that

> The wealth of commercial societies changes the constraints that individuals face. When the possibilities to gain approbation from wealth are large enough, they may incentivize more morally questionable actions and generate potentially disastrous consequences. It is after this realization

that *TMS* 1790 is changed. Behaviors and their consequences differ under different levels of wealth. This change in constraints has to be accounted for in the theoretical description of approbation. The model remains the same. It is just updated, given a case not previously considered, to account for all the circumstances.

Paganelli's conclusion is that the apparent contrast between the two editions of *TMS* is only apparent and that the Adam Smith Problem cannot be removed by reinterpreting the intentions of the 1790 edition.

In "The 'Adam Smith Problem' and Adam Smith's Utopia", Doğan Göçmen claims that Smith had only one conception of human nature with two complementary aspects: a general (developed in *TMS*) and a particular (used in *WN* as "human nature in the age of commercial society"). Previous scholars incorrectly took the Adam Smith Problem to be a conceptual failure of Smith's. But Smith had his own solution, a "utopia of a sympathetic society".

We know ourselves, Smith says, only by means of a mutual mirroring process with others. Therefore, we cannot be other than social individuals. In order to know how others see us, we must put ourselves into their situations. Moreover, others are mirrors, enabling us to have a self-image. Göçmen thus says that "we must aim necessarily and consciously at their happiness, because their happiness is also our happiness".

In *WN* commercial exchange-relations are power relations, having to do not only with the power to buy and sell commodities, but also with domination. "In short", says Göçmen, "in commercial society everybody is economically separated and isolated from one another, and the number of commodities that each individual potentially and actually possesses determines his power position in relation to others." But now if this is how we are seen by others, then everyone must have an interest in saving and accumulating possessions.

Given the division of labor, two forms of alienation arise: (1) Smith says that "the whole of every man's attention comes naturally to be directed towards some one very simple object", and such a person "generally becomes as stupid and ignorant as it is possible for a human creature to become" (*WN*, V.i.f.50). So they are in no position to judge anything impartially. (2) Göçmen says: "When we enter the sphere of production, we meet individuals no longer as individuals who are equals among equals. Rather, we meet them as representatives or personifications of different social classes." The three forms of revenue (wages, profit, and rent) correspond to three classes in commercial society: laborers, manufacturers, landlords.

Göçmen thus says that "there is always a contradiction between his [Smith's] conception of social individuality and social relations as developed in *TMS*, on the one hand, and his account of the situation of individuals and social relations in commercial society as described in *WN*, on the other. [...] [W]hen we examine his account of social relations in commercial society as well as at the level of commercial exchange-relations and production, there are no sympathetic relations at all. It is the principle of pure self-interest and mutual domination that serves to pervade social relations." Mutual advantage would characterize society framed on the principle of self-love whereas mutual happiness characterizes society framed on the principle of sympathy. As Göçmen says, "For most people in commercial society, the principle of respect is undermined by the very fact of the division of society into the 'poor' and the 'rich'". So "there is an essential contradiction between his theory of social individuality and his account of the situation of the self in commercial society". Does Smith have any solution to this contradiction?

Göçmen argues that he does, providing "a critique of commercial society, which serves at the same time as a kind of loose framework for his utopia". Smith uses what Göçmen calls a "realist utopia" "to overcome the contradiction between his concept of non-utilitarian ethics and the principle of utility that prevails in commercial society". This notion of utopia is not a detailed description of an ideal future society, but rather an immanent critique of existing social relations, on the basis of which we can infer a vague framework for a different society: "with his short-term aim, Smith wants"—though he does not formulate this explicitly—"to reform radically commercial society without questioning its essential logic, whereas with his long-term solution he essentially wants to overcome commercial society."

Attributing a moral end to Smith's economic theory is a common phenomenon. Indeed, in his "Modern Natural Law Meets the Market: The Case of Adam Smith", Amit Ron notes that "recent scholarship shows Smith's interest in economics to have been moral all the way down". But Ron has serious cautions about that: "understanding Smith's interest in economics solely from a moral perspective is too limiting". Commercial activity, for Smith, is "a political realm characterized by manipulation and coercion. His foray into political economy was in part motivated by an interest in better understanding the deceptive nature of the sense of fairness in commercial activity and its implication for the moral and legal regulations of commerce".

Ron "examines the roles played by these 'political' aspects of Smith's political economy in his understanding of jurisprudence by re-interpreting the discussion of prices in the first book of *The Wealth of Nations*". Smith compared "real value", "natural price", and "market price" to show that "only a system in which prices generated by the market appear morally justifiable can fulfill the needs of commercial societies, even though the market price system entails the most difficulty for making judgments about the fairness of economic transactions that take into account the broader social context in which these transactions are made".

"Real value", which uses labor as a measure, would probably be the first rule of exchange which an impartial spectator would turn to. But it would be too difficult to use as the legally institutionalized measure of value. Better would be the moral evaluation of value based on "natural prices", defined in terms of what was necessary to pay rent, wages and profit in bringing stock to market. But "natural prices" depend on a more elaborate social system, one based on unequal distribution of property—they emerge from struggles between labor and capital. Finally, there is "market price", which is the actual price at which something is sold. Ron says that using market price as the standard of moral judgment puts the impartial spectator in a weak position: it is possible to think that such prices are objective when in fact they can be manipulated and might hide the conditions which shaped the supply and the demand. What Smith thought of as the natural system of perfect liberty is one that would have a legal system which enforced certain rights so that ideally, market prices would tend in the long run to move towards "natural prices".

History has shown us that fashioning such a legal system while maintaining the idea of a free market as a means of moral regulation is a difficult political enterprise. Yet "successful legislation is an essential condition of the social transformation since it stabilizes and 'naturalizes' the predominance of new standards of impartial spectatorship".

Ron points out that Smith's theory of moral sentiments replaces contract theory as a basis for a distinction between perfect and imperfect rights, among other matters. Monica Gerrek's "Revisiting Sentimentalism: A Smithian Normative Moral Theory" furthers the argument for Smith's moral theory by introducing a normative ethic based on Smith's sentimentalism.

The heart of the ethic is this: "An act is wrong if an impartial spectator cannot sympathize with it and an act is right if an impartial spectator can sympathize with it." Gerrek gives an account of the role of sympathy (or empathy) and the sentiments in making moral judgments, discusses why we ought to make use of this moral theory, and shows how the theory applies to some cases which cause problems for some other normative theories.

Smith's basic definition of sympathy is "our fellow-feeling with any passion whatever" when people imaginatively put themselves into the shoes of others. When an impartial spectator does so and finds an "affect match between the spectator and agent, then the motive, and thus act, is said to be proper". The impartial spectator is capable of sympathetic accuracy "in the sense that reactions to particular acts are perfectly indicative of their moral quality". But we do not need some special ideal observer; ordinary persons are capable of being impartial spectators if they are not involved in the situation they are judging, if they possess a normal human nature, and if they know the relevant facts of the situation. But we obviously cannot always have an impartial observer telling us what we ought and ought not to do, and so we develop general moral rules as a substitute for the impartial spectator to guide our behavior and to which we appeal.

Gerrek says that there are points in favor of the ethic she has been describing: (1) Sympathizing is something we do naturally. (2) We need not be impartial spectators in every decision situation; it is easy to follow general rules. (3) "It accommodates our intuitions regarding partiality and impartiality." (4) It permits a degree of relativism. (5) "It accommodates our inclinations to judge actions based on both the motives (character) [...] and the consequences." (6) "It easily includes both moral agents and moral patients in the moral community." (7) "It finds a balance between the use of sentiments in making moral decisions and judgments and the use of reason in doing so." And (8) it works in a wide range of cases (both controversial and non-controversial). Gerrek examines how the sentimentalist ethic compares with deontology, utilitarianism and social contract theories in their application to two issues: murder and infanticide.

Unfortunately, as Tony Pitson points out in "*The Theory of Moral Sentiments* and Smith's Account of Sympathy", Smith's account of sympathy, as distinguished from the part played by sympathy in his moral theory, is far more complicated than it might at first seem. Pitson argues that sympathy, which is central to Smith's moral psychology, is two-staged. We are to imaginatively put ourselves in the place of other persons to form an idea of what they feel. This will be a basis for feelings. Sympathy also has an epistemological dimension, although Smith does not clearly distinguish it from the affective dimension. Smith's account of sympathy is thus no simple matter. Pitson raises and discusses several questions about Smith's account to begin to get clarity on its complexity.

1. We can distinguish between imagining what another feels and actually having a feeling like what the other feels. Is the second necessary? It seems that I can feel sorry for a suffering person without myself suffering, and even if I do feel any distress, why should this be, or lead to, concern for that other person?

2. What is the scope of the process of sympathy? Does it include cognitive states such as beliefs? If so, how does that play out in our feelings of sympathy for others?

3. Are the two stages of sympathy connected by an inference? Is this a version of the argument from analogy for other minds? If so, then Smith's account will be open to criticisms similar to those of the argument from analogy. Yet some of Smith's examples do not seem to fit the inferential model. For example, in response to seeing a stroke about to fall on another person, "we naturally shrink and draw back our own leg or our own arm". This seems to be spontaneous, not inferential. Or consider cases of "emotional transfusion" whereby we apparently have some fellow-feeling merely by seeing a smiling face.

"In general", Pitson says, "bodily feelings either excite no sympathy at all or only a relatively slight degree of it" so that some kinds of feeling do not seem to lend themselves to fellow-feeling: we do not feel hunger when we witness the suffering of a hungry person. Smith says that the correspondence of the feelings of others with our own is "a cause of pleasure, and the want of it a cause of pain" (*TMS*, 14). But Pitson suggests that there are counterexamples.

In *TMS* III.2 Smith considers the case of an innocent man about to be hanged for a crime he did not commit. Smith suggests that his "humble philosophy" might offer no consolation to such a man. "Religion can alone afford [...] any effectual comfort": "the all-seeing Judge of the world" can approve of the man's conduct (III.2.12).

In "'The most cruel misfortune': Suffering Innocence in *The Theory of Moral Sentiments*", Vincent Bissonette examines two mechanisms which Smith's "humble philosophy" describes. The first, which Bissonette calls the "causal imagination", makes use of Hume's notion of causality such that, as Bissonette says, "The individual sees connections in experience between virtue and praise, vice and blame; the ideas are habitually connected; eventually, his imagination begins to anticipate these connections. 'Conscience' here is merely an internalization of this habitual thinking".

Bissonette points out that in the first five editions of *TMS*, "Smith discusses praise without praise-worthiness; praise-worthiness without praise; and blame-worthiness without blame", and these can be described using Hume's naturalistic view of causality. The sixth edition of *TMS* adds the example of the innocent man on the scaffold—an example of blame without blame-worthiness.

Sympathetic imagination allows us to try to put ourselves in another's place. But it takes effort to imagine all the details of the other's position, and this sympathy is never perfect. No one knows that the man on the scaffold has been wrongly condemned. There is no consolation for this man because he cannot sympathize with persons who understand his situation. "He cannot sympathize with his hypothetical sympathizers", as Bissonette puts it. He can imagine them only as feeling shame (because they do not know of his innocence).

Bissonette suggests that Smith believes that doing without the fiction of religion is viable only if there is some consolation. The wrongly condemned man cannot take comfort in imagining how others can sympathize with him because they do not know that he is innocent. Who, then, is the spectator who can accurately sympathize with the wrongly condemned man? Perhaps the spectator of the innocent man on the scaffold can only be Smith himself, and we, the readers.

There is more to the morality of *The Theory of Moral Sentiments* than sympathy, however. Michael S. Pritchard's "Taming Resentment" is "an exploration of the role of resentment in Smith and Reid's accounts of morality". Resentment is an odd passion because, Smith claims, it is a principle of human nature that we care about other people: we often get pleasure from witnessing their happiness. Resentment is one of the "unsocial passions" which "excite no sort of sympathy, but before we are acquainted with what gave occasion to them, serve rather to disgust and provoke us against them" (*TMS*, 11). Resentment is "the greatest poison to the happiness of a good mind" (*TMS*, 37). It is a defensive response that "prompts us to beat off the mischief which is attempted to be done to us, and to retaliate that which is already done" (*TMS*, 79).

Resentment is also prone to excesses, and part of moral education involves the taming (but not the eliminating) of it. "Much of *The Theory of Moral Sentiments* is an account of what this requires and how it might be accomplished." A child has little self-control. In young children, anger is a form of resentment, but it is not yet a moral judgment, which requires, first, being concerned with how we seem to others, and, second, a desire for "what ought to be approved of" (*TMS*, 114). This desire can be satisfied only by seeing ourselves from the point of view of an impartial spectator.

The resentful person wishes support from others: misery loves company. But the person who resents another must try to view things as a spectator would, so resentment "must always be brought down to a pitch much lower than that to which undisciplined nature would raise them" (*TMS*, 34). And when resentment conforms to the requirements of propriety, it expresses the indignation of an impartial spectator.

A proper sense of resentment has to do with "real and positive hurt to some particular persons" (*TMS*, 79), and as an expression of justice it is not necessarily tied to utility (*contra* Hume). Consider Hume's "sensible knave", who understands the public benefits of justice but hopes to personally gain by breaking the rules. Hume claims that for persons with an "ingenuous nature", the aversion to deceit is stronger than the appeal of personal advantages.

Although Smith would agree, he may not have seen, as Reid did, that an account of resentment by Bishop Butler could be used to challenge Hume's response to such a sensible knave. According to Reid, we feel injured when our rights are violated; when the agent had the intention to produce hurt, we feel what Butler called a "deliberate resentment". Moreover, Reid claimed that "every man is conscious of a specific difference between the resentment he feels for an injury done to himself, and his indignation against a wrong done to the public" (*Essays on the Active Powers of the Mind*, 314). This is crucial to Reid's reply to the sensible knave.

Hume bases justice on public utility whereas Reid employs the notions of private favor (linked to gratitude) and private injury (linked to resentment) as embracing the conceptions of justice and injustice. And for Smith, too, the sensible knave's actions wrong individuals (even if his actions might not greatly harm public good).

But, as Pritchard says, Smith also claims, in *WN*, that the public good can be served (as if by an invisible hand) by persons aiming not at public good, but at their own private interests. Smith here avoids the problem of the sensible knave by distinguishing intentions (one's own gain) from constraints (considerations of justice). I can aim at my own profit and yet play within the rules in doing so. Violators of the rules can be expected to be met with resentment.

We may note here that Smith himself created conditions for resentment when he refused to ensure that Hume's *Dialogues Concerning Natural Religion* was published after Hume's death. Hume was obviously in no position to resent Smith's failure, but we must ask why Smith failed to do what he had apparently promised Hume he would do. Several plausible explanations—personal, political, and theological—have been advanced by scholars. In his "Skepticism and Imagination: Smith's Response to Hume's *Dialogues*", Ryan Patrick Hanley wishes to "supplement" them by suggesting a philosophical reason.

Hume's *Dialogues* was an assault not only on theology, but also on philosophy as a productive inquiry. Hume claimed that speculations which go beyond the limits of experience are illegitimate. But Smith wanted to encourage precisely that kind of philosophical inquiry, and this is seen in Smith's "The Principles Which Lead and Direct Philosophical Enquiries; Illustrated by the History of Astronomy".

For Hume, philosophy is a kind of refinement of common life. But according to Smith, wonder is a motive for speculation in order to understand phenomena beyond our ordinary experience; philosophy attempts to give such an account. "[P]hilosophy begins for Smith at precisely the point at which it ends for Hume", says Hanley.

In addition, wonder, for Smith, is both natural and necessary, and philosophical understanding is the only way to restore mental tranquility which is necessary for happiness. "Put differently", says Hanley, "where philosophizing is for Hume the cause of anxiety, and thus best abandoned for the study of common life, philosophizing is for Smith the only remedy for anxiety, and hence requires the abandonment of common life." A third difference between Smith and Hume, according to Hanley, is that "where Hume insists that the goal of philosophical investigation is to reveal the discrete nature of phenomena and to expose the lack of any substantive connection between them, for Smith the aim of philosophy is to synthesize and unite the formerly discrete into coherent wholes".

Thus, Smith could defend not publishing the *Dialogues Concerning Natural Religion* because philosophical speculation has potential utility both to promote scientific progress and to promote tranquility of the inquirer.

Hume's death occasioned not only the apparent obligation to publish which Smith refused to honor, but also a long letter to Strahan. Chad Flanders argues in "Hume's Death and Smith's Philosophy" that Smith's letter is worth studying not merely as paying tribute to Hume, but also as a philosophical document in its own right. The later revisions of *TMS* can be read as part of Smith's reaction to Hume's death.

Flanders first discusses how Smith's letter completes the biographical project which Hume began in *My Own Life*. How one dies is necessarily a part of assessing one's life, and so there is this curious fact: a complete life can in the end not be written by the one living it, but only by another. As Flanders puts it, "Paradoxically, a complete autobiography has to be a two person affair".

Flanders suggests that as a result of the public reaction to Hume's death, Smith put even more distance between his own philosophy and Hume's. In particular, Smith emphasized the separation of the impartial spectator from ordinary public opinion so that the impartial spectator becomes increasingly less dependent upon the judgments of people as they are and more tied to people as they might be. Moreover, the number of people who might qualify as impartial spectators shrinks to the point of being only hypothetical. "Smith had come to distrust human opinion, and his response was to place more and more the basis of ethics in something outside of the human, in God. The impartial spectator, to put the matter polemically, turns out to be God."

As another result of the public reaction to Hume's death, Smith became more convinced of the necessity in believing in an afterlife. What we end up with in Smith's later view is a non-Humean vision of an immortal afterlife, a vision that is "tied to the idea that the most appropriate inhabitant of such other world would be none other than David Hume".

As Flanders puts it, "It has been argued that the *Republic* is in a sense a response to the death of Socrates: Plato was creating a republic in which what happened to Socrates would not be repeated. Philosophers would be kings rather than being ruled by the many. Smith takes this same idea but puts it into a metaphysical key. The revisions in *TMS* are likewise a response to the death of the master. In Smith's afterlife, Hume will get the recognition he deserves, but was never fully granted in this life."

What Hume and Smith deserve in this life is recognition for their prose styles. In his "'A Delicate and an Accurate Pencil': Adam Smith, Description, and Philosophy as Moral Pedagogy", Colin Heydt argues that some kinds of prose can encourage ethical improvement and that Smith's description of prudence and vice in *TMS* functions as moral pedagogy.

Prudence is a virtue of commercial relations that has to do with care of health, fortune, rank, and reputation. Ancient writers are committed to moral ideals—the universal ideal of prudence, for instance. But this is not Smith's way. Smith gives the reader the features of prudence so that the reader will be able to recognize it, but he tries to find a balance between concreteness and abstraction. He does so by depicting a typified prudent individual rather than examining the attribute of prudence itself. Heydt contrasts Smith's approach to the more abstract approach of Reid and the more concrete approach of Addison.

Earlier versions of the papers in this volume were presented at a three day conference, "Adam Smith's *The Theory of Moral Sentiments*", at Rochester Institute of Technology on May 4–6, 2006. We are grateful to the Department of Philosophy and the Ezra A. Hale Chair in Applied Ethics for their support for that conference and for making this volume of essays possible.

SELECT BIBLIOGRAPHY

Grossman, Kathy Lynn. "Baylor Religion Survey Reveals Many See God Steering Economy". *USA Today*, September 20, 2011. (The Baylor Survey is at http://www.baylor.edu/content/services/document.php/153501.pdf.

Hume, David. *Dialogues Concerning Natural Religion*. Edited by Richard H. Popkin. Indianapolis: Hackett, 1980.

Hume, David. "My Own Life". In *Essays: Moral, Political and Literary*, revised edition, edited by Eugene F. Miller. Indianapolis: Liberty Fund, 1985.

Reid, Thomas. *Essays on the Active Powers of the Mind*. Edited by Knud Haakonssen and James A. Harris. Edinburgh: Edinburgh University Press, 2010.

Smith, Adam. *An Inquiry into the Nature and Causes of the Wealth of Nations*, 2 vols. Edited by R. H. Campbell and A. L. Skinner. Indianapolis: Liberty Fund, 1981.

———. "Letter to Strahan". In David Hume, *Essays: Moral, Political and Literary*, revised edition, edited by Eugene F. Miller. Indianapolis: Liberty Fund, 1985.

———. *The Theory of Moral Sentiments*. Edited by D. D. Raphael and A. L. Macfie. Indianapolis: Liberty Fund, 1984.

———. "The Principles Which Lead and Direct Philosophical Enquiries; Illustrated by the History of Astronomy". In *Essays on Philosophical Subjects*, edited by W. P. D. Wightman. Indianapolis: Liberty Fund, 1982.

SMITH ON TASTE AND CRITICISM:
TEXTS AND CONTEXTS

Peter Jones

By describing the contexts Smith inhabited I want to illustrate how very different they were from ours. This forces us to ask whether we can bridge the gap: can we "project ourselves imaginatively"—as the claim goes—into such an alien world? What are the criteria of success? Or, a different question: does it matter? Why do we not simply pretend Smith is one of us, and forget about his dismal context? The answer is simple: *traduttore traditore*.

I shall adopt one of Smith's own rhetorical devices: the juxtaposition of examples for comparison, but without authorial comment. Such "comparison" was, for Smith, a necessary condition for justifiable judgment on anything; moreover, the selection, and the arrangement of examples were, in his sense, a matter of taste. Like Hume, he held that all our ultimate judgments have what today we might call an aesthetic element; and these elements are not optional extras or detachable features of our moral life. Moreover, they were both intrigued by the dynamics of the thinking processes that form, dissolve, reform, enclose, disclose.

Although 18th-century thinkers welcomed the benefits of specialized investigation, many of them at the same time warned against the fragmentation of enquiry and understanding. Promoting an integrated, holistic approach very quickly became an urgent challenge, in philosophy as everywhere else. Indeed, they had to insist that confining philosophy merely to the work of the intellect, to the content of propositions, to the logic of argument, was to sell the moral pass.

In his prefatory "Epistle on Education and the Design of the Essay on painting" (*A Treatise on Ancient Painting*)[1], George Turnbull claimed that paintings had meaning only if they conveyed "into the mind ideas of sensible laws, and their effects and appearances" or "moral sentiments and corresponding affections"; moreover, in order to convey such meaning, they would have to "speak a language" (*Treatise*, ix). In the subsequent Preface, aimed at uneducated Grand Tourists, he emphasizes "how mean, insipid and trifling the fine arts are when they are alienated from their better and nobler, genuine purposes". Without rigorous preparation before one departs—he calls it "a truly liberal education"—one "goes abroad not knowing whither he goes, or what he goes to see; without any scheme; and absolutely unqualified to compare, or make

---

1   Bibliographic information for all references can be found in the Select Bibliography at the end of this essay.

judgments of men and Things". In a passionate plea to reverse the fragmentation of education, he tried to anchor the arts, and painting in particular, within a holistic approach to life. We need not follow his Platonic exploration of beauty, truth, and utility, or his analogies between moral and aesthetic beauty; what is important for us is his attempt to re-integrate the arts with all our other moral and epistemic concerns, and his insistence that only by making strenuous efforts to understand contexts can we take the arts seriously. Although he came to disagree with Turnbull's Platonism, Smith, as a fellow teacher, endorsed the central goal; however much we properly valued the pleasurable embellishments provided by the arts, the perpetual danger was that they seduced us into trivial trinketry. Society thus faced the deep moral task of maintaining the highest standards of appreciation, and of promoting only those artists who likewise strove to pursue the highest goals. By the mid-18th century, too, there was an additional, albeit contingent, task to insist that to take anything seriously was not the same as taking everything solemnly.

By the 17th century, many writers were underlining the importance of contexts in determining both what to do, and how to understand the past. The discipline that placed context at the center was rhetoric; everybody studied the *Port-Royal Logic*, Locke, Charles Rollin, or Isaac Watts. To European humanists, rhetoric was the core of education: it was an all-embracing concept, encompassing what we would call moral and mental philosophy, politics, and social psychology, as well as modes of communication and behavior. In modern jargon, it covered producer, process and product; it did not separate an artist from his work, nor the work from a spectator. Hume even described rhetoric as "l'art de vivre" ("Of Civil Liberty", in *Essays*, 91). Although rhetoric was concerned primarily with the fundamentally dynamic act of *speaking*, its prescriptions later extended to writing. It should not be forgotten, however, in the mid-18th century nine tenths of the world's population lived in an oral culture, with everything that entails.

Rhetoricians insisted that speakers who wanted to be understood needed to guide their listeners towards a desired interpretation. Smith's own first public lectures were on rhetoric and *belles lettres*, in Edinburgh and then Glasgow; and his first publications seem to have been his reviews of Johnson's *Dictionary* and a letter about the *Encyclopédie* in the *Edinburgh Review* of 1755 and 1756. This was the theatrical wing from which Smith entered onto the stage of *The Theory of Moral Sentiments* (*TMS*), concerned from the start to engage the sympathy of his audience. And his first challenge is enthralling. If the moral life is defined in terms of agency, or performance, what kind of agency characterizes artists, and what kind of agency is available to spectators? The answer is that artists can typically be regarded as *performers*, and spectators can avoid passivity only by participation, that is by becoming *quasi*-performers. And now the question is: will this work? More specifically, can the roles assigned by Smith to sympathy in the moral domain be projected into what we now call the aesthetic domain? To approach aesthetic questions from the directions of moral philosophy and its infrastructure of rhetoric is likely to place a high premium on thought, intention, and meaning; decorative activities are likely to be assessed as "merely" pleasurable, and beauties of nature, if at all, associated with utility. That, roughly was Hume's position, and Smith agreed—except that he said almost nothing about nature.

The world in which Smith lived was becoming increasingly textual, and this generated new challenges. Ephraim Chambers, in 1728, echoed an idea trumpeted by almost everyone since Bacon: that willful obscurity should be condemned because it gives a reader the spurious freedom to invent whatever meaning he wishes, and with it the seductive illusion of ownership. The human mind, he says, "in apprehending what was hid under a veil, fancies itself in some measure the author of it" (*Cyclopaedia*, "Fable"). The defining characteristic of impromptu speech is *improvisation*, which reflects the fluctuations of perception and thought as well as of the multiple contexts in which they take place. Writing and texts, however, stabilize such perpetual motion at the cost of distortion, even deception:

> There is something arbitrary and artificial in all writings: they are a kind of draughts, or pictures, where the aspect, attitude, and light, which the objects are taken in, though merely arbitrary, yet sway and direct the whole representation. Books are, as it were, plans or prospects of ideas artfully arranged and exhibited, not to the eye, but to the imagination; and there is a kind of analogous perspective, which obtains in them, wherein we have something not much unlike points of sight, and of distance. An author, in effect, has some particular view or design in drawing our his ideas [...] The case amounts to the same as the viewing of objects in a mirror; where, unless the form of the mirror be known, *viz.* whether it be plain, concave, convex, cylindric, or conic, etc., we can make no judgment of the magnitude, figure, *etc.* of the object. [*Cyclopaedia*, xvi]

In 1751, d'Alembert—later a friend of Smith and Hume, of course—forcefully endorsed Chambers's views. Two theoretical problems seemed to make the tasks of communication intractable: first, the puzzling relations of language to the world; and second, the ubiquitous implications of change.

> It is almost as if one were trying to express [a] proposition by means of a language whose nature was being imperceptibly altered, so that the proposition was successively expressed in different ways representing the different states through

> which the language had passed. Each of these states would be recognized in the one immediately neighbouring it; but in a more remote state we would no longer make it out. [*Mélanges*, 1.47]

D'Alembert feared, in other words, that across separated points in time, and in the absence of an intervening medium, we may be unable to work out what was being said. The meaning of even everyday expressions might change independently of any changes in their supposed objects. Action-at-a-distance might be doubtful, but meaning-at-a-distance impossible. We should ask ourselves why Smith valued the Abbé Girard's *Synonymes François* (1737) above all others in the field.

What devices are available to us for tackling these problems? To navigate the rich terrain we require maps of different kinds and of various scales. Several coordinates are needed to identify the contexts of writing—personal, historical, political, philosophical, religious, geographical: the publishing details and reviewing practices. Who were the intended and actual audiences? Who responded to what, how, when, why, and where? Most readers use what they read for their own purposes, in the present, and the further they are from the date of composition the less they are inclined to detect original intentions, meanings, implications. But can we sharply separate notions of "interpretation" and "use"? All texts operate within generic and rhetorical conventions peculiar to their contexts, and a knowledge of these is necessary to determine what meanings were derived by contemporary readers. Meanings only operate contextually, with the same words conveying different messages in different contexts. Eighteenth-century thinkers spoke to issues of their day in the language of their day; they were not addressing 21st-century issues in 21st-century language.

From the 1670s onwards anxiety was detectable among the newly leisured classes as they began to spend their time and money on pursuits formerly reserved for the privileged few. Two fundamental questions of thought and action fuelled their anxieties: "How am I supposed to behave?" and "What should I know?" The evolution of modern aesthetics since then is inseparable from the emergence of what I shall call such "essentially ignorant spectators"— the notion derives from the supporters of "les Modernes" against "les Anciens" in France, together with the proliferation of critics who acted as intermediaries between them and the works they encountered, and the eventual establishment of special locations for such encounters—museums, concert halls, galleries. Smith himself asserted that "in civilized nations, the inferior ranks of people have very little leisure"; but "wherever the Inhabitants of a city are rich and opulent [...] there are many who are not obliged to Labour for their livelihood and have nothing to do, but employ themselves in what most suits their taste" (*Essays on Philosophical Subjects* [*EPS*], 187; *Lectures on Rhetoric and Belles Lettres* [*LRBL*], 137).

Until the 19th century, only the middle and upper classes in great cities had opportunities for personal experience of such pleasures—elsewhere, they could only be *read about*, and that factor itself distorted the nature of both response and discussion. Texts dominated contexts, and talk was substituted for thought. Remarkably, some writers predicted these dangers at the very outset—Fontenelle, Claude Perrault, and the abbé Dubos in France, and their essentially Lockean acquaintances such as Shaftesbury and Addison. Parenthetically, we might note that, in contrast to painters who closely observed still life, almost no writers considered as *aesthetic* such ubiquitous aspects of poorer people's lives as the form, medium, color, texture, or arrangement of their clothes, utensils, or ornaments; indeed, Smith states that the lower orders who make their own clothes and furniture are not engaged in the fine arts (*Wealth of Nations* [*WN*], 407).

Two major factors combined to distort developments: in order to assert their social superiority over mere *doers*, and to disguise the fact that their amateur skills could no longer match the professional expertise now demanded, the new chattering classes inevitably exaggerated the importance of talk. Practitioners themselves soon abandoned hopes of instructing their potential audiences in anything regarded as technical, and critics followed them. Early in the century Jonathan Richardson tried hard to persuade people that looking at paintings was a learnable skill, but by the 1760s John Gregory's resigned complaint was commonplace: if we "cannot teach people to think and to feel" we can at least "teach them what to say", and a good way to retain their interest was to encourage them to talk about themselves. Discussion of merit, which is about public achievement, was surrendered to reports of private feelings, which are about biography—what *I felt* mattered more than what *you had done*; and self-absorption triumphed.

Gregory was in fact responding to things Smith and Hume had very recently said, and which was generating heated argument in Edinburgh and Aberdeen. By the time of Gregory's lament, all of the concepts central to discussions of "taste" or "criticism" had been identified: meaning, context, and interpretation; skill, tradition, and merit; learning, practice, and socialization; thought and feeling; reaction and response; the roles of theory and judgment; the oscillating relations between pleasure and utility; and, in more abstract discussions, the nature and roles of imagination, emotions, language, and symbols. Such a range of topics is surprising because, as philosophers and historians of science have pointed out, what counts as a legitimate question, and as a proper way of answering it, differs greatly across time and place. Problems, like the concepts in terms of which they are formulated, have histories, evolve, and become obsolete, and yet here are gathered together so many major issues that still interest us—although their meaning and import may well have changed. Much of this talk about taste and criticism occurred, over a period of barely ten years, in a stinking half-derelict medieval walled town, much of whose population went barefooted and lived close to starvation—Edinburgh; even more remarkably, among a group of its prominent citizens, at least ten published their views. This was remarkable because the topics were not immediately political or religious in their implications, and the disputants all subscribed to an empiricist account of response and judgment, however much they disagreed on epistemological issues.

Very briefly, they more or less all agreed that objective judgments are possible in every realm of experience and enquiry. As social beings anchored in our own contexts, we all have to learn what counts as objectivity in different realms of enquiry, but whether we bother to learn depends largely on how important we think the context is. Hume and Smith insisted that we can learn to make justifiable judgments about what is good—in art, for example—but that such judgments do not need to match our transient and personal likes. Everyone recognized that "taste" functioned as a metaphor—but then they failed to examine the consequences of the metaphor. Briefly: there can be no argument about tastes, understood literally, because these are sensory events; but there can and should be argument about misleadingly labeled *judgments*-of-taste, because such judgments are *not*, contrary to appearances, reports of those sensory events.

Here is Hume's friend Allan Ramsay, writing in 1755, urging readers to dissociate the concepts of "standard" and "taste":

> Whatever has a rule or standard to which it may be referred, and is capable of comparison, is not the object of taste, but of reason and judgment. On the other hand, the proper objects of taste, or feeling, are such as are relative to the person only who is actuated by them, who is the sole judge whether those feelings be agreeable, or otherwise; and being informed of this simple fact from himself, no farther consequence can be drawn from it; neither does it admit of any dispute. ["Dialogue on Taste"]

Four other features of the Edinburgh view, or the Ramsay-Hume-Smith view as we might call it, are worth mentioning here. The first is insistence that the causal relations between work and observer must be supplemented by the mental response of the observer *to* the work. The second is emphasis on the diverse *contexts* in which works are made and encountered and the consequences of such diversity for both our causal reactions and our mental responses. Thirdly, as empiricists, they all held that general principles could be legitimately formed only from particular cases—Burke held the same view. Fourthly, almost all of them deplored a growing tendency by critics and other talkers to impute theories to artists where none existed; one reason for this trend, detected by several artists and musicians, was the tyranny of the written text, which was proclaimed as the model and zenith of artistic achievement—but only by writers.

Consider some contextual dimensions of the year in which *TMS* was published, 1759. Such contextual anchorage should be undertaken periodically, in order to identify and dislodge any mis-projections that distort our understanding of what Smith either did, or could have intended to mean and do.

The Seven Years War (1756–1763) was raging to no one's benefit; Frederick was deeply embroiled, of course, but Catherine had not yet become empress. The scope for one's Grand Tour was tiresomely reduced during the interruptions. Handel died at the age of 74, a national hero but no longer the most popular opera composer; Voltaire, already in his mid-60s, published *Candide*, in the wake of the Lisbon disaster, and Samuel Johnson, also in his 60s, published his own moral tale *Rasselas*. In France, a gang of intellectuals in their mid-40s was about to confront authority, censorship, and imprisonment: with Volume 8 about to be published, the great *Encyclopédie* of Diderot and d'Alembert was banned by order of Louis XV, along with *De l'Esprit* of Helvétius. In Chapter 30 of Johnson's melancholy novel, Rasselas and his sister declare themselves to have little interest in history. They are firmly rebuked: "To see men we must see their works, that we may learn what reason has dictated or passion has incited, and find what are the most powerful motives of action. To judge rightly of the present we must oppose it to the past; for all judgment is comparative, and of the future nothing can be known" (*Rasselas*).

Such a view had been gathering support for more than a century, and in 1759 this had been conspicuously exemplified in the newly published Tudor volumes of Hume's *History of England*. He had already identified one unavoidable challenge: historians of the past know the outcome and consequences of actions but not the intentions necessary for understanding them. Agents, on the other hand, know their own intentions when they set out, but not the outcome. This interest in an historical approach to affairs, which outsiders saw as distinctive of the Scottish philosophers, defined their approach to everything human beings did, including the making of works of art (not, by the way, a phrase yet in currency). And it ineradicably re-instated the ancient insight that one fully knows *what* has happened, only when one knows why and how. This insight covers everybody—artists and critics, as much as politicians and philosophers.

To envisage the contexts in which our authors were living, however, is not a straightforward task. Pelion must be heaped on Ossa, for the past is a foreign country. Can we enter their mindset? They believed in almost none of the basic scientific beliefs that define our lives—they knew nothing, for example about forms of energy other than light and heat, or about the composition of air or water, or the nature of fire or breathing or procreation, or the age of the earth or the size of the universe, or about the nature of stars or the origins of life, or about the evolution of animals or genetic inheritance.

In trying to characterize differences in context, we should not limit our thoughts to size and scale; indeed, the distinctive sensory and emotional features of experience that are so hard to convey are precisely those that define events, are most cherished, and are perhaps most inaccessible to others. (James Beattie, in his *Essay on Poetry and Music*, published in 1776 but apparently "written in the year 1762" makes just this point.) Smith's sensory life must have differed in some respects from ours—could it matter philosophically? If so, how? Consider this. A sense of place is defined by a sense of space that is defined by light. That was why the light of Italy, and later of Egypt and India so enraptured the northern spirit. It was no accident that, in reflecting on health, wealth, and welfare, many 18th-century thinkers wondered about the influence of climate on character. Winter days in Scotland are nasty, British, and short. And at 56 degrees North, the level of southern Alaska, north of Moscow and the whole of China, Edinburgh in 1759 was a thoroughly sordid, crowded medieval town. It is true that for five months in the year the sun rises and sets in the North, so that all four sides of buildings can be lit and cast shadows—no landmass in the southern hemisphere enjoys that experience—but, for three months of the year there are barely five hours of daylight. Darkness enters the soul. In January 1697, for example, an Edinburgh student was executed for blasphemy, to the orgiastic delight of his professors—in fact, they probably organized it. More than 40 years later those same vicious purveyors of superstition petitioned the city to close all theatres and endorsed a church report that deplored "unprofitable converse, loud and noisy discourse, merriment and laughter". This referred to public conversations in the High Street. Terrified by rapid changes on all fronts, dour Calvinists expressed their fears in sullen disapproval of everything—costly display of any kind, together with theatre, music, and especially dancing—that lewd, lubricious, and deeply satanic depravity. In Glasgow, Hutcheson was painfully silenced by threats of ex-communication and ceased to laugh; 25 years later, the general assembly tried to take Hume and Kames on at the same time. Smith kept his head down—but continued to fear the terrorists long after failing to honor Hume's will in 1776.

In the 1750s, the walled city of Edinburgh covered an area less than 140 acres: about 55,000 people were crammed into 15-story buildings of minimal architectural merit. Edinburgh was twice as big as the next city, Glasgow, and ten times larger than any other town; but there were fewer people in the whole of Scotland than in London—under a million. There was, of course, no sewage anywhere. In 1756, the border market town of Jedburgh, near the family farms of both Hume and Kames, and with a population of around 5,000, boasted exactly two carpets. Except in the very wealthiest houses little meat was eaten, few vegetables, and no fruit; and there were never two courses at a meal. In 1748 the very first potatoes appeared in the city; there was neither cheese nor freshwater fish. Servants were bare-footed, as were postal runners; in today's vocabulary, Scotland was a third-world country, like most of the rest of the world. There were precisely two shops in the capital city, for luxury goods only; everything else was sold in markets. Until the 1730s all business, including legal affairs, was conducted in taverns, in which one could hire private rooms; social entertaining generally took place in these taverns well into the 1760s, not least because most dwellings had only one hearth. There was no concept of tourism, and a stranger without specific business was regarded with great suspicion. Travel, indeed, was both difficult and dangerous because of robbers; timid travelers took the terrifying boat to England, which could take one month. Although the Scotsman Tobias Smollett in 1770 declared that Edinburgh was "a hotbed of genius" and Glasgow "a perfect bee-hive in point of industry" (*Humphry Clinker*, II, 75, 92), these were recent developments, and did not yet extend to physical conditions. There should be no nostalgia about their living conditions. It is an unintended consequence of modern tourism that an obsession with manicured memorials to the past has anaesthetized our minds.

Smith lived when no music was heard as we hear it in concert halls; no paintings encountered as we today sniff at them in silent galleries; no building smelled like the sanitized wonders that hypnotize today's coach loads of shuffling automata. And remember the properties of candlelight: it animates the inanimate, dissolves the insoluble, mystifies the transparent, throws itself upwards—but never reaches the ceiling. And ask yourself this: how many penitents could see the *predella*-panels on Catholic or Anglican altars, so much treasured by today's connoisseurs? The answer is three—the celebrant, the cleaner, and, if they turned up, the patrons of the altarpiece. Everyone else was too far away, behind the altar rail, and in comparative darkness. The *predella* was a decorative addition to an overall pattern, or rather, to complex events, except between the prelate and the patron, for whom it was a private political engagement.

Still lagging economically behind England, the consumerization of leisure had barely started in Scotland by the 1760s, and Smith and Hume were well aware of the extent to which life in London and Paris was not mirrored in Edinburgh. There was one connecting link, however. From the mid-17th century, and inspired by French *salons*, discussion societies had sprung up throughout Europe; by the 1730s they even existed in most Scottish towns. They met in rented tavern rooms, typically under the banner of "improvement" and they explicitly sought to embody only the intellectual aspects of the salons, not their aristocratic social ambitions. This signified that they would discuss any matters which even indirectly might improve the health and wealth of the nation. Many such groups dedicated themselves to the special interests of their members. The three central topics in Edinburgh societies around the 1750s were agriculture, mining, and banking. But the range of topics was sometimes extensive. In such discussion groups—most prominently in Edinburgh and Aberdeen—the more radical ideas of Hume and Smith, for example, could be discussed in private by social equals, without upsetting the public or their religious guardians.

In 1755, The Edinburgh Society for the Encouragement of Arts, Sciences, Manufactures, and Agriculture (the similarity in name to the London

Society, founded in the previous year, was no accident) proposed a medal for "the best essay on taste". In fact they did not award the medal until 1757, when they gave it to Alexander Gerard of Aberdeen. The driving force of the discussion society was Allan Ramsay, who had already painted more than 400 portraits, half of which are still located in Scotland, and who later became the Royal portrait painter in London; the other founding members were David Hume, Adam Smith, Adam Ferguson, Lord Kames, and William Robertson. Many of their other intellectual friends were also members. Shortly before leaving for his second protracted visit to Italy in 1754, where he joined up with young Robert Adam, Ramsay had written his own essay on taste, partly to respond to Hogarth's *Analysis of Beauty*—which had come out in the previous year. Ramsay's essay was published in the spring of 1755, and Hume was delighted with it; it soon became the focus of discussion in Edinburgh, London, and Rome, and prompted plans for the competition. By the time Gerard's revised submission appeared as a book four years later, Hume in 1757, Smith in 1759, and Lord Kames in 1762 had also published their views; in Aberdeen, James Beattie, George Campbell, John Gregory, and Thomas Reid all wrote papers on the subject, although these were not published until later. In Italy itself, Robert Adam's younger brother James wrote from Rome to Kames in April 1761, with his views on architecture, taste, and criticism, and clearly had their mutual friend Ramsay's essay in mind. Ramsay's prominent choice of architecture to illustrate his main thesis not only echoed what Smith's own professor at Glasgow, Francis Hutcheson, had done 30 years earlier, but allowed him to naughtily pillory theologians: for they frequently referred to the Divine Architect, in order to bolster their design arguments for the existence and attributes of God. Ramsay, Hume, and Smith took their lead from Claude Perrault and would have none of it—with his brother Charles, Claude was a leader of the Moderns, against the Ancients. With the exception of Ramsay himself, who preceded them, the other authors took their cue from Hume's essay, "Of the Standard of Taste".

Gerard alone acknowledges the book from which Hume himself derived most inspiration—*Réflexions critiques sur la poésie et sur la peinture*, by the Abbé Jean-Baptiste Dubos, published in Paris in 1719. This was by far the most successful book on aesthetics—as we would call it—in the 18th century, and the most influential before Kant; it went through many editions and was translated into English in 1745. Hume himself quoted from Dubos in his 1742 *Essays*, and in several earlier manuscript Notes. All of the central concepts in his own essay on taste are derived from Dubos and are merely transliterated into equivalent or sometimes entirely new English terms: prejudice, delicacy, practice, comparison, and good sense. These terms, all with Cartesian baggage attached, formed the core of French critical discussions at the time of La Bruyère in the late 17th century. Hume uses these notions, with his own Humean foundation, to set out his views on fashion and the objectivity of critical judgments. His Scottish friends, all of whom had read Dubos, took up various aspects of his discussion, but as time went on, the reputations of Gerard, Kames, and Ramsay declined, and no one noticed that Smith had been involved. Hume's essay came to be treated as an isolated phenomenon, albeit one that provoked Kant into an influential response—the *Critique of Judgment*.

Debate about judgments of taste had raged in England since Addison's essays in the *Spectator* and had been further fueled by Pope's *Epistle to Burlington* (1731). To us, perhaps, Ramsay's most interesting remarks are about the influence of the socio-economic climate on fashion, and the sharp distinction between feeling and judgment, which the French had notoriously muddled up in the single term "*sentiment*". He argues that what we take to be standards in our judgments are neither more nor less than the effects of our "early education, and so early, that no man is able to remember its first establishment in his mind". Such cultural conditioning, as we would call it, is clearly contingent, but it is curiously re-enforced by another feature. Ramsay argues that something initially neutral, or even mildly disagreeable, can become agreeable simply through habit. And if habit is the main explanation of both original and changing fashion, judgments at neither time can be credited with the recognition of inherent qualities—a remark that Sir William Chambers, who knew Ramsay well, repeated, although ascribing it to Gerard (*Civil Arch.*, 54). "After-admiration" as Ramsay calls it, resulting from familiarity, is commonplace not only in cookery, dress, and furniture, "but also in things that are at first extremely nauseous and disagreeable, such as tobacco, coffee and other drugs". So called "good taste in architecture" can be explained similarly by reference to custom. For both architect and cook, Ramsay declares, the "rules are plainly no more than the analysis of certain things which custom rendered agreeable": "The fashions in building, tho' more durable than those in dress, are not the less fashions, and are equally subject to change. But [...] we must have recourse to history for the knowledge of those changes, which we can learn but very imperfectly from our own proper experience" ("Dialogue on Taste", 36).

Like Hume and Ferguson, Ramsay held that "the most extraordinary inventions were rather the effect of chance and subsequent trial, than of any profound forethought and contrivance"; moreover, "[t]he business of the bulk of mankind is not to think, but to act, each in his own little sphere, and for his own little purposes; and, this he may do, very completely, without much reflection, by the force of habit alone; leaving the conduct of the whole to the few of a more extended way of thinking" ("Essay on Naturalization of Foreigners", 5). Ramsay had discussed most of this with Hume and, like almost all British writers after Francis Bacon, argues that preferences based on first appearances rarely pass the test of time: we are often seduced by superficialities, and we fail to perceive subtleties or complexities, or compare the present case with other examples. "Comparative judgment", indeed, became one of the mantras of empiricist thought.

Did they think it mattered whether we settle discussions about taste?

Their view was that the behavior of other social beings matters to us on some occasions more than others; it especially matters if the metaphor of "taste" has disguised an essential distinction between "reaction" and "response", feeling and judgment. We are often interested in the causes of sensations, their intensity and duration; but "responses" are directed *at* or *to* something, and they therefore involve the mind. This was the point, arguably, at which the general thesis about the "aesthetic" element in all our evaluations is accidentally displaced by the narrower discussion of critical judgments of works of art—albeit that the analysis of the latter was supposed to be carried over to the former.

Hume holds that discussions of matters of taste require us to examine both the physical causes of pleasurable sensations and the thoughts of the maker and spectator—"thoughts" that, of course, embraced both cognitive and emotive elements. This is because works of art are not accidents, but are made intentionally by fellow human beings, for certain purposes, in certain contexts, using their minds and their skills to the utmost—they here resemble any other human activity; sometimes we may need to examine many aspects of the context, in order to establish the nature of an achievement. Thought, judgment, and the engagement of the mind are necessarily involved in such enquiry, and questions of meaning necessarily arise, at least twice, in connection with both the process and the product; for the agent may mean something by doing what he does, and the result itself may carry meaning. And, of course, there can be no meaning without interpretation. On this last point Smith completely changed his mind in the decade after the late 1740s—which is not surprising since his first position was incoherent by his own principles. He originally held that "the fine arts, matters of taste and imagination [...] require little labour" (*LRBL*, 55); this immediately rules out any didactic art, and detaches the arts from anything to do with rhetoric or communication. Notwithstanding all that, he placed the onus exclusively on the artist to engage, inform, entertain, and instruct. But by the time of *TMS* he clearly underlines the importance of a spectator correctly identifying the context and intention of the artist, and of comparing them with his own context of response.

Hume and Smith held that the foundations of all practices lie in the acquisition of learned skills, practiced, challenged, and modified over time in the public arena of comparative judgments made by those who are qualified to judge. Not everyone *is* qualified to judge, and few candidates for the accolade of "expert" ever achieve the highest standards attainable in their chosen fields. Nevertheless, all of us have to learn what the standards are in any given field, and we are taught by the current experts; we are not qualified to judge by ourselves until we have proved ourselves over time by means of discriminating perception and rational discussion—only then are we entitled to modify the existing repertoire of judgments and seek endorsement from our peers. Are there no occasions for someone to express "a purely personal opinion" and "a mere matter of taste"? Certainly, but they are rarely of interest to anyone else:

reports of likes, as Ramsay declared, are about private biographies inaccessible to others, discussions of merit are about public achievements.

Learning is at the center of our socialization as human beings. Only from other people can we learn about the practices, attitudes, and beliefs transmitted from one generation to another—in brief, about our culture; that was always one goal of formal apprenticeships throughout history. Moreover, there can be expression only when there is both content and skill—something to express and the command to achieve it—Turnbull and Gerard (*An Essay on Taste*, III.ii) made just this point. This is partly because relevant skill is a necessary condition of merit in any field, and knowledge of the inherited traditions is a necessary condition of intelligible and justifiable departure from them. Contrary to the seductive lie trumpeted from the 1770s onwards, a lie that released the ignorant from embarrassment only to condemn them to self-deception, artists cannot afford to be ignorant of other artists' work, because what has gone before *alone* provides the conditions of both understanding and merit. Artists are neither solipsists nor ego-trippers. Nor is everything they make of equal value; in truth, very little of anything made by anyone, was, is, or ever will be of any great merit. But to apprehend *their* achievement requires *us* to use *our* minds—first and last.

In the presence of a possible human artifact, several questions help us decide precisely what it is: who made it, for whom, how, when, why, where, of what? By providing us with perceptual coordinates, answers to such questions help us to place the thing in one or more contexts. Yet meaning and value cannot themselves be sensorily perceived, since neither is worn on the face: their detection requires thought and interpretation. Some philosophers (e.g., Collingwood) claim that focused attention entails contextual detachment; but appropriate verdicts are syntheses of many processes and must not disregard the contexts in which the achievements are embedded. Let us return to Smith's text.

Smith's contribution to the Ramsay-Hume debate is in *TMS* Part V; he takes up Ramsay's precise example and alludes to its source in Claude Perrault (who was also the source of Hume's remarks in *EPM*; Robert Adam subsequently acquired Hume's own 1673 edition of Perrault). The example illustrates how our preferences and critical judgments are embedded in our social lives and can be both understood and justified only by reference to such contexts. Notions of an "impartial spectator" or "disinterested" observer do not usher in the allegedly detached and pure aesthetic judgments normally imputed to Kant; they merely define the conditions for mutual understanding and social cohesion. Smith then states three times that "whatever is in any respect the object of taste" is "entirely under the dominion of custom and fashion" (*TMS*, V.1.4). He cleverly contrasts this view with those rhetoricians who claimed that there were unique forms "naturally expressive of that character, sentiment, or passion, which ought to predominate in it". Indeed, manifest cultural variations between the French and English verse forms were to be largely understood in terms of prevailing, even if longstanding, customs. Artists who are already acknowledged as "eminent" or "masters", can and do "bring about considerable changes in the established modes" of their art, thereby establishing a new "fashionable style"; but it remains the case that the "production" of the arts, as well as our judgments of them, are under the dominion of custom and fashion. Ramsay and Smith are right. Unless spectators take up what seems new to them, little credit will be given to an innovator. When challenging our expectations and in order to extend their range, established artists trade on reputation and familiarity; indeed, they must do so, because we all necessarily encounter the new through the lens of the old. Innovative artists nevertheless still intend to please, to be understood, to be applauded. Smith was writing before the lunacies of Romantic dogma bullied nervous spectators into mute surrender before the self-indulgence of manic solipsists.

Like Hume, Smith was attracted by Buffier's notion that the criteria of beauty are derived from the usual characteristics of a species—or, at least, those with which we have become familiar; black swans and one-humped camels were especially discomfiting to those expecting something else. Smith wonders, nevertheless, whether some sensory stimuli might be naturally, and thus universally, agreeable or disagreeable, although he agrees with Ramsay that custom and fashion can reconcile us to anything. With one exception—Smith's note of panic is evident: those "brought up" amidst the worst depravity do not lose "all sense of impropriety", because that is grounded in the strongest of natural instincts—James Beattie made the same point, and remained close to the views of Ramsay and Smith. Real experience of other cultures, however, and gradually less fearful scrutiny of their own, increasingly dislodged such pieties among 18th-century thinkers.

At the end of his memorable description of the writhing mob, entranced by the slack-rope dancer, Smith concludes: "the emotions of the by-stander always correspond to what, by bringing the case home to himself, he imagines would be the sentiments of the sufferer" (*TMS*, I.i.1.3). Proper sympathy arises "from the situation which excites it", and in theatrical contexts this is not too difficult to achieve. Indeed, in all publicly dedicated spaces, one goal is to secure shared points of view and appropriate behavior—every joker derided spectators who tried to clamber onto the stage to prevent murder in *Othello*. In churches as in arenas, theatres and, for later generations, museums, one has to learn how to behave, and in all of them we must pay attention to the proceedings; our minds must be engaged. After that, similarity of response calls for explanation of the ways in which critical judgment works.

In Smith's fascinating essay on music, probably begun in Paris in the mid sixties, but not completed until 20 years later, two points are of immediate relevance to us. First, "in civilized nations, inferior ranks […] have very little leisure" to "spend much of their time in Music and Dancing"; second, "the human voice, as it is always the best, so it would naturally be the first and earliest of all musical instruments" ("Of the Nature of that Imitation", Part II)—this was a commonplace view, prominently advocated also by Beattie. Both remarks are concerned with agency—that is, with making music, not passive listening. Since the early 1700s there had been lively debate about whether accompanying words were necessary in order for music to have meaning—Addison had famously lampooned the new craze for Italian opera on the grounds that no one could hear or understand the words; in fact, English audiences only *thought* they could hear the words in English, because they had them on paper on their knees. Smith fully concedes that "instrumental music" does "subsist" apart from poetry or dancing, and he eventually canvasses a French view that our emotional responses to such music do not involve sympathy at all. This seemed to follow from the intentionality of sympathy: we are sympathetic with, about or towards something, and this requires us to have at least an idea of what we are attending to. After considering many of the contemporary French views, Smith concludes that instrumental music does require close intellectual attention; but it is to the music itself, not to any mimetic or other relationships between music and something else—Beattie agreed entirely. But this conclusion posed special problems for spectators. Until the mid to late 18th century, people who gathered specifically to listen to music were the very same as those who made it—so that interest in and estimation of *what* was done was closely tied to focus on *how*. Indeed, membership of musical societies throughout Europe required everyone to perform at some regular stages in the year. The so-called "amateur" musician was displaced only by the emergence of supremely skilled professionals who began to tour urban centers to display their skills, much like acrobats. The burgeoning bourgeois classes with both money and leisure to spend it eagerly responded to the pyrotechnics, and composers themselves happily obliged. But there was something else, which modern audiences tend to forget: the composer or his scribe would not try to write the music out in full—it was extremely expensive to print—because every performer was expected to improvise; improvisation defined performance, its nature and its quality. Throughout 17th and 18th centuries, improvisation played a central role in opera and sonata form from Corelli onwards; all the most admired singers, keyboard players and organists were famous for their improvisatory skills—Bach, Handel, Mozart, to name only a few.

The supreme quality of improvisation is propriety—Cicero's *decorum*; he, of course, is the key—and the factor that conditions propriety is context. Improvisation presupposes extensive preparation, a mnemonic repertoire and intense concentration on the present, momentarily extinguishing its temporality—why else is it regarded as central to children's aural education? It is the ultimate art that disguises art.

In "Of the Nature of that Imitation" Smith was keen to supplement Rousseau's discussion of operatic scenery and welcomed Metastasio's reforms of Italian opera, which greatly served "to determine the character, and explain the meaning of the Music". The "sensual pleasure" enjoyed in opera derives from music that "supports the imitation of both the poet and the actor, as well as of the scene-painter". For example, "the overture disposes the mind to the mood which fits it to the opening of the piece"; and "the correctness of the best vocal Music is owing in a great measure to the guidance of instrumental". But in all these cases, "imitation" recedes as a consideration and disappears altogether in "pure" instrumental music. Once he makes this admission, however reluctantly, Smith waxes lyrical about music in ways unfamiliar to most of his readers. He concludes that the "meaning" of truly great music "may be said to be complete in itself, and to require no interpreters to explain it". He insists:

> An object so agreeable, so great, so various, and so interesting, that alone, and without suggesting any other object, either imitation or otherwise, it can occupy, and as it were fill up, completely the whole capacity of the mind, so as to leave no part of its attention vacant for thinking of anything else. In the contemplation of that immense variety of agreeable and melodious sounds, arranged and digested, both in their coincidence and in their succession, into so complete and regular a system, the mind in reality enjoys not only a very great sensual, but a very high intellectual, pleasure, not unlike that which it derives from the contemplation of a great system in any other science. ["Of the Nature of that Imitation"]

Another factor lay behind Smith's discussion of instrumental music. Opera, to literary scholars, seemed an uncomfortably hybrid genre; and yet in some contexts its appeal exceeded that of traditional plays. Indeed, for 50 years at least, between 1730 and 1780, the dominant musical form throughout much of Europe was opera: possibly as many as 10,000 operas were composed during that period. Many composers used the same basic story, and almost all re-worked their most successful tunes into different works: more than 50 composers wrote an opera on Metastasio's *L'Olimpiade* and 80 on his *Artaserse*. Josef Haydn (1732–1809) directed 80 operas by Anfossi (1727–1797) at Esterhazy. Such works were performed in several operatic centers, the influence of which moved ever northwards: Naples, Rome, Venice, Paris, Dresden, Vienna, and Stuttgart. But no core repertory existed, and the modern convention of a classical canon does not contain them. Of the vast output, most can be identified today only by means of fragmentary manuscripts, advertisements, and private or theatrical archives. In brief, they were loved, and lost.

It is sometimes forgotten that the most widely performed *opera buffa* in the whole 18th century was *La buona figliuola*, which arrived in London in 1766. Such was the musical context in which Smith was writing. He was alluding to works unknown to us, performed in ways unfamiliar to us, and in locations quite alien to his own; indeed, he himself had witnessed almost none of them. London was *not* on the list of operatic centres because Italian operas faced financial crisis in the capital throughout the century, and although many works were performed in the six-month seasons, most were composite anthologies of successful tunes (*pasticcios*) for different voices or instruments, sometimes from works by different composers. In other words, Smith learned of the vibrant Italian scene mainly by reading Charles Burney. And in such cases one must ask whether a more extensive experience than he actually enjoyed would have led him to revise any of his claims. We do not know what concerts or operas Smith heard and saw in France and London. But during his London visits in 1782 and 1787, Piccinni was still enjoying success, and works by Paisiello, Traetta, and Sacchini were regularly performed; the repertoire, however, in no respect mirrored London's continental rivals. We do know from Boswell that Smith discussed several aspects of "imitation" with Reynolds in 1782 at The Club in London, and was talking about music in 1783–4.

There are, nevertheless, important features of the works he was writing about that warrant reflection.

Opera buffa, or comic opera, bridged the categories of both "art" and "entertainment": it was immediately accessible because of its topical allusions, and it enjoyably echoed the practices of improvisational comedy. Human foibles typically caricatured included vanity, cowardice, miserliness, hypocrisy—and plain stupidity. The central features of topicality and improvisation mean that the "contexts" in which comic operas were written, revised, performed, and encountered are so integral to "the work" that they must be regarded as elements of it, rather than detachable surroundings for it. For example, although a successful work might receive some 30 productions, no two would be identical: new titles might be given to works, major characters re-named, minor characters added or dropped, cut-and-paste procedures regularly adopted, and arias transposed between voices and registers for entirely practical reasons. Commercial necessity might force a work to be pruned by as much as half after an unsuccessful staging, as happened with Gaetano Latilla's (1711–1788) *La Finta Cameriera*. From its first performance in 1738 this opera was hugely popular, yet the 44 arias it contained at its opening were reduced to only 15 arias after a Paris production in 1752.

Comic opera, as a genre, flourished throughout Europe and evolved quickly because it was unhampered by either theory or tradition. It was typically devised for a local market, runs in Italy were short (a season, with three mandatory works, lasted six weeks), and novelty was its prime attraction to audiences; even keen opera goers would see dozens of operas only once or twice, all of them contemporary works. Obviously, experiences of novelty can never be recaptured, and by the 1750s critics and philosophers worried about the significance and reliability of first impressions; in the domains of the performing arts, and of paintings and buildings which, to a degree, were crucially defined by their precise contexts—for example, church ceremonies—most 18th-century spectators would encounter such works only *once*. In this respect, published literature was entirely different. Certainly, attentive musical audiences were capable of noticing, absorbing, and remembering a great deal more during a single hearing than most of us can today—partly because they were still living within a generally oral culture. Moreover—and this is the key—Italian audiences especially were deeply, if insensibly, grounded in music as a result of attending church since infancy; countless visitors remarked on this between 1700 and 1780. Plots were easy to follow and, in any case, performances took place in fully candlelit theatres; audiences were given not only small books containing the full texts—the *libretto*—but, where necessary, translations.

The overall point to underline is that Italian opera theatres of Smith's day were nothing like ours. They were small, noisy, and during the short season, the center of social life in the community—many people, including everyone's servants, attended without paying. The theatre was a substitute for a parliament or a free press. Always on the move, the world of opera was like a medieval troupe or circus—indeed, it had evolved from them. The chattering audiences, spellbound by excellence as well as by daring, resembled those at an Indian festival witnessing the offerings of sitar players and dancers—commenting, encouraging, applauding, concentrating; Smith's own choice of the slack-rope dancer was perfectly judged. Charles de Brosses, in his famous letters of 1740, remarked that "society assembles at the opera" but "nobody wants to see again a play, a ballet, a setting, or an actor from the previous season, unless it may be some excellent opera by Vinci (1690–1730) or a very famous singer". Above all, however, "music is not seen a second time and is neither printed nor engraved; consequently people remember only the most famous passages" (de Brosses, *Letters*, 20–22).

Opera, however, brought one problem into sharp focus. The increasing complexity of the works that they enjoyed, along with the phenomenal skills demanded by those works, widened the gap between audiences as virtual co-performers, and audiences as merely passive witnesses. This trend, combined with a transition from *social events* where music was *heard*, to *musical occasions* when *listening* was demanded and had to be *learned*, further detached music both from everyday life and from the playing capacities of mere listeners. Indeed, in almost all domains, the Enlightenment, in all its diverse national and cultural forms, typically reduced widespread participation, because expertise was now a requirement. To spectators, discouraged by highly skilled performers, passivity became an attractive option; before long, the stifling 19th-century practices that we all inherited from Germany had annihilated 18th-century ebullience and dare-devil, and fostered attitudes of solemn submission.

Hume's view that because of the inert character of reason a theory never motivated anyone was readily appropriated by Smith, together with another insight. They both realized that the search for intelligibility, which is itself an act of the understanding, inclines us to *project* on to events the influence of the understanding—our own intellectual efforts over-intellectualize our interpretation of other people's actions.

There had always been a challenge to those who had no first-hand experience of what they read about. In the present case, and to predominantly literary audiences, printed commentary about the non-verbal and the performing arts seemed more durable than the works themselves; Kant's friend J. G. Sulzer (1720–1779), who translated Hume for him, made this very point, as did Charles Burney independently, here, in the 1770s:

> To the reputation of a Theorist, indeed, longevity is insured by means of books, which become obsolete more slowly than musical compositions. Tradition only whispers, for a short time, the name and abilities of a mere Performer [...] whereas, a theory once committed to paper and established, lives, at least in libraries, as long as the language in which it was written. [*A General History*, Vol. 1, 705]

The temporal character of wordless music lacked the fixity of painting or literature. Because the new public for painting and music really did lack relevant know-how, commentaries explicitly avoided reference to technical aspects of the works and concentrated on their emotional effects. Such talk about responses *to* the arts was intended to re-direct attention back to the works themselves; but it did the opposite. Criticism and theory became autonomous.

Another issue made matters worse. During much of the 18th century, almost everyone assumed that the arts had meaning because they involved *mimesis* or representation. But, since meaning was itself assumed to be a property only of languages, either music itself would have to *be* a language—which few then wanted to claim—or music could acquire meaning only when *attached* to a genuine language. The preferred solution was to regard music as enhancing the force of linguistic meaning. Smith, as I have mentioned, was still worrying about the possible meaninglessness of wordless music in the 1780s.

It had been a central observation of practicing painters, architects, and composers, from at least the 1650s, that their works could not justifiably be detached from their general context of making, and that critics who lacked first-hand understanding, tended to substitute theory for practice, where no theory in fact existed. This mainly consisted in attributing pretentious intentions to the works, for if they were not pretentious and thus in need of deciphering, what jobs were left to the critics? The Ramsay-Hume-Smith view of the late 1750s identified several important variables in the equation. Gregory, for example, underlined the consequences of allowing contextual detachment to flow from focused attention. He noted that when "music, dancing and poetry" are experienced as constituent parts of complex events and processes, we neither typically, nor justifiably focus on them as isolable elements. If such focus does occur, however, audiences inevitably demand higher standards of performance. Music contributes to social ceremonies in many ways, together with numerous other elements such as food, dress, and decoration; the decorative features are not less significant, but spectators are primarily intended and invited to respond to the whole sequence of events. The examination of often arbitrarily selected elements of the whole may be necessary and rewarding, for a range of purposes—to establish quality of workmanship or appropriateness of inclusion, for example; but, in the domain of *events*, overall responses are directed towards overall results.

If our vision remains clouded by 19th-century Germanic theory and practice, we misread Smith's interest in the spectatorial domain of the moral life as well as his analogies with Italian opera-theatre. This can perhaps be more positively illuminated by returning to an earlier point. The sociability fostered in the discussion clubs was sustained and monitored by conventions mutually agreed upon by their members; the rules of attendance and behavior were enforced, and the defining criterion of membership was *participation*. It was regularly and explicitly insisted that conversation was the cement of society, and that the art of conversation had to be learned and practiced. Indeed, if I may offer my own definition: *conversation was a sacred art in which the duty to listen preceded the right to speak*. The term "sacred" signals that the practice embodied and conveyed the values of society, and therefore requires the fullest attention of which participants were capable. Here is Smith (*TMS*, VII.iv.23): "The great pleasure of conversation and society […] arises from a correspondence of sentiments and opinions, from a certain harmony of minds, which like so many musical instruments coincide and keep time with one another". Once again, his reference to music—all his French sources use the analogy—and his allusions to rhetoric underline my point: the making of music was an essentially *improvisatory* skill, constantly alert to the changing needs of the *context*. No Scots fiddler at the dance, no folksinger, no piper always stuck to the minimal scores available. Similarly, properly educated and engaged conversationalists improvised throughout their performance, which would be centrally colored by all the elements studied in rhetoric, such as breathing and posture, pace and pitch, gesture and tone.

In brief: the moral domain is a theatre of conversations in which the context contributes as much to the performance as the mood, the skills, and the journeys of the audience. *Traduttore traditore*: to translate is to betray. To overlook a context is to misplace it, literally to "trans-late" it from one location to another. Only by the exercise of sympathy in determining the contexts can the character, identity, meaning, and quality of conversations be sensed; only then can the implications and benefits of improvisation be grasped; only then can the propriety of judgment and behavior be assessed.

SELECT BIBLIOGRAPHY

D'Alembert, Jean. *Mélanges de littérature, d'histoire et de philosophie.* Amsterdam: Zacharie Chatelain & Fils, 1770.

Beattie, James. *Essays on Poetry and Music*, 3rd ed. London: E. and C. Dilly, 1779.

De Brosses, Charles. *Letter on Italian Music.* Translated by D. S. Schier. N.p., 1978. Originally published 1799.

Burney, Charles. *A General History of Music from the Earliest Ages to the Present Period.* London: Constable, 1957. (Originally published 1776–1779.)

Chambers, Ephraim. *Cyclopaedia.* London: D. Midwinter, A Bettesworth, C. Hitch, et al., 1738.

Chambers, William. *A Treatise on Civil Architecture.* London: J. Haberkorn, 1759.

Dubos, Jean-Baptiste. *Réflexions critiques sur la poésie et sur la peinture.* Utrecht: E. Neaulme, 1732. First edition 1719.

Gerard, Alexander. *An Essay on Taste.* London: A. Millar, 1759.

Girard, l'Abbé Gabriel. *Synonymes François.* Paris: Veuve d'Houry, 1737.

Gregory, John. *A Comparative View of the State and Faculties of Man.* Dublin: Sleater, Chamberlaine, et al., 1768. (Originally published 1765.)

Hogarth, William. *The Analysis of Beauty.* Edited by Ronald Paulson. New Haven: Yale University Press, 1997. (Originally published 1753.)

Hume, David. *Essays, Moral, Political, and Literary.* Edited by Eugene F. Miller. Indianapolis: Liberty Fund, 1985.

———. "Of the Standard of Taste". In *Four Dissertations.* London: A. Millar, 1757.

Johnson, Samuel. *Resselas*, 1759. (Many editions.)

Perrault, Claude. *Les dix livres d'architecture de Vitruve.* Paris: Jean-Baptiste Coignard, 1673.

Ramsay, Allan. "Dialogue on Taste". *The Investigator* CCCXXII (London, 1762).

———. "Essay on the Naturalization of Foreigners". *The Investigator* CCCXXII (London, 1762).

Smith, Adam. *Correspondence of Adam Smith.* Oxford: Oxford University Press, 1977.

———. *Essays on Philosophical Subjects.* Oxford: Oxford University Press, 1980.

———. *An Inquiry into the Nature and Causes of the Wealth of Nations.* Oxford: Clarendon Press, 1976.

———. *Lectures on Rhetoric and Belles Lettres.* Oxford: Oxford University Press, 1983.

———. "Of the Nature of that Imitation which takes place in what are called The Imitative Arts/Of the Affinity between Music, Dancing, and Poetry". In *Essays on Philosophical Subjects.* Oxford: Oxford University Press, 1980.

———. *The Theory of Moral Sentiments.* 1759. Oxford: Clarendon Press, 1976.

Smollett, Tobias. *Humphry Clinker.* N.p., 1770.

Sulzer, Johann Georg. "Architecture", "Art", "Esquisse", in d'Alembert and Diderot, *Supplément à l'Encyclopédie.* Amsterdam: M. M. Rey, 1776.

Turnbull, George. *A Treatise on Ancient Painting.* London: A. Millar, 1740.

THEORY OF MORAL SENTIMENTS 1759 VS. THEORY OF MORAL SENTIMENTS 1790: A CHANGE OF MIND OR A CHANGE IN CONSTRAINT?

Maria Pia Paganelli[1]

The name of Adam Smith is more often than not associated with *The Wealth of Nations* (*WN*). But his first book was *The Theory of Moral Sentiments* (*TMS*). The place *TMS* holds in the literature on Smith is problematic. When it was first published, *TMS* was a success. Then, for a long time, *TMS* tended to be disregarded as an uninteresting book. But ignoring *TMS* to concentrate on *WN* did not erase *TMS* from the list of Smith's works. Indeed, in recent years, *TMS* has been (re)discovered and its richness is now being (re)appreciated.

Laurence Dickey ("Historicizing the 'Adam Smith Problem' "[2]) is one of many scholars who analyze how the relation between Smith's two books is treated in the literature (see also Montes, *Adam Smith in Context* and Peters-Fransen, "The Canon"). Dickey claims that the Adam Smith Problem", the problem of the consistency or lack of thereof between *WN* and *TMS*, can take at least four forms. In one approach, *TMS* and *WN* are two separate and non-reconcilable entities—this is the Adam Smith Problem traditionally understood (Oncken, "The Consistency of Adam Smith"). In a second approach, *TMS* swallows *WN*, with *WN* being like a long footnote to *TMS*—this is the approach exemplified by A. L. Macfie and D. D. Raphael ("Introduction"). In the third approach, *à la* Viner ("Adam Smith and Laissez Fair"), *WN* and its system of natural liberty is the major focus of Smith's attention, and *TMS* just sits close by, in *WN*'s shadow, as an additional source of support. The fourth approach, the one of Dickey himself, considers "three rather than one or two motivating centers" ("Historicizing", 587); one center is *WN*, the other one is *TMS* 1759 (*TMS* 1st–5th edition), and the third one is *TMS* 1790 (*TMS* 6th edition), the edition finalized after the completion of *WN* and with major changes.

With this paper, I address Dickey's challenge, showing that *WN*, *TMS* 1759, and even *TMS* 1790 are consistent with one another. I do not compare the three books as a whole, or the entirety of their themes, approaches, styles, focuses, etc. Rather, I slice one common issue out of *TMS* 1759, *WN*, and *TMS* 1790 and compare its treatment in the three books. My conclusion is that *TMS* 1759 and *TMS* 1790 are one and the same book, and they are one book that is not in contradiction with *WN*. In their differences they are intertwined,

---

1 This paper was originally published in *Studi e Note di Economia* XVI.2 (2011): 105–114, and it is reproduced with permission.

2 Bibliographic information for all references can be found in the Select Bibliography at the end of this essay.

complemented, and strengthened by one another.

The single common thread I follow is the approbation gained from having material possessions, an issue covered both in *TMS* (1759 and 1790) and in *WN*. By focusing exclusively on the approbation generated by showing off material possession, I propose that *WN* and *TMS* can be read as having a symbiotic relationship in which neither book has dominance over the other, and that *TMS* 1790 is just an updated edition of *TMS* 1759, not a different book. I propose that all four approaches to the problem summarized by Dickey have some validity, but none of them is complete by itself. Similarly to Macfie and Raphael's approach of seeing *WN* as the applied version of *TMS*, I see *TMS* (1759 and 1790) as the "theory" book and *WN* as the "practice" book. But differently from them, I do not see *WN* as a simple application of *TMS* and its consequent lack of autonomy—I think that one feeds off the other. To better understand "practice" we need a "theory", and to have a good "theory", we need a "practice". As proposed by the original formulation of The Adam Smith Problem, one book stands independent from the other but, at the same time, in contrast to that reading, combining the two (or three) makes a better and stronger case, rather than generating an incoherent picture.

If we look at the approbation generated by material possession in the three-center Adam Smith Problem of *TMS* 1759, *TMS* 1790, and *WN* that Dickey presents as well as to the original Adam Smith Problem, we may come to opposite conclusions. In *TMS* 1759, approbation from material possessions seems to generate a moral and prosperous individual and society—in *TMS* 1790, less so. But in *WN*, that same desire for approbation is described as a potentially destabilizing force for individuals and society, not always bringing prosperity or morality. *TMS* 1759, and even *TMS* 1790, seem to present a more favorable account of this form of self-interest than *WN*, which may sound counterintuitive given some of the previous expositions of The Adam Smith Problem.

On the other hand, if *TMS* (1759 and 1790) and *WN* are somehow read together in terms of theory and practice, the contradiction is only apparent, and we can see the same approbation, and the same consequences of it, in all three books. *TMS* describes the general mechanism through which man gains approbation—a combination of moral and material approbation—and in *WN*, the same principle works in a world where the amount of wealth and the involvement of government in the economy change. The constraints that the individual faces in *WN* change, and they are meant to change given the historical narrations of *WN*. But a change in constraints changes the observed behaviors. The individual actions and their consequences are therefore going to be different depending on what constraint the individual faces. In *WN*, indeed, the more prosperous a society is and the more a government grants monopoly powers, the more incentives there are to rely on wealth to receive approbation and the higher is the risk that individual would dismiss moral conduct to achieve that wealth. Actually, it is only in *WN*, when Smith describes societies with increasing commerce, wealth, and government-granted monopolies, that the consequences of the natural desire of approbation generate the potential ruin of some individuals, as well as the socially disastrous mercantilist policies, rather than the betterment of the individual and of his society (Paganelli, "Approbation and the Desire").

The treatment of approbation in one book can stand independently from the exposition of it in the other book. But at the same time, combining them makes a much better and stronger case. If we look at the revisions that Smith makes, rather than seeing The Adam Smith Problem with three centers *à la* Dickey, with the sixth edition of *TMS* being the major source of the Problem, we can see the feedback mechanism often present when theories are put into practice and practices are analyzed through theories. The theory is updated, given some practical results. Updating is not changing. The general idea still holds. But now we are able to account for the "difficult" cases as well as for the general case. Seen in these terms, what may look like contradicting results is in fact conciliated as the two faces of the same coin.

The paper develops as follows. The next section describes the theoretical mechanism through which one can gain approbation as presented in *TMS*. The following section illustrates the practical consequences of acting in a world with "politics, revenue, and arms" as described in *WN*. Concluding remarks end the paper.

APPROBATION IN *THE THEORY OF MORAL SENTIMENTS*

In *The Theory of Moral Sentiments* 1759, Smith explains how approbation works. Approbation comes from two different channels: an appropriate moral conduct and the social status associated with the possession of wealth.

The approbation generated from appropriate moral conduct generally gives us incentives to behave morally as well as, unintentionally, to generate moral rules of conduct that are the embodiment of behaviors that give moral approbation (Muller, *Adam Smith in His Time and Ours*). Rules of appropriate moral conduct come from the habit of "adjusting the pitch of our passions" to the level we think others would show if they were in our place (*TMS*, III.i–iii). We want to "adjust the pitch of our passions" to what we think the expectations of others are, because one approves the presence in others of the same feeling that one has (*TMS*, I.i.2.1 and I.ii).[3]

In addition, the desire to be approved of is also fulfilled by the visible accumulation of wealth. And indeed, the reason why men accumulate wealth is to receive the approbation of others (*TMS*, I.iii.2.1). Wealth is a visible and

---

3   For a recent attempt to formally model it, see Khalil, "Naturalizing the Sacred". For Smith the development of fellow-feelings is an imperfect process, the accuracy of which decreases as social distance increases.

easily distinguishable sign of distinction. The more wealth one has, the more attention he attracts, and the more approbation he gains. Furthermore, the approbation deriving from possessing fortunes is strengthened by the process through which the fortune is accumulated. He who wants to pursue "wealth and greatness" will gain not only the approbation granted to possessors of wealth, but also the admiration and the esteem of the observers when he acts in a morally appropriate way (*TMS*, IV.2.8).

Our desire to be approved therefore can have positive consequences for the individual—individuals can both learn how to be virtuous and moral and can gain material fortune. Under these circumstances, the positive consequences of the desire to gain approbation at the individual level extend to the social level as well. The desire to gain approbation drives man not only to generate rules of moral conduct but also to transform natural challenges into useful things (*TMS*, IV.1.9–10).

TMS 1759 therefore describes how approbation generates positive outcomes both for the individual and for society. Dickey claims that *TMS* 1790 is a different book from *TMS* 1759 because Smith changes his mind, among other things, regarding what approbation from material possession can do. Holding constant the effects of approbation due to moral behaviors, Smith introduces some potential negative effects of our desire for approbation achieved through the accumulation and parade of riches in I.iii.3 and in part VI, all added in the last edition. But even with these considerations, if one reads *TMS* by itself, approbation does not seem to generate major negative material consequences for individual or society, especially when compared to what *WN* portrays.

Smith describes the potential negative consequences of the desire for approbation from wealth accumulation in *TMS* 1790, in a chapter titled "Of the corruption of our moral sentiments, which is occasioned by this disposition to admire the rich and the great and to despise or neglect the persons of poor and mean condition" (I.iii.3). Here Smith notices that the greater admiration for men of fortune may induce individuals to take great moral risks (*TMS*, I.iii.3.8). If the results of the morally questionable actions are positive, they gain the approbation from the higher level of wealth, and their immoral misbehavior will be ignored. Similarly, in Part VI of *TMS* we find that reproachable behaviors generate great admiration when the resulting gains are great, while they generate contempt if the gains are "petty" (*TMS*, VI.i.16.217). What Smith is telling us, then, is that we are willing to gamble moral approbation for wealth approbation. We are willing to give up moral approbation if we think that we can gain a lot of material approbation. The higher the gain in material approbation, the more we will be willing to risk in terms of moral approbation.

This is not surprising given that material possessions are easier to recognize, and therefore approve, than moral (mis)behaviors (*TMS*, I.iii.3.4). Thus, given the high recognizability of wealth and the difficulties with which virtue is distinguished from morally questionable behaviors, we tend to rely more on wealth than on morality when we give approbation to others (*TMS*, VI.ii.1.20). Similarly, we rely more on wealth than on morality when we seek approbation from others. The frequency of moral gambles is even less surprising when one considers that in *WN* Smith claims that people systematically overestimate their probability of success and underestimate their probability of failure. Gambling morality does not seem too different from gambling fortunes through a lottery or (lack of) insurance (*WN*, I.x.b).[4]

A couple of considerations are relevant here. First, despite the possible disillusion at the end of one's life, the anxiety, and the infamy of a dirty conscience of an individual (*TMS*, I.iii.3.8), the consequences of trading off moral approbation for material gains at the social level do not appear to be devastating.[5] Second, the ease with which one is willing to give up moral approbation for material approbation depends on the amount of material gains one makes. The larger the material gain, the more likely one is willing to behave in morally disapprovable ways.

If one stops here, two contradictions emerge, like the ones Dickey points to. First, Smith changed his mind from *TMS* 1759 to *TMS* 1790, because now approbation from moral possession has high costs, not just high benefits. Second, despite these differences within the various editions of *TMS*, the consequences of gaining approbation through the accumulation of wealth remain generally positive. The disruptive consequences of gambling morality for material wealth remain on a private and moral level. The end result is still, generally, a betterment of an individual's material condition as well as of his society. This, however, is not always the case in *WN*, where pursuing approbation through material possessions has more ambiguous consequences, being dependent on how rich society is. In *WN* Smith is frazzled about how disruptive the consequence of pursuing material approbation can be, if a society is rich. But he is not, if the society is not rich.

What I propose here is that these differences are not due to a different perspective or a different motivation at the base of human behavior. They are simply due to the development of an awareness of differences in the constraints that individuals face. *WN* introduces differences in the environment in which an individual operates. The mechanisms are the same, but the outcomes are different if we are in a poor society or in a rich society, as the incentives in these different environments vary. *TMS* 1790 accounts for the possibilities of differences in the constraints within the same model, differences that were overlooked in *TMS* 1759.

Let us see how Smith explains how approbation works in the real

---

4 For an analysis of the consequences of overestimation of the probability of success in the loanable funds market in Smith see Paganelli, "In Medio Stat Virtus".

5 Even factions, where local moral approbation is favored over the general good, do not seem to be a serious or permanent threat (*TMS*, VI.ii.2.13–14, VI.iii.12.19–20).

world, in a world with "police, revenue, and arms", as described in WN.

APPROBATION IN *THE WEALTH OF NATIONS*

The Wealth of Nations is well known, correctly, for the idea that pursuing one's interest to better oneself would generate not only individual prosperity, but also social prosperity. There is no need to restate this argument here. Yet, contrary to what is often presumed, WN does not always match the depicted picture or the optimism present in TMS. In WN, the people "whom heaven in its anger has visited with ambition" are not always gaining social status and benefiting society. Smith, in WN, talks about unambiguously ruinous consequences both for individuals and for society when the desire for approbation meets the enormous commercial fortunes. WN indeed describes how consequences of our desire for approbation may potentially become increasingly negative as society becomes richer. When a society is poor, there is not much to show off and not much to gain with questionable behaviors. But the wealth of a rich society generates perverse incentives that may lead to the ruin of the individual or of society itself. If read in isolation, the analysis for approbation in WN is sound, yet dark (Paganelli, "The Adam Smith Problem").

WN has a first explanation of how we are willing to gamble away morally approvable behaviors to gain material fortune in its account of wage determination in Book 1, Chapter 10. David Levy ("Adam Smith's Katallatic Model of Gambling") highlights how large changes in money are able to change one person's rank and the social approbation that comes with it. People are therefore willing to take large risks, such as attempting to succeed in some very competitive professions, to try to improve their material status.

The trading off of moral approbation for material application under different constraints is explicit in WN, II.iii.38–42. Here Smith describes how every man suffers from a "base and selfish disposition". When the wealth and the riches of commerce and manufactures are introduced, they bring along durable goods, such as "frivolous trinkets". Spending on durable goods is more directed toward oneself than toward others. The "selfish disposition" in us is unleashed with morally questionably behaviors. Indeed "where he can spend the greatest revenue upon his own person, he frequently has no bound to his expense, because he frequently has no bounds to his vanity, or to his affection for his own person" (WN, III.iv.16). This "base and selfish disposition" is present even in poor non-commercial societies. But because there is very little on which to gratify one's "most childish vanity", the temptations of human "folly" are less and weaker. Indeed when a man can spend his fortune only on consumption goods, such as sumptuous meals and numerous servants, his "selfish disposition" is well constrained. When spending one's fortune implies spending on others as well as on oneself, as consumption goods usually imply, only very few people will go bankrupt. This is the case in "nations to whom commerce and manufactures are little known" (WN, III.iv.5). Indeed, Smith repeats, in non-commercial societies "seldom [one has temptations] so violent as to attempt to maintain more than he can afford" (*WN*, III.iv.16).

The increase of wealth, changing the constraints, increases the incentives for reckless behavior. The glitter of wealth blinds prudence. The negative consequences will also be more severe. With the introduction of commercial wealth, indeed, individual ruin becomes more common, as individual behavior becomes less prudent. Proprietors are willing to sell their birthrights in exchange "for a pair of diamond buckles [...] for the gratification of the most childish, the meanest and the most sordid of all vanities, they gradually bartered their whole power and authority" (*WN*, III.iv.10–15). They think that they would gain approbation by showing off their unique trinkets, even if they lose moral approbation because of their sordid, childish, and vain behaviors. They think they are "bettering their condition" by buying "trinkets and baubles". In reality, by so doing, they are bound to become poor. True, this drive for approbation is the cause of the dismantling of feudal institutions—which is a good thing for society (Rosenberg, "Adam Smith, Consumer Tastes, and Economic Growth", and Rosenberg, "Adam Smith and the Stock of Moral Capital"). But the "folly" and the gratification of "the most childish vanity" tear away the stability of land property and generations of family riches, and bring individuals and their families to ruin (*WN*, III.iv.16–17).

When the sovereign faces the same change in constraints, differences in behavior are parallel. The consequences, though, are felt not just at the individual level but at the societal level as well. Smith explains:

> The ignorance of the times [among nations to whom commerce and manufactures are little known] affords but few of the trinkets in which that finery consists [...]. In a commercial country abounding with every sort of expensive luxury, the sovereign, in the same manner as almost all the great proprietors in his dominions, naturally spends a great part of his revenue in purchasing those luxuries. His own and the neighbouring countries supply him abundantly with all the costly trinkets which compose the splendid, but insignificant pageantry of a court. [*WN*, V.iii.2–3]

And since the sovereign will spend his revenue on futile things when there is peace, when war comes, he will go into debt. Unfortunately, "[t]he progress of the enormous debts which at present oppress, and will in the long run probably ruin, all the great nations of Europe, has been pretty uniform" (*WN*, V.iii.10). Even if Smith is not very preoccupied by it, the ruin of a country is a possible threat of commercial society caused by the possibilities that commerce itself offers.

The change in constraints that commercial society brings about is also felt at the policy level. Merchants and manufacturers, in their desire to improve their image in the eyes of others, now have opportunities to do so in a grand manner. The wealth generated by commerce is unprecedented and can be concentrated in their hands, if only the government grants them monopolies. Merchants and manufacturers are willing to take the moral tradeoff—to increase their fortune and status at the expense of the rest of society; they are willing to elbow their way over their competitors, even if these are reproachable behaviors, because with monopoly power, they will gain much wealth and approbation. The increase in personal wealth brings an increase in social approbation sufficient to outweigh any possible disapprobation for the methods used to achieve it. In *WN*, given the perverse incentives that large commercial wealth can create, the social consequences of our desire for approbation can be devastating (Evensky, *Adam Smith's Moral Philosophy*). Mercantilist policies deform, distort, and impoverish society (*WN*, IV.viii.c.43; I.xi; IV.i.10; IV.ii.38; IV.iii.c.9–10). Merchants and manufacturers are able to extort ferocious laws from the legislature (*WN*, IV.viii.17; IV.ii.43; IV.viii.53).

The wealth of commercial societies changes the constraints that individuals face. When the possibilities to gain approbation from wealth are large enough, they may incentivize more morally questionable actions and generate potentially disastrous consequences. It is after this realization that *TMS* 1790 is changed. Behaviors and their consequences differ under different levels of wealth. This change in constraints has to be accounted for in the theoretical description of approbation. The model remains the same. It is just updated, given a case not previously considered, to account for all the circumstances.

CONCLUSIONS

Focusing on a single common issue among *TMS* 1759, *TMS* 1790, and *WN* may help us better understand the relationship between the books and the different editions of *TMS*. Looking at approbation deriving from material possession suggests that *TMS* (1759 and 1790) and *WN* are two distinct books, each standing alone on its own feet, yet feeding off the other. *TMS* can be interpreted as the "theory" book—the book containing the positive description of the mechanism through which approbation works—and *WN* as the "practice" book—the book that looks at how man lives in a world with "police, revenue, and arms", where the level of wealth changes through time, and where the government is a concrete player of tangible force.

The same desire to gain the approbation of others motivates the man of *TMS* 1759, the man of *WN*, and the man of *TMS* 1790. But while in *TMS* 1759 the desire of approbation does generally make the individual and society better off, in *WN* this result is questioned, and the desire to gain approbation is described as potentially generating individual and social disruption. This is not because the two books are inconsistent with each other, but rather because one book has individuals facing the different and changing constraints of a world of "police, revenue, and arms" and the other one, describing a theoretical model, does not. The additions in *TMS* 1790 can be interpreted as a simple update of the previous description of approbation, rather than a change of mind. The man of *WN* is the same as the man of the various editions of *TMS*. The mechanisms through which he gains approbation are the same in *TMS* 1759 and in *WN*, *TMS* 1790 presenting a more complete account of it than *TMS* 1759. The differences appear as a synergic point when the two books in their various editions are read together. Reading *TMS* and *WN* together allows one to interpret Smith as explaining that approbation derives both from appropriate moral conduct and from wealth, but that enough wealth can trump moral conduct in achieving approbations and can generate social malfunctions. The strength of the incentives in poor pre-commercial societies is different from the strength of the incentives in rich commercial societies and as a consequence behaviors and consequences will differ. The apparent contrast between the two editions of *TMS* can therefore be interpreted as only apparent.

SELECT BIBLIOGRAPHY

Dickey, Laurence. "Historicizing the 'Adam Smith Problem'": Conceptual, Historiographical, and Textual Issues". *The Journal of Modern Issues* 58, no.3 (1986): 579–609.

Evensky, Jerry. *Adam Smith's Moral Philosophy*. Cambridge: Cambridge University Press, 2005.

Khalil, Elias L. "Naturalizing the Sacred". Summer Institute for the Preservation of the Study of the History of Economics, George Mason University, Fairfax, VA, May 30–June 3, 2005.

Levy, David. "Adam Smith's Katallatic Model of Gambling: Approbation from the Spectator". *Journal of the History of Economic Thought* 21 (1999): 81–91.

Macfie, A. L., and D. D. Raphael. "Introduction" to Adam Smith, *The Theory of Moral Sentiments*. Edited by D.D. Raphael and A.L. Macfie. Indianapolis: Liberty Fund, 1984.

Montes, Leonidas. *Adam Smith in Context: A Critical Reassessment of Some Central Components of His Thought*. New York: Palgrave Macmillan, 2004.

Muller, Jerry Z. *Adam Smith in His Time and Ours*. Princeton: Princeton University Press, 1995.

Oncken, August. "The Consistency of Adam Smith". *Economic Journal* 7 (1897): 443–50.

Paganelli, Maria Pia. "The Adam Smith Problem in Reverse: Self-Interest in Adam Smith's Wealth of Nations and Theory of Moral Sentiments". *History of Political Economy* 40, no. 2 (2008): 365–382.

———. "Approbation and the Desire to Better One's Condition in Adam Smith: When the Desire to Better One's Conditions Does not Better One's Condition and Society's Condition…". *Journal of the History of Economic Thought* 31, no.1 (2009): 79–92.

———. "In Medio Stat Virtus: An Alternative View of Usury Law in Adam Smith's Thinking". *History of Political Economy* 35, no.1 (2003): 21–48.

Peters-Fransen, Ingrid. "The Canon in the History of the Adam Smith Problem". In *Reflections on the Classical Canon in Economics*, edited by Evelyn L. Forget and Sandra Peart. London: Routledge, 2000.

Rosenberg, Nathan. "Adam Smith, Consumer Tastes, and Economic Growth". *The Journal of Political Economy* 76, no.3 (1968): 361–374.

———. "Adam Smith and the Stock of Moral Capital". *History of Political Economy* 22, no.1 (1990): 1–17.

Smith, Adam. *An Inquiry into the Nature and Causes of the Wealth of Nations*. Edited by R. H. Campbell and A. A. Skinner. Indianapolis: Liberty Fund, 1981.

———. *The Theory of Moral Sentiments*. Edited by D. D. Raphael and A. L. Macfie. Indianapolis: Liberty Fund, 1984.

Viner, Jacob. "Adam Smith and Laissez Fair". *Journal of Political Economy*. 35, no.2 (1927): 196–232.

THE "ADAM SMITH PROBLEM" AND ADAM SMITH'S UTOPIA[1]

Doğan Göçmen

For Michael Freudenberg

I. INTRODUCTION

The Adam Smith Problem concerns the relationship between Smith's two major works, *The Theory of Moral Sentiments* (*TMS*) and *An Inquiry into the Nature and Causes of the Wealth of Nations* (*WN*).[2] Two passages in particular, one in *TMS* and the other in *WN*, triggered off the whole debate some 150 years ago. In *TMS*, Smith asserts:

> How selfish soever man may be supposed, there are evidently some principles in his nature, which interest him in the fortune of others, and render their happiness necessary to him, though he derives nothing from it except the pleasure of seeing it. [*TMS*, I.i.1]

Yet in *WN* he observes:

> It is not from the benevolence of the butcher, the brewer, or the baker, that we expect our dinner, but from their regard to their interest. We address ourselves, not to their humanity but to their self-love, and never talk to them of our own necessities but of their advantages. [*WN*, I.ii.2]

In these two statements Smith makes two fundamentally different claims about human nature. In the quotation from *TMS*, Smith suggests that in human nature there are some original principles that make us interested in the happiness of our fellow creatures. If our fellow creatures are unhappy, we feel sorrow and want to help them to overcome their unhappiness. If they are happy, we enjoy their happiness without expecting anything except seeing their happiness. By contrast, in the passage from *WN*, Smith describes human beings

---

1 This essay draws upon my PhD dissertation (*Adam Smith's Utopia: Society as an Open and Progressive System of Mutial Sympathy*), which I presented to the College of Humanities and Social Sciences at the University of Edinburgh in 2005.

2 Bibliographic information for all references can be found in the Select Bibliography at the end of this essay.

merely as self-interested or egocentric beings. It is not the pleasure of seeing others' happiness that primarily motivates them but pure self-interest. The conception Smith relies on here is a conception of pure utilitarian *self-interest* or *self-love*. Accordingly, we have to expect our dinner from the butcher, brewer, or baker not from their benevolence or humanity, but solely from their regard to their own self-interest.

It is this seeming paradox in Smith's anthropological and in effect social theoretical accounts that gave rise to the whole debate about the "Adam Smith Problem".[3] The main question in this debate is whether Smith's work contains two fundamentally different conceptions of human nature. If it does, how should this contradiction be explained?

In this paper I make two fundamental claims. *First*, unlike many scholars, I claim that Smith has one conception of human nature. But I suggest that his conception has two complementary aspects—a general and a particular. The aspect of human nature he develops in *TMS* I take for his general conception, and the one in *WN* I regard as his particular conception of human nature in the age of commercial society. *Second*, I claim that all attempts to explain the contradiction between these two aspects of Smith's conceptions of human nature have failed because they approached it merely as a conceptual problem of Smith's.[4] Unlike these scholars, I suggest that this is a historical-practical problem arising from social relations in commercial society. Moreover, I suggest that Smith is very well aware of this problem and that he develops a solution to it. In this paper, I endeavor, therefore, to show Smith's own solution to the Adam Smith Problem. To do this, I will *first* reconstruct the problem by working out Smith's theory of social individuality in *TMS*. I move on then, *secondly*, to explore Smith's account of the situation of the individual in commercial society as is given in *WN*. And *finally*, I shall refer to Smith's utopia of a sympathetic society as his projected solution to the problem.

II. SMITH'S THEORY OF SOCIAL INDIVIDUALITY IN
THE THEORY OF MORAL SENTIMENTS

1. Where to Begin?

To show that Smith's anthropological view is not an individualistic one, many scholars begin their analyses with the first paragraph of *TMS*, which is a general conclusive statement. At first sight, its objective methodological and analytical background is not obvious. To bring this to the fore, I suggest, unlike

---

3   For an account of the history of the Adam Smith Problem, compare Neili, "Spheres of Intimacy and The Adam Smith Problem", 611–616, and Raphael and Macfie, "Introduction", 20–21.

4   I have discussed different approaches at some length in my book *The Adam Smith Problem*.

many scholars, we begin our analysis with Smith's only explicit mirror passage in *TMS*, III.1.3. This approach is consistent with Smith's overall work and is in fact suggested by Smith himself. When he asserts, for example, in the first paragraph of *TMS*: "[t]hat we often derive sorrow from the sorrow of others" (*TMS*, I.i.1.1), he explores a mirror theory. His assertion that we derive sorrows from one another's sorrows implies a mirror theoretical approach as there is a mutual mirroring process. The sorrow we observe in others calls forth a similar feeling in us, and vice versa: the sorrow others observe in us gives rise to a similar feeling in others. This is an ontological necessity. What I am suggesting, therefore, is merely putting a principle at the beginning of our exploration, which works as an organizing principle implicitly throughout *TMS* until we come to his explicit mirror paragraph. In doing so we may be able to show why Smith thinks that human beings cannot be anything other than social individuals.

2. Smith's Mirror Theoretical Approach to the Constitution of the Self

I would like to work out theory of social individuality under the heading of the constitution of the self, because Smith himself discussed this issue explicitly under the heading of "the constitution of human nature" (*TMS*, III.3.29).

To find out what kind of a theory of the constitution of the self Smith explores in *TMS*, in European philosophy we may need to differentiate methodologically between two grand traditions. We may call them, in agreement with Lacan, theories that derive from Descartes's *Cogito*-principle and theories that originate in *Mirror*-principle.[5] The theorists relying on the *Cogito*-principle begin to develop their theories of the self with the self that is usually called the *I*. By contrast, the theorists starting from *Mirror*-principle start to develop their theories with the constitution of the other self.

This can best be seen in the subtitle of the sixth edition of *TMS*, which runs as follows: "THE THEORY OF MORAL SENTIMENTS; OR, An ESSAY towards an Analysis of the Principles by which Men *naturally* judge concerning the Conduct and Character. *First of their Neighbours, and afterwards of themselves*" (italics mine). This statement aims at an essential critique of Cartesian tradition, and Smith obviously thinks that in any situation of communicative action human beings necessarily first judge others before they can come to judge themselves.

Smith's mirror theoretical approach may become clearer when we turn to his mirror passage. In his mirror passage (criticizing the *Cogito*-principle) Smith asks rhetorically,

> [w]ere it possible that a human creature could grow up to manhood in some solitary place, without any communication with his own *species*, he could no more think of his own

---

5   Lacan, "The Mirror Stage", 1–8.

character, of the propriety or demerit of his own sentiments and conduct, or of beauty or deformity of his own mind, than of the beauty or deformity of his face. All these are objects which he cannot easily *see, which naturally he does not look at*, and with regard to which he is provided with no *mirror* which can present them to his view. Bring him into society, and he is immediately provided with the *mirror* which he wanted before. It is placed in the countenance and behaviour of those he lives with, which always mark when they enter into, and when they disapprove of his sentiments; and it is here that he first views the propriety and impropriety of his own passions themselves, the desires or aversions, the joys or sorrows, which those objects excited, though of all things the most immediately present to him, could scarce ever be the objects of his thoughts. [*TMS*, III.1.3; italics mine]

What does Smith say in this passage?

First of all, Smith defines human beings as mirrors of one another, which reveals also his inter-subjective approach. As opposed to the *Cogito*-principle, Smith suggests that without the mirror of the other selves, the self would be lacking any instance by means of which he/she can judge his/her character, sentiments, or aesthetic and moral values. It is only through the mirror of others that the self can look at these aspects of his/her character and define him/herself.

Second, the self does not produce from within values by means of which he/she defines him/herself in relation to others as the *Cogito*-principle implies but he/she gains them from without, that is, from others. By means of their criticism, others provide the self with a mirror. Thus the self becomes aware of whether his/her values, passions, projects, and actions are appropriate. Therefore, "[o]ur *first ideas* of personal beauty and deformity are drawn from the shape and appearance of others, not from our own" (*TMS*, III.1.4; italics mine).

Third, according to Smith's mirror theoretical approach, it is only by means of others that the self becomes self-reflexive and self-critical, and consequently possesses a kind of self-corrective capacity. So, it is by means of others that he first views the propriety and impropriety of his own passions themselves, the desires or aversions, the joys or sorrows, which those objects excited, though of all things the most immediately present to him, could scarce ever be the objects of his thoughts. The idea of them could never interest him so much as to call upon his attentive consideration (*TMS*, III.1.3).

Fourth, others not only provide us with a mirror that makes us self-critical, that looks at our passions, thought, and actions critically and draws from this our values, but it is also by means of others only that there arise in us new passions, projects, and aims. It is only by means of the mirrors of others, that is, by means of their critical assessments, that we move forward in our lives and produce new pieces of art, create new ideas, and write new books or pursue whatever else is the object of our lives. Therefore, without others, no one can become self-critical and create in him/herself new energy to move forward in his/her life and improve his/her bodily and intellectual capacities. Therefore, without others the "consideration of his joy could excite in him no new joy, nor that of his sorrow […]. Bring him into society, and all his own passions will immediately become the causes of new passions" (*TMS*, III.1.3).

3. Smith's Theory of Mutual Constitution of the Selves

Let us now illustrate how this mutual mirroring process takes place. In all situations of communicative action, we are always spectators and agents in an ongoing open process. In this process, we constantly change our roles as spectators and agents—at one minute we may be spectators and at the next agents. If we are spectators, we judge the agent, and if we are agents we are judged by others. Smith describes this process of mutual understanding and judgment as a process of mutual constitution. Smith makes use of three concepts to explain the process of mutual constitution.

First, according to Smith's theory of the constitution of the self, the self is always embedded into a situation. Smith's conception of situation comprises the whole process of the socialization of individuals. It has three components. In one's social relations every person is always embedded in a general, concrete, and actual situation. The first and second comprise the totality of objective and subjective conditions of experience and action in space and time; they refer to natural, social, and material conditions; social rank and class; socialization in its most general sense, including education; and thereby durably form a person's internal world, that is, their emotional and intellectual capacities. They actualize themselves in any new situation of action in the form of value judgment; differing from the first, the second gives to these durable emotional and intellectual dispositions a particular turn and brings them into play according to the immediate situation in which the agent (or "person principally concerned" as Smith would put it) is in this actual moment of consideration and action embedded. Based on their durable emotional and intellectual dispositions, everybody acts according to his/her actual situation and aims at the satisfaction of his/her bodily and/or intellectual passions or needs.

Second, Smith regards the situation of the self as the genesis of what he calls the "impartial spectator" within, or conscience; in other words, it is the product of all social relationships. It is the critical mirror of the situation of the self. Smith does not deal with conscience merely as an ethical capacity. Rather, he employs a broad conception of conscience, which also involves the theory of cognition, knowledge, judgment, and decision. It is an internal cognitive, judging, and deciding capacity that leads to actions. It critically collects, unifies, and synthesizes all general social values involved in the process of socialization of human beings. Conscience, therefore, critically mirrors in each individual from his/her particular perspective the common sense that prevails in a given society.

Third, sympathetic sentiments depend on how conscience is formed according to external circumstances. He seems to define sympathy, on the one hand, in a particular sense as a passion. In this sense, sympathy is a social need, namely we want to be able to sympathize with others and we want others to be able to sympathize with us. In this sense of mutual need, sympathy embraces all original passions of human nature. On the other hand, he seems to use it in a more general sense as a cognitive and epistemological capacity. Let us now apply these concepts to Smith's theory of the constitution of the self.

3.1. How do we constitute others?

Smith's theory of the constitution of the self faces a huge challenge. It concerns the question of the authenticity of mutual mirroring between the agent and the spectator. In a situation of communicative action, the mutual mirroring process may involve discrepancy and consequently conflicts between the agent's self-image and his/her mirrored image in the spectator. There may sometimes be distortions involved in the situation of communicative action. Therefore, the process of mutual mirroring may not work or may work in a distorted way.

To meet this challenge, Smith suggests that we have to gain mutual objectively valid cognition and understanding of the passions. To do this we must trace passions back to their objective sources—to the external situation or circumstances of the agent, because the inner world is the mirror of the external situation. Smith formulates this more explicitly in the context of his theory of character (*TMS*, V.2.7). "Sympathy, therefore", says Smith, "does not arise so much from the view of the passions, as from that of the situation which excites it" (*TMS*, I.i.1.10). Once the passions are traced back to their external sources the conflict between self-image and reflected image may be resolved in one way or another.

But how do we do that? If we understand and judge others on some kind of reliable objective foundation, we trace passions back to the situation of the agent. Therefore, to understand or to constitute others we must place ourselves by means of imagination in their situation and bring their cases "home to ourselves" (*TMS*, V.2.5) and view the world from their point of view. Only after having endeavored as much as we can to put ourselves in the situation of others, after having brought home to ourselves "every little circumstance" they are placed in, after having adopted their whole case "with all its minutest incidents" (*TMS*, I.i.4.6), can we begin to feel almost the same feelings, sentiments, emotions, passions, to think almost the same thoughts and to have almost the same projects as correspond to the situation of the agent. This is the only way, according to Smith, in which we can become undistorted mirrors of one another.

Smith subsumes this process of putting on the "looking-glass" of the agent, under his term of "sympathy" or "fellow-feeling". If we place ourselves in fancy into the situation of the agent, if we become in some measure the same person and endeavor "to regard it with his present reason and judgment" (*TMS*, I.i.1.11), there arises the correspondence of others' internal worlds with our own (*TMS*, I.i.2.2). That is to say that there arises between the spectator and the agent those "sympathetic sentiment[s]" (*TMS*, I.i.4.7), "sympathetic emotions" (*TMS*, I.i.3.1), and "sympathetic passions" (*TMS*, I.ii.5.3). After having gained this correspondence, we can begin to constitute, that is, to cognize, understand, and make judgments about others.

3.2. How do we constitute ourselves in the mirror of others?

Smith thinks that the same principle also applies to the question of how we constitute ourselves in the mirror of others (*TMS*, III.1.2). We methodologically cognize and understand and judge ourselves in exactly the same way as we cognize and understand and judge others.

When we cognize, understand, and judge ourselves in relation to others, our look is directed towards ourselves. When we cognize and understand others in relation to ourselves we place ourselves by means of imagination in their situation and make judgments about their passions and actions from their objective perspective. When we cognize and understand ourselves in relation to others, however, we place ourselves into the situation of other selves and thereby gain a kind of distance from ourselves; we "put" ourselves before ourselves and judge our motives and passions from their point of view, that is, from a distance to ourselves.

> We can never survey our own sentiments and motives, we can never form any judgment concerning them; unless we remove ourselves, from our own natural station, and endeavour to view them as at a certain distance from us. [*TMS*, III.1.2]

> We begin, upon this account [of an actual inter-subjective situation of communicative action] to examine our own passions and conduct, and to consider how these must appear to them, by considering how they would appear to us if in their situation. [*TMS*, III.1.5]

But how do we do this if there is not an actual other person present?

We suppose ourselves the spectators of our own behaviour,

and endeavour to imagine what effect it would, in this light, produce upon us. This is the only looking-glass by which we can, in some measure, with the eyes of other people, scrutinize the propriety of our own conduct. [*TMS*, III.1.5]

But how can we suppose ourselves the spectators of our own behavior? Smith gives the following answer to this question:

> When I endeavour to examine my own conduct, when I endeavour to pass sentence upon it, either to approve or condemn it, it is evident that, in all such cases, I divide myself, as it were, into *two persons*; and *that I*, the examiner and judge, represent a different character from that *other I*, the person whose conduct is examined into and judged of. The first is the spectator, whose sentiments with regard to my own conduct I endeavour to enter into, by placing myself in his situation, and by considering how it would appear to me, when seen from that particular point of view. The second is the agent, the person whom I properly call myself, and of whose conduct, under the character of a spectator, I was endeavouring to form some opinion. The first is the judge; the second the person judged of. [*TMS*, III.1.6; italics mine]

This is the only device by means of which we can constitute, that is, "approve" and "disapprove" of ourselves in relation to others. It is because of these analytical considerations about the mutual mirroring process that Smith comes to his statement in the first paragraph of *TMS* and suggests that

> How selfish soever man may be supposed, there are evidently some principles in his nature, which interest him in the fortune of others, and render their happiness necessary to him, though he derives nothing from it except the pleasure of seeing it. [*TMS*, I.i.1.1]

For if others are our mirrors who enable us to have a self-image, we must aim necessarily and consciously at their happiness, because their happiness is also our happiness.

But this whole system of mutual constitution can work only if the situational differences do not admit alienation between the agent and the spectator. They must have similar interests and they must be able, despite the situational differences, to produce corresponding or similar sympathetic sentiments in relation to one another and consequently there must be mutual respect. To meet all these criteria they must be able, without any regard to loss and gain, "to examine" their "own conduct as [...] any other fair and *impartial spectator* would examine it" (*TMS*, III.1.2; italics mine). In short, everybody must be able to listen to his/her second self or conscience; otherwise, Smith's principle of *seeing oneself as others would or are likely to see one* would not work.

III. SMITH'S ACCOUNT OF THE SITUATION OF THE SELF IN THE AGE OF COMMERCIAL SOCIETY AS MIRRORED IN *THE WEALTH OF NATIONS*

Smith draws his theory of social individuality in *TMS* on the basis of his observations about non-commercial social relations. To reconstruct the other side of the Adam Smith Problem let us turn to Smith's account of the situation of the self in commercial society as accounted for in *WN*.

1. How to Approach The Wealth of Nations

The approach to *WN* that I am going to suggest differs from most other interpretations. Two important methodological principles may be of great help in approaching *WN*. The *first* one is Smith's explicit use of critical Common-Sense realism as a methodological principle, which means that the subject under examination must be analyzed and presented critically as it really *is*. The *second* one was formulated again by Smith more or less explicitly by utilizing the categories of "essence" and "appearance" throughout his work. These two categories are fundamental to Smith's scientific concerns not only in *WN*. I take Smith's category of appearance as referring to market relations, that is, to the relation between buyers and sellers, and his category of essence I take as referring to social relations in the sphere of production in commercial society. Taken together, these two methodological principles mean that we must explore his examination of the constitution of the self in commercial society in the sphere of production as well as in that of market relations.

2. Smith's Account of the Situation of Individuals in Commercial Society
2.1. Smith's account of the situation of the self in market relations

In his account of market relations, Smith identifies a causal relationship between the division of labor and the genesis of market society. The division of labor not only gives rise to "a proportional increase of the productive powers of labour" but at the same time it brings about the "separation of different trades and employments from one another" (*WN*, I.i.4). It is this separation of trades and employments that give rise to commercial exchange relations and "[e]very man thus lives by exchanging, or becomes in some measure a *merchant* and the society itself grows to be what is properly called a commercial society" (*WN*, I.iv.1). Though the division of labor gives rise to market relations, they, in turn, set limits to the division of labor. There is a causal relationship between the division of labor and the extension and the depth of market relations.

Smith deals with commercial exchange-relations as *power relations*. He uses this term sometimes in a neutral way in the sense of potentiality to buy and sell commodities. But he uses it also in the sense of domination. He asserts, for example, that "it is the *power of exchanging* that gives occasion to the division of labour, so the extent of this division must always be limited by the extent of that *power*, or, in other words, by the extent of the market" (*WN*, I.iii.1; italics mine). Therefore, unlike many contemporary scholars' fascination with market relations, he introduces his analysis of commercial exchange-relations with the assertion that "EVERY man is rich or poor according to the degree in which he can afford to enjoy the necessaries, conveniences, and amusements of human life" (*WN*, I.v.1).

Smith identifies commercial exchange-relations as power relations because he thinks that when the market comes to serve as the basis of all fundamental social relations, it expresses a kind of social inequality that turns all forms of equality and difference into relations of mutual domination. He seems to suggest that commercial society exhibits already at its very "surface", that is, in commercial exchange-relations, those inequalities that arise from social class relations originating in the sphere of production.

The division of labor gives rise to the "separation of different trades and employments from one another". This has at least three implications. *First*, with this separation there also arise private property-relations; *second*, due to this and to the rise of private property-relations, there also arises a kind of economic *isolation* of individuals from one another and as a result each individual works solely for him/herself; *third*, because of all these reasons there also emerge commercial exchange-relations, which are nothing but quantitative power-relations. In short, in commercial society everybody is economically separated and isolated from one another, and the number of commodities that each individual potentially and actually possesses determines his power position in relation to others. If one possesses a large amount, he commands a large number of commodities, and if one possesses a small amount, he/she commands a small number of commodities. At worst, if one possesses nothing, he/she commands nothing and, therefore, counts *absolutely* as nothing in the views of others. It is this mutual command-relation (or relations of mutual domination) in commercial exchange relations that Smith calls the "power of exchanging".

It is because of this analysis that Smith comes to his assertion in the butcher-baker passage. By any offer like "[g]ive me that which I want, and you shall have this which you want" we mean that it is above all in your own interest if you accept our offer (*WN*, I.ii.2). By any such offer we appeal to each other's self-love or self-interest rather than to each other's conscience or benevolence, because, if one's possession of the number of commodities is existential, if it determines our position in relation to one another, if it determines whether we count and how we count in the "eyes" of one another, everyone must be very keen to save and accumulate possessions.

2.2. Smith's account of the situation of the self in the sphere of production

Smith describes the historical development towards commercial society as the growth of the wealth of society, which originates in the increasing division of labor. But at the same time he points out two forms of alienation arising from the division of labor. The *first* relates to his conception of alienation caused by the technical division of labor and the *second* to his theory of class conflicts caused by the social division of labor.

First, in *WN* Smith is not only concerned about the growth of wealth as originating from the increase of the division of labor. He accounts also for its effects upon the intellectual and social qualities of individuals. "But", he says, "in consequence of the division of labour, the whole of every man's attention comes naturally to be directed towards some one very simple object" (*WN*, I.i.8). He outlines then, with soberness, the consequences of the concentration on "some one very simple object":

> The man [or "the great body of the people"] whose whole life is spent in performing a few simple operations, of which the effects too are, perhaps, always the same, or very nearly the same, has no occasion to exert his understanding, or exercise his invention in finding out expedients for removing difficulties which never occur. He naturally loses, therefore, the habit of such exertion, and generally becomes as *stupid* and *ignorant* as it is possible for a human creature to become. [*WN*, V.i.f.50; italics mine]

He concludes then further down that the "great body of people" acquires their dexterity at the cost of their "intellectual, social and martial virtues. But in every improved and civilized society this is the state into which the laboring poor, that is, the great body of people, must necessarily fall, unless government takes some pains to prevent it" (*WN*, V.i.f.50). Smith's reference to intellectual and social virtues is the most important one for the issue in question, because without these intellectual and social virtues, that is, when they "become as *stupid* and *ignorant* as it is possible for a human creature to become", they can hardly be in a position to judge impartially in any case—even in the simplest cases in everyday life.

Second, market society gives rise not only to the separation and differentiation of trades and employments and consequently to the economic isolation of individuals from one another, it also separates and squeezes them into the structure of social classes in accordance with their position vis-à-vis the means of production and their source of revenue. When we enter the sphere of production, we meet individuals no longer as individuals who are equals among equals. Rather, we meet them as representatives or personifications of different social classes.

Smith's main aim in *WN*, particularly in the first book, is to provide an answer to the questions as to what the wealth of nations is, how it comes about, and how it is distributed among different social classes. In this connection, Smith defines three main social classes in commercial society that compete with and fight against one another in order to have a greater share of this wealth. He asserts that "[t]he whole of what is annually either collected or produced by the labour of every society [...] is in the manner originally distributed among some of its different members. Wages, profit, and rent, are the three original sources of all revenue derived from one or other of these" (*WN*, I.vi.17). These three forms of revenue correspond to three different social classes in commercial society: that of laborers, that of manufacturers, and that of landlords.

Smith divides the historical development of society into four stages. The first stage is the stage of hunters and gatherers, which he sometimes refers to as the "original state of things". "In that original state of things, which precedes both the appropriation of land and the accumulation of stock, the whole produce of labour belongs to the labourer. He has neither landlord nor master to share with him" (*WN*, I.viii.2). However, "[a]s soon as the land of any country has all become private property, the landlord, like all other men, love to reap where they never sowed, and demand a rent even for its natural produce" (*WN*, I.vi.8). Smith calls what the laborers must pay to the landlords *rent,* and this form of revenue constitutes landlords as a social class. The emergence of manufacturers as a social class has to do with the monopolization of the means of production, which Smith calls "stock", and their revenue "profit" (*WN*, I.vi.5). This form of revenue constitutes manufacturers as a social class.

To work out what Smith means by wages, we must qualify further what he means by "stock". He defines stock first as a means of subsistence that is just enough to survive (*WN*, II.i.1). However, when stock is accumulated in the hands of "particular persons", and if it is employed in order to make "profit", it becomes "capital". The "whole stock, therefore, is distinguished into two parts. That part which, he [the manufacturer] expects is to afford him this revenue [profit], is called his capital. The other is that which supplies his immediate consumption" (*WN*, II.i.2).

From what has been said about the constitution of landlords and capitalists as social classes, we may be able to deduce which circumstances determine the constitution of laborers as a social class. The main circumstance that constitutes laborers as a social class is above all their separation from all the means of production, that is, from the land and all other means of production. Laborers as a social class are those people of a given country who possess nothing except for their labor power. Smith calls the revenue that laborers receive for their work *wages*.

In his analysis of the relationship between these three social classes, Smith seems to draw a line between the laborers and manufacturers on the one hand, and the landlords on the other. He appears to assert an antagonistic relationship between the former and the latter. The last mentioned two social classes own all the means of production and live at the expense of laborers by appropriating the value that the laborers add to the material by their work. He is, of course, very well aware of the fact that the interests of the landlords and the manufacturers are by no means the same. Each of them tries to appropriate the bigger portion of that new value. However, in relation to the class of laborers, they have similar interests. In short, from whichever angle we approach the relationship between these social classes, a permanent fight exists against one another for the bigger portion of the value that has been originally produced by laborers.

3. Some Comparative Conclusions

Now, from whichever angle we approach Smith's analysis of social relations in commercial society, there is always a contradiction between his conception of social individuality and social relations as developed in *TMS*, on the one hand, and his account of the situation of individuals and social relations in commercial society as described in *WN*, on the other. If we approach, for example, his account of the situation of individuals in commercial society from the standpoint of his conception of sympathy: within the framework of his general conception of social individuality, he defines sympathy not only as a means of communication but also as a mutual need. But when we examine his account of social relations in commercial society as well as at the level of commercial exchange-relations and production, there are no sympathetic relations at all. It is the principle of pure self-interest and mutual domination that serves to pervade social relations.

Let us for example refer back to the passages from *TMS* and *WN* that triggered off the debate. In the first passage from *TMS*, Smith refers to human nature. It is a general statement about human nature as such. By contrast, in the passage from *WN* he describes human beings in a particular historical stage in their development, namely in commercial society. Despite the fact that some scholars claim that the concept of sympathy can be reconciled with commercial exchange-relations, most seem to agree that Smith's account of sympathy is at odds with principles that serve as the foundation of commercial exchange-relations, for social theoretical frameworks that are implied by his conceptions of sympathy and self-love are entirely different ones. It is the principle of *mutual sympathy* and *mutual happiness,* that would define the social theoretical framework for all sorts of social relations if we rely on the concept of sympathy. But if we rely on the principle of self-love, the framework for all kinds of social relations would be defined by the principle of *mutual advantage*. The former is a portrayal of a non-utilitarian society, whereas the latter is a description of a utilitarian society. From whichever aspect we approach the relationship between *TMS* and *WN* we seem to have to reassert the Adam Smith Problem.

All in all, if we examine Smith's account of social relations in any sphere of commercial society, we observe that there is no general morality, that there is no impartiality, that there is no mutual sympathy, that there is no mutual love and mutual respect. In whichever sphere we examine his account of social relations in commercial society involving commercial exchange, we find that there prevail the principles of nihilism, utility, pure self-interest, and, as a consequence of all these, that there is alienation; we observe that there prevail only those principles that are opposed diametrically to Smith's most fundamental principles laid down in his general theory of the constitution of the self in *TMS*.

Smith is, of course, very well aware of this fact. To see that there is a contradiction between his concept of social individuality in *TMS* and his account of merely self-interested and egoistic individuals in commercial society, we did not have to wait until the so-called "Adam Smith Problem" was formulated. Moreover, in order to find out that there is a dualism between his conception of social individuality and his account of the situation of the self in commercial society, we did not have to wait until *WN* was published. Smith himself deals already in *TMS* with different forms of this dualism throughout history. Already in *TMS*, he asserts that

> [e]very independent state is divided into many different orders and societies, each of which has its own particular powers, privileges, and immunities. Every individual is naturally more attached to his own particular order of society, than to any other. His own interest, his own vanity, the interest and vanity of many of his friends and companions, are commonly a good deal connected with it. He is ambitious to extend its privileges and immunities. He is zealous to defend them against the encroachments of every other order or society. [*TMS*, VI.ii.2.7]

Because of the same analysis in *WN*, he asserts that "[i]n every civilized society, in every society where the distinction of ranks has once been completely established, there have been always two different schemes or systems of morality" (*WN*, V.i.g.10). Smith seems even to say that due to this distinction of ranks and orders within a society, there are also two different languages within a language, with severely distorting consequences for communication (*Lectures on Rhetoric and Belles Lettres*, 4–5).

Though Smith observes this fact that in commercial exchange-relations there prevails the only principle of "absurd self-love" (*TMS*, II.iii.1.5), he is not prepared to accept that the principle of self-love and utility is the sole principle of all social relations. In *TMS*, I.i.2.1, where he argues explicitly for the first time against those philosophers whose starting point in their ethics is the principle of self-love and utility, Smith asserts that "[t]hose who are fond of deducing all our sentiments from certain refinements of self-love, think themselves at no loss to account, according to their own principles, both for this pleasure and this pain. [...] But both the pleasure and the pain are always felt so instantaneously, and often upon such frivolous occasions, that it seems evident neither of them can be derived from any such self-interested considerations" (*TMS*, I.i.2.1).

If it is true, some of you may ask, that Smith sees this contradiction clearly, why does he, instead of formulating a fundamental critique, like Marx for example, justify commercial society?

To understand Smith's justification we must first of all bear in mind that he analyzes commercial society before the French Revolution. Nonetheless his justification of commercial society is not an unconditional one. Rather he justifies it because he regards its establishment as a historical advance in the history of humanity in almost all respects. In particular, his comparative historical studies in *Lectures on Jurisprudence* (*LJ*) give a very accurate account of this. He approaches it above all from a historical point of view. In this context, we may be able to deal with his justification in many respects. I am going to point to his closely connected economic and sociological aspects.

Firstly, Smith formulates his historical, economic justification already in his "Introduction and Plan of the Work" of *WN*. According to Smith's account, in relation to earlier social formations, commercial society is wealthier. Smith compares, for example, "savage nations of hunters and fishers" with "civilized and thriving nations". There he asserts that though in savage nations "every individual who is able to work, is more or less employed in useful labour", they are, however, "so miserably poor, that, from mere want, they are frequently reduced, or, at least think themselves reduced, to the necessity sometimes of directly destroying, and sometimes of abandoning their infants, their old people [...]". In commercial society, by contrast, "though a great number of people do not labour at all, many of whom consume the produce of ten times, frequently of a hundred times more labour than the greater part of those who work; yet the produce of labour of the society is so great, that all are often abundantly supplied, and a workman, even of the lowest and poorest order, if he is frugal and industrious, many enjoy a greater share of the necessaries and conveniences of life than it is possible for any savage to acquire" (*WN*, 10). A similar comparison occurs in the main text of *WN*. He makes a comparison between the accommodation of a "frugal peasant" and an "African king" who is "the absolute master of the lives and liberties of ten thousand naked savages" and asserts that the accommodation of the former exceeds many times that of the latter (*WN*, I.i.11).

Secondly, Smith thinks that commercial society is not only relatively wealthier but also more dynamic. According to Smith's historical account, commercial society destroys the communitarian structures of feudal society and thereby admits less social control of the lives of individuals. He thinks that commercial society, instead of limiting the "good office" of individuals within a tribe or a clan, frees them from communitarian structures and enlarges thereby their relative scope for freedom of action, despite all the forms of alienation deriving from the structure of the division of labor. Due to this historical-social development, commercial society enables individuals to meet one another, at least in their non-commercial social relations, as particular individuals, instead of as members of this or that tribe or clan. As opposed to all earlier social formations, commercial society brings to individuals more anonymity, more tolerance and indulgence, and therefore also more variety in their social relations, which enriches also their capacity for sympathy (*TMS*, VI.ii.1.13). Therefore, he observes: "[a]mong civilized nations, the virtues which are founded upon humanity, are more cultivated than those which are founded upon self-denial and the command of the passions. Among rude and barbarous nations, it is quite otherwise, the virtues of self-denial are more cultivated than those of humanity" (*TMS*, V.2.8; cf. also *TMS*, V.2.9).

IV. SMITH'S CRITIQUE OF COMMERCIAL SOCIETY AND HIS UTOPIA OF A SYMPATHETIC SOCIETY

I have outlined above, *firstly*, Smith's theory of social individuality. I have presented *secondly* his account of the situation of individuals in the age of commerce. I have then shown *thirdly*, in my preliminary conclusions, that there is an essential contradiction between his theory of social individuality and his account of the situation of the self in commercial society. Now, we have to turn to the question whether Smith formulates any solution to this contradiction. I am going to claim that Smith's solution lies in his critique of commercial society. When I worked out Smith's theory of social individuality I concentrated on *TMS*, and when I worked out his account of the situation of individuals in commercial society I relied on *WN*. Now I am going to consider them together. Let me therefore say something about how I approach their relationship to one another.

Almost all scholars suggest that *TMS* and *WN* should be read in one way or another as complementary works. Smith himself regards them as complementary parts of a more comprehensive project that may be seen from the last paragraph of *TMS* and the "Advertisement" for the sixth edition of *TMS* from 1790. Up to this point there is a more or less explicit agreement among scholars who are concerned with Smith's overall work. But this is also the point where the controversy begins. Many scholars read *TMS* and *WN* as if they have no terminological and conceptual relation. There are others who see between *TMS* and *WN* a conceptual relation, but they suggest taking Smith's conceptions from *TMS* (particularly his conception of sympathy) as devices to improve or perfect commercial exchange-relations. I suggest that there is a close terminological and conceptual relationship between Smith's two major works. But I suggest regarding *TMS* as providing a critical perspective or "window" from which *WN* should be considered.

In what follows, I am going to suggest that Smith develops an essential critique that may be described as an early attempt at an immanent critique. To see this we must take into account not only *that* he describes the problems but also *how* he describes them. If we approach his analyses, most of his justifications quite often turn out to be an implicit critique of commercial society. If Smith had remained merely descriptive and justificatory in his analysis, we may have been entitled to claim that the Adam Smith Problem was a conceptual problem of Smith's. But Smith clearly formulates, in almost all respects, a critique of commercial society, which serves at the same time as a kind of loose framework for his utopia.

1. Smith's Essential Critique of the Division of Labor in and Social Class Structure of Commercial Society

Smith's critique of the situation of the self as affected by the division of labor may be explored best if it is considered in the light of his account of the distribution of time (time-structure) in commercial society. As a solution to the alienation arising from the social division of labor as described above Smith proposes a universal education. This education should enable laborers to understand not only their professional world but also "the great society of mankind".

But Smith thinks that any educational measure to be taken against the alienation arising from the social division of labor would be undermined by the distribution of time among social classes. Unlike the "common people", for example, who start working at age seven or eight, the "people of some ranks and fortunes" start working when they are approximately eighteen or nineteen. The work the people of some ranks and fortune do is not simple and uniform. Unlike the common people whose intellectual and emotional capacities "grow torpid" from their work, they can develop their intellectual capacities while they work. They too have enough spare time to acquire what Smith calls "ornamental knowledge". But the common people, who carry on their "shoulders the whole of mankind, and [are] unable to sustain the load" are "buried by the weight of it and thrust down into the lowest parts of the earth, from whence [they support] all the rest" (*LJ*, 341), are harassed by their work from morning to night. They have therefore "little time to spare for education. Their parents can scarce afford to maintain them even in infancy. As soon as they are able to work, they must apply to some trade by which they can earn their subsistence". As a result of this they become "stupid and ignorant" (cf. *WN*, V.i.f.52 and 53). In civilized or commercial countries their "labour and time […] is […] sacrificed to the maintaining the rich in ease and luxury" (*LJ*, 340).

But it is exactly this "leisure" that common people need in order to enjoy a universal education. Therefore, Smith thinks that time-structure must essentially be changed by redistributing the whole work of society. This problem with regard to time-structure would cease to exist if "labour was equally proportioned to each". "That is, if we should suppose that of the 10,000 whose labour is necessary to the support of one individuall, each was maintained by the labour of the rest, there would here be the reciprocall proportion of one bestowed upon him" (*LJ*, 341). This proposal of Smith as a solution to time-dilemma in commercial society essentially challenges the social class structure of commercial society.

2. Mutual Respect, Trust and Free Communication as the Sign of an Open Society

We can approach Smith's critique of commercial society also from the standpoint of his theory of communicative action. When Smith deals with the problem in commercial society, he operates with two models of society that are contrary to each other. The one is a harmonious and open society, in which everybody is potentially entitled to access to all spheres of society. The other is a society fragmented by the division of society into social classes with their resulting contradiction of interests. It is, therefore, closed and restricts everybody throughout their lives to only certain spheres. The former is based on the principle of mutual respect, trust, and unreserved communication, whereas the latter is based on the principle of distrust and reserved communication or even, more probably, manipulation.

A harmonious and open society may form our emotional and intellectual dispositions in a different way than a closed one. In an open and harmonious society, the general intellectual and bodily capacities can be formed in such a way that the agent can act spontaneously, i.e. without any long and deep considerations, on the basis of the principle of impartiality, spontaneously taking both general and particular interests into account. In a fragmented and therefore closed society, the intellectual and emotional dispositions of the agent will be formed partially, so that the agent can act only from a partial point of view, being unable to approach issues in question from a general point of view.

Let us, for example, refer back to Smith's conception of situation. According to Smith, we are always, in all situations of communicative action, embedded in a three-dimensional situation, both in an open and in a closed society. However, in an open society, we can easily imagine that there is a social world that is much broader than our concrete or actual situation. We can imagine the whole, either because of our experiences in different spheres of social life, or due to the universal education that we have enjoyed. In our concrete situation we know that we are entitled to enter into all other spheres. We can receive information about their functioning, and we can rely on it. If we are involved in an interaction with individuals from other spheres, we do not need to hide our feelings, emotions, and internal considerations, we do not need to submit ourselves to self-censure as there is mutual sympathy; we can reveal our internal world, our intimacy, without any fear; we do not need to be afraid of being abused because we trusted blindly and revealed ourselves without any reason.

Smith points, therefore, to "trust" and "free communication" as the main features of an open society. If we can trust, he says, "[w]e see clearly [...]

the road by which" our partner in conversation "means to conduct us, and we abandon ourselves with pleasure to his guidance and direction" (*TMS*, VII.iv.28). "We all", Smith continues, "desire, upon this account, to feel how each other is affected, to penetrate into each other's bosom, and to observe the sentiments and affections which really subsist there" (*TMS*, VII.iv.28). In an open conversation, Smith adds: "[t]he man who indulges us in this natural passion, who invites us into his heart, who, as it were, sets open the gates of his breast to us, seems to exercise a species of hospitality more delightful than any other" (*TMS*, VII.iv.28).

In a closed society, by contrast, even though we know that there is a much broader world than our own, we cannot involve it in our considerations of our world, because we are excluded from it; we cannot care about it as we are not a part of it. We must check all information many times before we can trust it. "Reserve and concealment, on the contrary, call forth diffidence. We are afraid to follow the man who is we do not know where" (*TMS*, VII.iv.28). Therefore, if we necessarily get involved in interaction with individuals from different spheres, we cannot easily reveal ourselves. We must remain formal and reserved.

What about mutual respect in commercial society? What is the "great purpose of human life which we call bettering our conditions?", Smith asks. In all of our life, he seems to respond, everything that we do aims at mutual respect: "[t]o be observed, to be attended to, to be taken notice of with sympathy, complacency, and approbation" (*TMS*, I.iii.2.1), this is the real end of all our life. "For to what purpose is all the toil, and bustle of this world? What is the end of avarice and ambition, of the pursuit of wealth, or power, and preheminence? [*sic*] Is it to supply the necessities of nature? The wages of the meanest labourer can supply them" (*TMS*, I.iii.2.1). However, in commercial society for the "great body of the people" the principle of respect is undermined by the very fact of the division of society into the "poor" and the "rich", because "[t]he man of rank and distinction [...] is observed by all the world" (*TMS*, I.iii.2.1), but the "poor man, on the contrary, is ashamed of his poverty. He feels that it either places him out of the sight of mankind, or, that if they take notice of him, they have, however, scarce any fellow-feeling with the misery and distress which he suffers. [...] The poor man goes out and comes in unheeded, and when in the midst of a crowd is in the same obscurity as if shut up in his own hovel. [...] They turn away their eyes from him, or if the extremity of his distress forces them to look at him, it is only to spurn so disagreeable an object from among them" (*TMS*, I.iii.2.1).

V. SMITH'S UTOPIA AS A SOLUTION TO THE ADAM SMITH PROBLEM: SOCIETY AS AN OPEN AND PROGRESSIVE SYSTEM OF MUTUAL SYMPATHY

Because of these considerations, Smith regards the division of society into the "rich" and the "poor" as "the great and most universal cause of the corruption of our moral sentiment" (*TMS*, I.iii.3.1). This is in fact the greatest challenge to the sort of ethics that Smith teaches. I claim however that Smith employs a concept of future-history as a solution to overcome this challenge.

That is to say that he employs a certain concept of utopia to overcome the contradiction between his concept of non-utilitarian ethics and the principle of utility that prevails in commercial society.

Now, the claim that Smith delineates in his work a certain concept of utopia may astonish many scholars more than the claim that there is a critique of commercial society, because Smith seemingly rejects explicitly the possibility of utopia in his only invisible-hand paragraph in *WN*. The term "utopia" is usually explained in terms of a visionary social and political system. Obviously, Smith did not rely on this kind of a concept of utopia. This does not mean, however, that Smith discarded the concept of utopia as such, for originally utopia was meant to be an essential critique of existing conditions. Had Smith discarded the concept of utopia, he would have probably ended in positivism. However, without sticking to the traditional concept of utopia, Smith endeavors to rescue its critical intention and give to it a new turn. Unlike the traditional concepts of utopia (which I call here "ideal utopia"), Smith employs a certain concept of utopia, which I would like to describe as a "realist utopia". In other words, instead of detaching critique from reality or *ought* from *is*, as is common in traditional concepts, Smith endeavors to integrate the conception of critique into his account of commercial society. As opposed to traditional concepts of utopia, Smith does not give a detailed description of an ideal society to come. Rather, he prefers to develop an immanent critique of existing social relations and deduces thereby a kind of vague framework for a society to come.

If we take the term "utopia" in this Smithian sense as described above, then we can assert that we have been in fact already dealing with Smith's utopia, since by working out his critique of commercial society, I referred to the most essential principles of his ethics and social and political theory, such as mutual sympathy and trust, and to his critique of alienation behind which there lies implicitly his conception of authenticity.

In what follows, I am going to claim that Smith employs a certain type of utopia to criticize commercial society. That my suggestion is consistent with Smith's overall work can be shown in many ways. Here I will refer to the debate between Smith on the one hand, and Hume and Mandeville on the other, regarding whether it is possible to establish an ethical society based on the principles of mutual sympathy and virtue.

1. Smith against Hume's and Mandeville's Moral Skepticism

One of the most important aims of Smith's moral philosophy is to show that morality is possible. Smith defines the aim of any theory of ethics as endeavoring to "direct the judgements" of the impartial spectator. This is, according to Smith, "the great purpose of all systems of morality" (*TMS*, VII.ii.1.47). He thereby challenges both Hume's skeptical claim about the impossibility that human beings should regard one another as their second selves and Mandeville's claim that a virtuous life is impossible. Both of them claim it is *utopian* to aim to establish a non-utilitarian ethical society. Both of these claims culminate, from Smith's point of view, in the claim that morality based on sympathetic social relations (and utopia in this sense) is impossible. Therefore, in his account of ethics, Smith responds to both Hume's and Mandeville's skeptical challenges.

Mandeville's main argument, in *The Fable of the Bees or Private Vices, Publick Benefits*, is that there is no distinction between virtue and vice. He seems even to claim that the distinction between virtue and vice would hinder the progress of civilization. Therefore, in the second part of his poem "The Grumbling Hive: or, Knaves *turn'd Honest*", which is entitled "The Moral", he makes a programmatic assertion that a virtuous life without vices is "EUTOPIA", that is to say that it is impossible.

In his discussion of the question whether benevolence is possible, Hume formulates a similar skeptical challenge to Smith's account of ethics. If benevolence were possible, Hume asserts, then everybody would regard one another as his/her second self. However, as the conception of benevolence is impossible, then it is also not possible that human beings should regard one another as their second selves (Hume, *Enquiries*, 185). From this consideration Hume concludes that the principle of justice in the sense of the distinction between *mine* and *thine* is absolutely necessary.

Mandeville's and Hume's skeptical accounts of ethics present, of course, huge challenges to Smith's moral philosophy. For if it should be impossible for human beings to see themselves as others would or are likely to see them, then the most essential foundation of Smith's moral philosophy would be undermined, since it is exactly this principle upon which his whole system is built. Therefore, his response to Hume's challenge may be seen also as a response to Mandeville's, since it is in exactly this context that he formulates also his account of propriety and virtue (which are in Smith's account, in most cases synonymous).

Smith does not differ much from Hume in his assessment of the oppositional relation between the concepts of benevolence and justice. According to Hume, as well as to Smith, the concepts of benevolence and justice are built upon entirely different principles. Whereas the concept of benevolence is built upon the principle of commonness, that of justice is built upon the separation between *mine* and *thine*. They differ, however, in their assessment of whether benevolence is possible. Unlike Hume, Smith's aim in his discussion of the relation between justice and benevolence is to show that benevolence is possible. According to Smith's approach it is an epistemological necessity. Otherwise, there can hardly be any communication in any given society.

In his account of commercial exchange relations, Smith does not differ much from Mandeville; his description of commercial exchange relations is very similar to Mandeville's. However, they differ in their normative assessment of these relations. Like Smith, Mandeville asserts that "[t]o expect, that others should serve us for nothing, is *unreasonable*; therefore all Commerce, that Men can have together, must be a continual bartering of one thing for another. The Seller, who transfers the Property of Thing, has his own Interest as much at Heart as the Buyer, who purchases that Property" (Mandeville, *Fable*, Vol. 1, 349; italics mine). This normative assessment of commercial exchange relations of Mandeville's refers to his utilitarian conception of reciprocity, as explored elsewhere (Mandeville, *Fable*, Vol. 1, 341), and it recalls immediately Smith's initial paragraph of *TMS*, in which he formulates a *non*-utilitarian conception of reciprocity.

But Smith approaches the utilitarian concept of reciprocity historically. Let us look at a paragraph from *LJ*, for example, in which he compares two historical hypothetical examples: a poor and a rich country with social class distinctions:

> In a poor country there can be no great difference betwixt the master and the slave in any respect. They will eat at the same table, work together, and be cloathed in the same manner, and will be alike in every other particular. In a rich country the disproportion betwixt them will [...] make the rich men much more sevr [sic] to their slaves than the poorer ones. A man of great fortune, a nobleman, is much farther removed from the condition of his servant than a farmer. The farmer generally works along with his servant; they eat together, and are little different. The disproportion betwixt them, the condition of the nobleman and his servant, is so great that he will hardly look on him as being of the same kind; he thinks he has little title even to the ordinary enjoyments of life, and feels but little for his misfortunes. The farmer on the other hand considers his servant as almost on an equall with himself, and is therefore the more capable of feeling with him. [*LJ*, 184]

Smith concludes from these considerations: "[t]hose persons most excite our compassion and are most apt to affect our *sympathy* who most *resemble* ourselves, and the greater the difference the less we are affected by them" (*LJ*, 184; italics mine). Thus, as we may see, Smith refers implicitly to a form of society without social classes as the most important precondition for the principle of sympathy's becoming actuality. For in both of the countries, whether rich or poor, there are no sympathetic relations because of the division of society into different social classes. In a poor country, there may still be some remnants of sympathetic relations because it does not admit of a great difference in fortune. But even in a poor society with social classes the principle of sympathy no longer serves as the foundation of all social relations. But in his moral philosophy Smith teaches us that without sympathetic social relations there can hardly be communication and morality, and to establish this, I think, is Smith's utopia.

2. Smith's Conditional Justification of the Possibility of Utopia

Now, suggesting that there is a utopia in Smith's work sets a challenge for us. It reminds us of Smith's "scepticism" about the possibility of utopia, which he formulates in WN, IV.ii.43. He says explicitly: "[t]o expect, indeed, that the freedom of trade should ever be entirely *restored* in Great Britain, is as absurd as to expect that an Oceana or Utopia should ever be *established* in it" (*WN*, IV.ii.43; italics mine). In this assertion Smith refers to three types of utopia at the same time: *freedom of trade*; *Oceana* pointing to James Harrington's *The Commonwealth of Oceana*; and *Utopia* referring to Thomas More's *Utopia*.

Here it seems as if Smith would assert that whichever utopia we take, its realization is impossible. In order to respond to the challenge, we must consider how Smith justifies his skepticism. Smith does not commit himself to skepticism in principle. When we glance at this sentence and consider Smith's choice of words, especially the strong connotations of "absurd", for example, we might well think that Smith commits himself to the principle of skepticism without any reservation.

However, unlike Hume and Mandeville, Smith is not questioning the possibility of utopia as such. He says it is impossible because the "prejudices of the publick" and "the private interests of many individuals", that is, "master manufacturers", stand against it (*WN*, IV.ii.43). At first sight, Smith appears to reject the possibility of utopia as such. On closer examination, however, he does in fact formulate at least two preconditions that should be fulfilled so that utopia may become possible. He refers to "public prejudices" and "master manufacturers" as presenting fundamental obstacles to the realization of utopia. For if public prejudices can be overcome by enlightening them, if "master manufacturers" as a social force can be overcome, there is no reason why utopia should be impossible. Therefore, on closer examination, the reasons that Smith gives in order to justify why he thinks that utopia would not be possible turn themselves into historical, social and political challenges that must be overcome if the existing social conditions become a burden and if the realization of utopia appears to be the only way out of these.

If my reading of this paragraph is correct, Smith's seeming skepticism with regard to the possibility of utopia turns out to be in fact a conditional justification. This would, in turn, mean that Smith seems to put before us at least three types of utopia: that of free trade, that of Harrington, and that of More. This may indeed be seen as a problem in Smith's formulation of his utopia.

There may be many ways of interpreting the paragraph quoted above, and any suggestion about how the problem in Smith's formulation should be solved can only be a speculative one. But I suggest that these three forms of utopia must be taken together and set in relation to one another.

The scholars of Smith's work who dealt with his utopia were, implicitly or explicitly, mostly concentrated on his idea of freedom of trade. However, reading Smith's work in the light of what I suggest would mean that his utopia consists of three complementary elements: freedom of trade, *Oceana,* and *Utopia*. Smith's conception of freedom of trade seems to refer to the equal distribution of commodities in the market. His reference to James Harrington's *Oceana* points to the equal distribution of land. That is to say, both the principle of freedom of trade and *Oceana* are developed on the basis of the principle of distributive justice and may be taken together. His reference to Thomas More's *Utopia* refers to the common use and administration of all means of production and subsistence.

The Harringtonian version of utopia and the idea of freedom of trade are above all concerned with the division of land and the distribution of wealth among the citizens. The Morean version of utopia, by contrast, is concerned primarily with the socialization of land and wealth. Philosophically speaking, Harrington wants to establish a society on the principle of distributive justice, i.e., merit and demerit. More, by contrast, aims at establishing a society on the principle of mutual respect.

How do these two types of utopia relate to Smith's utopia? How can this apparent interpretive dilemma be solved? I suggest differentiating within Smith's utopia between short-term and long-term aims. I especially suggest that what Smith discusses under the terms of freedom of trade and *Oceana* refers to his short-term solution and *Utopia* to his long-term solution to the problems arising from the division of labor in commercial society. This would mean that, with his short-term aim, Smith wants to reform radically commercial society without questioning its essential logic, whereas with his long-term solution he essentially wants to overcome commercial society.

I am not claiming that Smith formulates this explicitly. But I am maintaining that this may be a more reasonable explanation of the above-formulated interpretative problem, when we take seriously the most fundamental conceptions of his social and political theory such as mutual sympathy and mutual love. This reading would also conform to his non-utilitarian conception of ethics.

However, apart from all these arguments, in my reading I am inspired particularly by two passages in *TMS*. *Firstly,* when Smith comes to deal with the sense of merit and demerit in part two of *TMS,* he defines merit and demerit as "species" of criteria of approbation and disapprobation distinct from propriety and impropriety (*TMS*, II.intro.1). The main difference between these two sets of criteria is this: whereas the former are to be seen within the paradigm of justice, which is according to Smith a negative virtue, the latter can hardly be confined to the conception of justice and therefore it must be placed within the paradigm of mutual sympathy and respect. *Secondly* and more importantly, Smith says:

Society may subsist among different men, as among different merchants, from a sense of its utility, without any mutual love or affection; and though no man in it should owe any obligation, or be bound in gratitude to any other, it may still be upheld by a mercenary exchange of good offices according to an agreed valuation. [*TMS*, II.ii.3.2]

But

[w]here the necessary assistance is reciprocally afforded [not based on the principle of utility but,] from love, from gratitude, from friendship, and esteem, the society flourishes and is happy. All the different members of it are bound together by the agreeable bands of love and affection, and are as it were, drawn to one common centre of mutual good offices. [*TMS*, II.ii.3.1]

The former principles refer to the system of justice and utility, that is, to the idea of freedom of trade and the Harringtonian version of utopia, whereas the latter points to the system of mutual sympathy and respect and the Morean version of utopia. The establishment of the last-mentioned utopia may also be seen as Smith's own projected solution to the Adam Smith Problem.

SELECT BIBLIOGRAPHY

Göçmen, Doğan. *The Adam Smith Problem: Human Nature and Society in* The Theory of Moral Sentiments *and* The Wealth of Nations. London: I. B. Tauris, 2007.

Hume, David. *Enquiries Concerning Human Understanding and Concerning The Principles of Morals*. 3rd ed. Reprinted from the 1777 edition with introduction and analytical index by L. A. Selby-Bigge. With text revised and notes by P. H. Nidditch. Oxford: Oxford University Press, 1989.

———. *A Treatise of Human Nature*, 2nd ed. With an analytical index by L. A. Selby-Bigge. With text revised and notes by P. H. Nidditch. Oxford: Oxford University Press, 1978.

Lacan, Jacques. "The Mirror Stage as Formative of the Function of the I as Revealed in Psychoanalytic Experience". In: *Écrits: a selection*. Translated by A. Sheridan, and with a foreword by M. Bowie. London: Routledge Classics, 2001.

Mandeville, Bernard. *The Fable of the Bees or Private Vices, Publick Benefits*, 2 volumes. With a commentary critical, historical, and explanatory by F. B. Kaye. Indianapolis: Liberty Fund, 1988.

Neili, Russell. "Spheres of Intimacy and The Adam Smith Problem". *Journal of the History of Ideas* 47 (4) (1986): 611–624.

Raphael, D. D., and A. L. Macfie. "Introduction" to Smith, *The Theory of Moral Sentiments*, edited by D. D. Raphael and A. L. Macfie. Indianapolis: Liberty Fund, 1984.

Smith, Adam. *An Inquiry into the Nature and Causes of Wealth of Nations*, 2 vols. Edited by R. H. Campbell and A. L. Skinner. Indianapolis: Liberty Fund, 1981.

——. *Lectures on Jurisprudence*. Edited by R. L. Meek, D. D. Raphael, and P. G. Stein. Indianapolis: Liberty Fund, 1982.

——. *Lectures on Rhetoric and Belles Lettres*. Edited by J. C. Bryce. Indianapolis: Liberty Fund, 1985.

——. *The Theory of Moral Sentiments*. Edited by D. D. Raphael and A. L. Macfie. Indianapolis: Liberty Fund, 1984.

MODERN NATURAL LAW MEETS THE MARKET: THE CASE OF ADAM SMITH[1]

Amit Ron

I. INTRODUCTION

"In *The Wealth of Nations* the impartial spectator puts in no appearance, unless perhaps Smith cast himself in that role" (Bitterman, "Adam Smith's Empiricism", 520).[2] Much has changed in the scholarship on Adam Smith since Henry Bittermann has made this observation in 1940 echoing the long-debated "Adam Smith problem": a conspicuous absence of the impartial spectator, the main theoretical device of Smith's moral philosophy, from his political economy and, more generally, perceived thematic and stylistic differences between his two major works. The Adam Smith scholarship of recent decades, sparked in part by the discovery of another set of notes from lectures on jurisprudence given by Smith, offers us a better understanding of how seemingly divergent components of Smith's work—his moral philosophy, jurisprudence, and political economy—are tied together and embedded in the traditions of modern natural law and of civic humanism.

Generally speaking, recent scholarship shows Smith's interest in economics to have been moral all the way down. Like his contemporaries Francis Hutcheson, Jean-Jacques Rousseau, Bernard Mandeville, and David Hume, Smith struggled with redefining the idea of a virtuous life in the nascent commercial society.[3] Against the backdrop of his interlocutors, Smith's position appears to be a cautious *via media* between wholesale enthusiasm and principled objection to the pursuit of self interest through the activity of commerce. He saw commerce as an inevitable and effective, yet dangerous vehicle for promoting virtuous conduct. Furthermore, examination of his views on law and justice in the context of the tradition of modern natural law reveals that for Smith the regulation of justice by the state was an end in itself, not just a burden reluctantly assumed in order to ensure economic efficiency. The extent of the difference between the Adam Smith depicted by recent scholarship and the traditional portrait is illustrated by Keith Tribe's observation of a modish trend toward supplementing Marx's *Capital* with *The Wealth of Nations* as sourcebooks for

---

1 Reprinted from *European Journal of Political Theory*, vol. 7, no. 2 (April 2008): 117–136, with minor changes to style and grammar.

2 Complete bibliographic information for all sources can be found in the Select Bibliography at the end of this essay.

3 Force, *Self-Interest before Adam Smith*; Hont and Ignatieff, *Wealth and Virtue*; Rothschild, *Economic Sentiments*; Winch, *Adam Smith's Politics*.

the moral critique of capitalism (Tribe, "Adam Smith: Critical Theorist?").

While drawing upon the new scholarship, I nevertheless argue in this article that understanding Smith's interest in economics solely from a moral perspective is too limiting. Such an understanding overlooks his interest in the "political" dimensions of economic activity, a form of interaction involving asymmetric and often hidden forms of power relations. In particular, I argue that Smith sought to understand how skilled and powerful players can manipulate commercial activity to their own benefit while maintaining an appearance of fairness. Smith was interested in these political aspects of economic activity not because he envisaged an "ideal economic situation" free from political power, but because the economic market played a crucial role in his theory of jurisprudence. Smith needed to find a way of accounting for the political aspects of economic activity in order to make a theory of jurisprudence based on impartial spectatorship applicable to modern commercial society. Allow me to explain why.

Reading *The Theory of Moral Sentiments* (*TMS*) and *The Wealth of Nations* (*WN*) in light of the Glasgow lectures on jurisprudence reveals that Smith situated his views in a tradition of modern natural law originating with Grotius and transformed (with a Scottish twist) by Smith's mentor Francis Hutcheson and his close friend David Hume. Philosophers within this tradition sought new philosophical foundations for legal systems in place of what they took to be an unnecessarily complicated legacy of medieval jurisprudence. The problem with the medieval tradition of scholastic disputation was that it overburdened a legal system by making any violation of a moral conduct redressable through courts. This resulted in an overly ambitious attempt to regulate all sorts of moral conduct, culminating in the generation of a behemoth of self-contradictory rules. The solution offered by natural law philosophers was to restrict the scope of legal and juridical authority to the protection of what they termed perfect, or legal, rights, which they associated with the concepts of justice, property, and injury.[4] Thus, for example, theft is a form of injury to one's property that can be forbidden by law. On the other hand, a right to receive proper gratitude in return for a gift is an imperfect, or moral, right. Its determination should not be resolved by laws, nor can any claim that one has been deprived of this right be enforceable by courts.

The best-known versions of modern natural law are theories of the social contract, which attempted to explain how the notion and content of perfect rights can be derived from such a contract. However, recent scholarship demonstrates that the social contract was only one theoretical device among others for justifying and specifying natural rights.[5] In fact, *The Theory of Moral*

---

4 Gordley, *The Philosophical Origins of Modern Contract Doctrine*; Tuck, *Natural Right Theories*.

5 Buckle, *Natural Law and the Theory of Property*; Haakonssen, *The Science of a*

Sentiments can be read as presenting an alternative to social contract theory by showing how the principle of sympathy can explain the origin of the distinction between perfect and imperfect rights. In this reading, the *Lectures on Jurisprudence* provide an analytic and historical account of a gradual shift in European systems of law toward a legal system founded on such a distinction.[6] Perfect rights emerged from a long historical process, during which nations realized that in order to organize and stabilize their commonsense moral judgments they needed no more than simple and easy to adjudicate rules of justice.[7] *The Wealth of Nations*, as Hont and Ignatieff have shown, explains why a legal system that focuses on the protection of justice and shies away from the regulation of commerce is better suited to solving the problem of providing for the poor in times of famine.[8]

Questions about the appropriate regulation of market activities, which were seen as falling within the boundaries of justice and perfect rights, were central to the natural law tradition. To begin with, much of the philosophical burden posed by the contention that a lean legal system could sufficiently regulate conduct rested on a subsidiary claim that the institution of the market, with its "invisible hand", could regulate economic activity in a morally satisfactory, if not fully harmonious, way. At the same time, however, these philosophers also held a different and more complicated image of economic activities. Economic activities were seen as a "political" realm characterized by manipulation and deceit, wherein hidden forms of domination could make unjustifiable economic exchanges appear legitimate.[9] In this latter image, legal regulations of the market were largely deemed ineffective, since the regulations themselves could be subjected to manipulation. Nor were manipulable and excessive regulations the only problem. We shall see that Smith described economic activity as taking place within an environment characterized by asymmetries of power that affected economic outcomes.

Thus, the problem Smith faced, emblematic of that posed to all participants in the discourse of modern natural law, was that of taming the political character of economic activity to fit a moral and legal paradigm that understood any injustice related to economic activities as a form of theft. The problem was that while economic exchange could, in theory, be thought of as subject to commonsense moral evaluations aided by simple rules of justice, Smith acknowledged that, in practice, the sense of fairness in commercial

---

Legislator; Haakonssen, *Natural Law and Moral Philosophy*; Hochstrasser, *Natural Law Theories in the Early Enlightenment*; Pack and Schliesser, "Smith's Humean Criticism".

6   Haakonssen, *The Science of a Legislator*, chapter 7; Adam Smith, *Lectures on Jurisprudence* [*LJ*].

7   Otteson, *Adam Smith's Marketplace of Life*, 178–180.

8   Hont and Ignatieff, "Needs and Justice in *The Wealth of Nations*".

9   See also Ron, "The 'Market' and the 'Forum' in Hobbes's Political Philosophy".

transactions could be easily manipulated. This problem became all the more difficult in commercial society because commerce played a central role in securing moral foundations. Thus, Smith realized that the two components of his jurisprudence—an impartial spectator's distinction between perfect and imperfect rights, and a free market as the main mechanism of moral regulation— were in tension with one another. Economic exchange defied the vision of moral judgment Smith planned for commercial societies.

This article examines the roles played by these "political" aspects of Smith's political economy in his understanding of jurisprudence by reinterpreting the discussion of prices in the first book of *The Wealth of Nations*. This discussion is commonly perceived as a scientific theory intended to explain the formation of prices.[10] However, I interpret the explanation of price to be part of a broader enterprise. Smith was in fact interested in examining different reference points for judging the fairness of economic exchange so as to determine the one best suited to serving as an organizing principle for the legal foundation of commercial societies. The focus of his discussion was a comparison of the susceptibility of each way of thinking about value to manipulation by powerful interests.

The interpretive approach I use here follows that of Richard Ashcraft. In the context of his study of John Locke, Ashcraft argued that "writing a work of political theory is a complex action", and therefore the meaning of any particular argument is open to interpretations at different levels. Furthermore, "since the meaning of a particular argument [...] is referable, in part, to the multiple intentional objectives of the author, what the interpreter of the text offers the reader is a plausible reconstruction of the evidence".[11] In a similar vein, I believe Smith's discussion of prices is open to multiple interpretations corresponding to multiple objectives Smith had in writing the text. Thus, even though at one level Smith must have intended to engage in an analysis of the formation of prices, I offer a "plausible reconstruction of the evidence" to show that at another level, Smith's discussion of prices struggled to reconcile a tension within his account of the legal basis of commercial society.

To substantiate this interpretation, the following section explicates Smith's "science of the legislator" and the place of "systems" and "mechanisms" within it, all three of these being terms often used but never fully explained by Smith. The section makes the following two claims. First, when legislators turn existing social practices into laws, they generate regularities that make a society appear to operate like a machine, or a social system. This, in turn, allows

---

10   See, for example, Blaug, *Economic Theory in Retrospect*, chapter 2. Exceptions include Young, *Economics as a Moral Science*; Fitzgibbons, *Adam Smith's System of Liberty, Wealth, and Virtue*, 176–182; and Montes, *Adam Smith in Context*, chapter 5.

11   Ashcraft, "Locke's Political Philosophy", 227.

a scientific re-description of the social practices as mechanisms. In a sense, if we understand ideology to be a hegemonic discourse embedded in institutions and social practices, Smith treated legislation as an ideological construction. Second, legislators' freedom to shape social practices is limited since their menu of choices is limited to standards of moral judgment already practiced by members of society.

My main thesis, presented in the third section, is that the discussion of prices in Book I of *The Wealth of Nations* is part of such an ideological construction. When Smith compared the "real value" based on labor, the "natural price", and the "market price", he was not only explaining price formation. Instead, each measure represents a different way to evaluate economic transactions from a moral perspective. Smith needed to compare them in order to show that only a system in which prices generated by the market appear morally justifiable can fulfill the needs of commercial societies, even though the market price system entails the most difficulty for making judgments about the fairness of economic transactions that take into account the broader social context in which these transactions are made.

SMITH'S SCIENCE AND THE LEGISLATOR

The science, according to Smith, which is "by far the most important, but hitherto, perhaps, the least cultivated" is that of natural jurisprudence (*TMS*, VI.ii.intro.2). Its aim is to give precise rules for regulating human behavior in four areas: police, revenue, arms, and justice (*TMS*, VII, iv, 37). As Smith explained in the advertisement to the last edition of *The Theory of Moral Sentiments* published during his lifetime, the first three had been discussed in *The Wealth of Nations*, while the last remained an unfinished project (*TMS*, advertisement to the sixth edition). The lectures on jurisprudence are thought to provide an elaborate sketch of what he intended to write on justice. While *The Wealth of Nations* does not explicitly mention a science of natural jurisprudence, it does refer to a "science of a legislator" (*WN*, IV.2.39) that includes "political economy", the science dealing with the "nature and causes of *The Wealth of Nations*" (*WN*, IV.9.38, but also the title of *WN*) as one of its branches (*WN*, IV.introduction).

Smith's interest in the activity of legislation and his own advocacy for legal reforms in *The Wealth of Nations* might seem puzzling given his account of the "origin and use of general rules" in *The Theory of Moral Sentiments*. This account seems to leave very little room for legislative agency in explaining the development of systems of law (*TMS*, III.4). Rather, he argued there that general rules of morality and their codification develop as a result of "habitual reflection" as to their suitability for the conditions in which they arise, not from the initiatives of any legislators (*TMS*, III.4.12).

Apart from these comments and other scattered notes, Smith did not offer any explicit account of connections between legislation and science. None of his works begins with a "methodological introduction", and whenever he did discuss questions of method, he often used analytically loose metaphors such as "machine", "system", and, most famously, the "invisible hand".

My aim in this section is not to explicate fully the meaning of a "science of a legislator", but to highlight the role of the activity of legislating in creating conditions that make the scientific study of society possible. The main claim I seek to make is that, according to Smith, the system of law generates regularities that make society a fit subject matter for scientific inquiry. It does so by delineating the forms of "habitual reflection" already prevailing in a society, thereby making certain standards of moral judgments appear natural, or in Smith's terminology of impartial spectatorship, "fixed in our mind" (*TMS*, III.4.12). Legislation is related to science, therefore, not only because legislators ought to be guided by scientists, but also because legislators create through the act of legislation conditions that allow the formation of shared expectations regarding the activity of subjects.

Edward Cohen has made a compelling case for a unity of method between *The Theory of Moral Sentiments* and *The Wealth of Nations* that can serve as a useful summary of Smith's view and a starting point for our discussion. Smith's science, according to Cohen, "provides an analysis of the workings of commercial society that will guide the legislator in the cultivation of justice" ("Justice and Political Economy in Commercial Society", 53). Thus, "Smith's picture of commercial society is one of a number of 'spheres' constituted by a set of invisible mechanisms that tend naturally to turn the pursuit of self-interest to the public advantage" (ibid., 53). Scientific activity is the activity of identifying these mechanisms and showing how, taken together as a "system", they promote the public advantage. Smith's analysis of competitive markets "demonstrates that the pursuit of economic gains by individuals has the unintended consequence of maximizing the opulence of society as a whole" (ibid., 54). However, these mechanisms function most efficiently only if supplemented by positive actions by the magistrate in enforcing security, justice, and certain "public works" (*WN*, IV.ix.51). "The conclusions of moral philosophy and political economy", therefore, "are the tools used by this 'mechanic' to ensure the achievements of justice as the central goal of natural jurisprudence" (Cohen, "Justice and Political Economy", 69). Eric Schliesser is therefore right to note that for Smith "[t]heories not only attempt to explain and predict economic behaviour, but through the actions of rulers also deliberately or unintentionally influence it" (Schliesser, "Adam Smith's Benevolent and Self-Interested Conception", 341).

Cohen correctly argues that his explication of Smith's science "presents an understanding of commercial society that is more complex and skeptical than is often recognized" (Cohen, "Justice and Political Economy", 69, n. 21). However, Smith's use of the terms "system" and "machine" is even more complicated than Cohen allows. In Cohen's view, the "scientific" aspect and the legislative aspect are analytically separate. The "scientist" hands her findings to the magistrate, who then puts them into use. But this is not quite the case for Smith. The constitutive parts of social systems are not springs and cogs but social practices. Consequently, the making of a system cannot be simply an act of describing or explaining existing mechanisms. Rather, it requires a re-description of existing social practices that situates them as parts of a system. These practices look like "mechanisms" to participants in social interactions only after they have been institutionalized in a way that makes them seem "natural", that is to say, unquestionable, a matter of common sense. Perhaps counterintuitively, one of the locutions of "natural" denotes for Smith the fact that standards of moral judgment that members of society find "natural" are, in fact, socially constructed and that this construct is instrumental in making certain forms of power relations appear as natural.

Comments made by Smith in an early essay, "History of Astronomy", can help us understand the process of creating a social system. There, he posits that three cognitive interests (so to speak) underlie scientific activities: wonder, surprise, and admiration (*Essays on Philosophical Subjects* [*EPS*], 35). We wonder when we encounter an extraordinary or uncommon object; we are surprised when things that commonly occur together do not occur together and vice versa, and we "admire the beauty of a plain or the greatness of a mountain" (ibid., 35).[12]

Scientific explanations, for Smith, are always motivated by a combination of these interests. Of the three, the admiration of beauty is of particular importance for his concept of a social mechanism, as it is "the love of system" and the "beauty of order" that "convince a leader to promote the public happiness". As Smith illustrates in *The Theory of Moral Sentiments*, "[w]hen the legislature establishes premiums and other encouragements to advance the linen or woollen manufactures, its conduct seldom proceeds from pure sympathy with the wearer of cheap or fine cloth, and much less from that with the manufacturer or merchant". Instead:

> The perfection of police, the extension of trade and manufactures, are noble and magnificent objects. The contemplation of them pleases us, and we are interested in whatever can tend to advance them. They make part of the great system of government, and the wheels of the political machine seem to move with more harmony and ease by means of them. We take pleasure in beholding the perfection of so beautiful and grand a system, and we are uneasy till we remove any obstruction that can in the least disturb or encumber the regularity of its motions. [*TMS*, IV.i.11][13]

---

12 In *TMS*, I.i.4.3 Smith provided a slightly different classification. There, admiration is the result of "approbation heightened by wonder and surprise".

13 See also *TMS*, VI.ii.2.15: "The great body of the party are commonly intoxicated

Smith was most likely being disingenuous here, not offering an implausible and rather naïve account of the process of legislation, but countering Hume's strictly utilitarian account. For our purpose we can leave aside the question of the motivation underlying legislation and simply note that legislators are here responsible for making "the wheels of the political machine" move. A social system appears to operate like a machine because legislators made it to appear this way.

So far, I have argued that legislators adjust social norms in a way that makes society appear to function like a machine that can therefore become the object of scientific study. However, Smith understood legislation to be taking place, not in a vacuum, but against existing historical experience and social practices.[14] To see the effect of history, we first need to introduce properly the main devices of Smith's moral philosophy: sympathy and the impartial spectator. Stephen Darwall aptly describes Smith's usage of sympathy as "a specific form of fellow-feeling, a sharing of another's feeling or motive as a result of projecting into his perspective and seeing his situation in the same emotionally or motivationally laden way we imagine he does" ("Sympathetic Liberalism", 144). For Smith then, sympathy is the ability to put oneself in the situation of the other person and to feel (with reduced intensity [*TMS*, I.I.47]) what he or she is feeling. The ability to sympathize with another person allows us to evaluate the propriety of the other person's feelings for his or her situation. We would disapprove of a person who laughs excessively upon hearing a marginally funny joke. On the other hand, we would approve of a person who laughs at a funny joke even if we ourselves are in a bad mood and do not laugh (*TMS* I.i.3.1–3). Therefore, sympathy is a mode of moral judgment that is not only projective, but also situational and contextual. It is based upon the evaluation of the propriety of a person's actions in the light of his or her situation and context.

Smith further described the way the principle of sympathy works by introducing an "impartial spectator". The impartial spectator serves both descriptive and evaluative purposes. Descriptively, the impartial spectator represents a communal standard against which moral evaluations of a person's own actions are being made. The impartial spectator represents the "reaction of an ordinary person when he is in the position of a non-involved spectator".[15] Smith argued that when we act, we do so in a way that seeks the approval of such a hypothetical spectator.

---

with the imaginary beauty of this ideal system".

14   Stephen Buckle's *Natural Law and the Theory of Property* is attentive to the historical dimension of the natural law tradition. See also Haakonssen, *The Science of a Legislator* chapter 7, for a discussion of "Smith's historical jurisprudence", and Meek, *Social Science and the Ignoble Savage*.

15   Campbell, *Adam Smith's Science of Morals*, 135. See also the discussion in Otteson, *Adam Smith's Marketplace of Life*, chapter 6.

The principle of sympathy and the idea of the impartial spectator allow Smith to explain a large number of complex moral evaluations. However, when he applied the impartial spectator to the understanding of the system of law, the crux of his argument lay in the way he put the impartial spectator into use. Smith's argument was inherently historical. He used the impartial spectator to explain the interaction between social and legal changes.

Smith's discussions of the development of the law of primogeniture in *The Wealth of Nations* and the *Lectures on Jurisprudence* (*LJ*) is instructive of the general gist of his views.[16] While Smith did not explicitly use the "impartial spectator" in this particular discussion, the spectator's frequent appearance elsewhere in the *Lectures* makes it plausible to assume that Smith applied the same mode of reasoning to the primogeniture discussion. Under ancient Roman law, inherited land was divided equally among all children of a family (*WN*, III.ii.3; *LJ*, (A).i.94). Such a "natural law of succession" can be seen as the default or commonsense view of an impartial spectator when land "is considered as the means only of subsistence and enjoyment" (*WN*, III.ii.3). However, the collapse of the Roman Empire led to the usurpation of uncultivated lands by barbaric nations, and in response, land became consolidated into large units. This consolidation could have been "a transitory evil" had land not become a means of "power and protection" (*WN*, III.ii.2; ii.3). Since concentration of power was viewed as a necessity, an impartial spectator would agree that it made sense to change the law so that all land would be inherited by one child. Given these circumstances, the law of primogeniture developed "in the process of time" (*WN*, III.ii.3). Thus, Smith's account of inheritance law in *The Wealth of Nations* is consistent with his suggestion in *The Theory of Moral Sentiments* that laws emerge through a process of "habitual reflection" on existing social circumstances.

However, Smith adds, "[l]aws frequently continue in force long after the circumstances, which first gave occasion to them, and which could alone render them reasonable, are no more" (*WN*, III.ii.4). The law of primogeniture itself became counterproductive once security was no longer the duty of large landowners who, furthermore, fail to take sufficient care of the land (*WN*, III.ii.6.8). While the right of primogeniture relied on presuppositions that had become "absurd", it remained respected in Smith's day and was, in his opinion, "likely to endure for many centuries" since people habituated to viewing this right of succession as natural approved of it morally (*WN*, III.ii.6.4).

Generalizing from this example, Smith's view of history can be described as follows. Although he did not portray primitive society in idyllic terms, he found the presumed simplicity of primitive social relations useful

---

16 His discussion of customs is another prime example of his deployment of the impartial spectator. See *TMS* V, and particularly V.2.15, where he explains how infanticide could have received moral approval in ancient Greece.

for enlightening later social relations. However, he does not treat the primitive state or any other stage as an ideal. Each society emerges from its historical predecessor and should be understood against it.[17] In response to changes external to the legal system, rearrangements of an existing distribution of the means of subsistence hold out the possibility of enhancing stability and progress. These changes, in turn, affect the balance of power among groups in a society, such that some groups possess greater access to the means of controlling power. Changes in the legal system, specifically, changes in the definitions of what constitutes a right to property, follow social changes. These legal changes occur spontaneously, yet benefit newly powerful groups by making their superior position appear natural and unquestionable. Nonetheless, successful legislation is an essential condition of the social transformation since it stabilizes and "naturalizes" the predominance of new standards of impartial spectatorship.

A note made by Smith in a different context captures the essence of his view of legislation: "man", he suggested, "the only designing power with which they were acquainted, never acts but either to stop, or to alter the course, which natural events would take, if left to themselves" (*EPS*, 49). Smith's legislator is not a platonic philosopher-king. He has some power to "alter the course" of conventional standards of moral judgment, but he cannot create them from scratch. Legislation must rely on an empirical and sociological understanding of the standards of moral judgment followed by members of society and the feasible ways of altering them. Change is achieved by adjusting definitions of property rights in order to make the power relations deemed desirable by the legislator appear natural, a matter of common sense.

Legally instantiated forms of unequal power relations outlast their usefulness, however. As we saw with the two changes in European inheritance law, a legal system that once served the "real interests" of the people eventually comes to hamper them.[18] Smith's science, as part of what Knud Haakonssen called "critical jurisprudence", evaluates the usefulness of existing laws and institutions by asking whether they still serve an advantageous social function.[19] Historical inquiry is a device that helps critical jurisprudence argue against certain laws and institutions that once served the "real interests" of society under different social conditions, but no longer do so.

Nevertheless, Smith was not the young Marx, and his science did not consist only of "ruthless criticism of everything existing". Science was not a value

---

17 Don Herzog makes this the cornerstone of Smith's notion of moral justification, which Herzog sees as a commendable form of justification that does not rely on an unnecessarily foundational view of human nature (Herzog, *Without Foundations*, chapter 4).

18 *WN*, III.ii.4, where Smith talks about "the real interests of a numerous family".

19 Haakonssen, *The Science of a Legislator*, chapter 6. See also, Teichgraeber, "Free Trade", 140.

neutral enterprise, for Smith, and he put it to the task of ideological construction. Legislators can effect change to the extent that legislation can encourage certain standards of moral judgment and repress other forms. Eventually, the forms institutionalized through the legal system end up appearing natural. In this second manifestation, Smith put his science in the service of legislators seeking to construct a successful ideology. Science can be used to determine which standards of moral evaluation can best serve as a foundation for legislation in a particular society. *The Wealth of Nations* provided a theoretical argument in support of the minimalist legal system he called the "system of natural liberty".

LEGAL FOUNDATIONS FOR COMMERCIAL SOCIETY

Following the explication of Smith's "science of the legislator" in the previous section, the interpretation of Smith offered below maintains that in Book I of *The Wealth of Nations* Smith followed the latter path of the "science of legislation", that of ideological construction. My interpretation is innovative in that it takes the different measures of value discussed by Smith to be part of a study of possible legal foundations for modern commercial societies. Smith argued for the system of natural liberty by examining different standards of moral judgment, i.e., of impartial spectatorship, that people in commercial societies seem to follow (summarized in Table I). He examined these sets of rules, or "the maxims of common life", to determine which are the most useful as building blocks for the legal system of commercial society.[20] He argued that a legal system dealing exclusively with violations of injustice and operating within a free market economy was capable of producing distribution that, under conditions of perfect liberty and continued growth, would be satisfying from the perspective of the other standards of moral judgment he examined: that of the real value and that of the natural price.

Table I: Standards of Moral Judgment—a summary

	Real Value	Natural Value	Market Value
Standard of Moral Judgement	Labor	Compensation for wage, rent, and profits	Negotiation in the marketplace; supply and demand (which are based on the subjective and socially constructed perception of needs)
Scope	Universal, accurate	Assumes unequal ownership	Conducted with the assistance of money
Difficulties	Not convenient for buying and selling	Based upon political struggle	Not sensitive to contextual aspects (esp. value of money)

20 *WN*, V.i.f, where Smith argues that systems of moral philosophy deal with arranging the "maxims of common life".

The obvious difficulty with the interpretation I offer is that Smith does not present the discussion in Book I as a study of conventional forms of moral judgment. However, I believe this is not a serious obstacle for my aim here, which is to present a "plausible reconstruction of the evidence" to support such a reading. As argued in the previous section, the understandings of Smith and his contemporaries regarding connections among politics, economics, and political economy differ greatly from ours. First, political economy was a subordinate branch of jurisprudence dealing not only with wealth creation, but also with the relationship between legislation and the creation of wealth. Second, legal discourse of Smith's era understood market prices as commonsense, moral guidelines used by judges in cases of commercial disputes, not as spontaneous outcomes of commercial interactions. They were the explaining variable, not the variable to be explained (Gordley, *Philosophical Origins*, 97–98). For these reasons, I believe that my reading of Smith's theory of prices, while conjectural, is neither anachronistic nor implausible.

At the beginning of the first book of *The Wealth of Nations* Smith set up the following question for inquiry: "what are the rules which men naturally observe in exchanging them [goods] either for money or for one another?" (*WN*, I.iv.12). For each of three rules that he examined, Smith essentially asked, if this rule were to be the underlying organizing principle of the legal system for a commercial society, how would economic exchanges be morally judged by members of society, once they had been habituated to view the rule as the natural standard of moral judgment? In particular, Smith seemed to be asking whether commerce itself would be deemed a morally neutral or an inherently corrupt social practice.

What first rule of exchange might appear morally fair to an impartial spectator in an environment without any power asymmetries or pre-established property rights? No negotiating party would agree to barter his or her product for something he or she could produce with less effort. The first standard of moral judgment Smith identified was therefore the use of labor time, or "toil and trouble" as a measure of value (*WN*, I.v.2). Labor, "the first price, the original purchase-money", "is the real measure of the exchangeable value of all commodities" (*WN*, I.v.1).[21] Now, to be sure, Smith was inconsistent in the way he described labor as a measure of value; he swayed between viewing the amount of labor that goes into an object as the measure of value and viewing its value as the amount of labor that an object can command. Nonetheless, labor is described as the "first price" since it seems likely to be the first rule an impartial spectator would follow (*WN*, I.v.2; *WN*, I.v.4). Under such circumstances, considerations of factors such as "hardship or ingenuity" are dealt with not by economic theory, but by the "haggling and bargaining of the market" above or below the standard set by labor time (*WN*, v.4).

---

21 See Fleischacker, *On Adam Smith's* Wealth of Nations, 124–131.

Smith often used primitive societies to illustrate the possibility of social interactions devoid of asymmetric power relations. This is the case with his use of a society of hunters to illustrate the notion of labor as a source of value.[22] If, in such as society it takes twice the amount of labor to kill a beaver than a deer, "one beaver should naturally exchange for or be worth two deer" (*WN*, I.vi.1).[23] Even though Smith discussed labor as the "real" measure of value in the context of a primitive society, this standard of moral judgment is not timebound. It is still available to commercial societies and thus deserves consideration by legislators.[24] Indeed, Smith deemed labor "the only universal, as well as the only accurate measure of value, or the only standard by which we can compare the values of different commodities at all times and at all places" (*WN*, I.v.17).

However, Smith argued that using labor as the legally institutionalized measure of value is impractical for any legal system. Labor, or the real price, exists alongside nominally priced commodities in societies using money. Since labor cannot be easily quantified, it is of no use as a measure of value in "buying and selling, the more common and ordinary transactions of human life" (*WN*, I.v.18). Commodities are "more frequently exchanged for, and thereby compared with, other commodities than with labor", and therefore, "it is more natural" to estimate their values in monetary terms (*WN*, I.v.5). As is often the case with Smith, an assertion that some standard of moral judgment is "natural" does not imply that it is also morally neutral. To the contrary, as we shall see, Smith shared with Locke and others a traditional view that money corrupts our ability to make commonsense moral evaluations. The "naturalness" of nominal prices turns out to favor the interests of those who make their living from commerce.

The political implications of being perceived as "natural" are central to the second standard of moral judgment Smith examined: the moral evaluation of value based on natural prices. In *The Wealth of Nations*, the natural price is achieved when it is "neither more nor less than what is sufficient to pay the rent of land, the wages of the labour, and the profits of the stock employed in raising, preparing, and bringing it to market". It is based on an "average" specific to "every society or neighbourhood" (*WN*, I.vii.4.2).[25] Unlike the "real value" of goods, their "natural price" presupposes a more elaborate social background

---

22 John Elliott suggests that this example should be seen as a "hypothetical mental experiment" ("Adam Smith's Conceptualization of Power, Markets, and Politics", 430).

23 And see Young, *Economics as a Moral Science*, 57.

24 For the way Smith used history to model different forms of behavior, see Samuel Hollander, "The Historical Dimension of *The Wealth of Nations*".

25 Notice that in the *Lectures on Jurisprudence* Smith defines the "natural price of labor" as the wages sufficient for the maintenance of the person, as well as recompense for the cost of education and the risk of dying (*LJ*, (A).vi.63–64).

in which rights for property are distributed unequally.²⁶ Smith discussed the reasoning behind the "natural price" in the following way:

> As soon as stock has accumulated in the hands of particular persons, some of them will naturally employ it in setting to work industrious people, whom they will supply with materials and subsistence, in order to make a profit by the sale of their work, or by what their labour adds to the value of the materials. In exchanging the complete manufacture either for money, for labour, or for other goods, over and above what may be sufficient to pay the price of the materials, and the wages of the workmen, something must be given for the profits of the undertaker of the work who hazards his stock in this adventure. The value which the workmen add to the materials, therefore, resolves itself in this ease into two parts, of which the one pays their wages, the other the profits of their employer upon the whole stock of materials and wages which he advanced. [*WN*, I.vi.5]²⁷

Smith was notoriously vague regarding the conditions that lead to the accumulation of capital. He seems to reject, albeit implicitly, the possibility that an historical "difference of natural talents" can be responsible for the existing accumulation of stock (*WN*, I.ii.3). Perhaps inequality is an unintended, yet advantageous, result of the propensity to admire the rich described in *The Theory of Moral Sentiments*.²⁸ At any rate, when natural price is discussed in *The Wealth of Nations*, the legitimacy of inequalities of wealth is not questioned. What is important for Smith is that in commercial societies natural price is a commonsense—indeed, to the participants themselves a "natural"—standard of moral judgment of prices.

While "real value" is accurate and universal, "natural price" results from a political struggle between laborers and owners of capital.²⁹ This struggle

---

26 Jan Peil captures this essence of natural prices, which Smith interpreted as "social values which people recognize as being adhered to in producing and distributing wealth" (*Adam Smith and Economic Science*, 146).

27 See also I.viii.5.

28 *TMS*, I.iii.2, but notice the ironic twist in *TMS*, IV.1.7 (the parable of the poor man's son) and in *TMS*, I.iii.3. For a discussion, see Khalil (2005) "An Anatomy of Authority".

29 See Herzog, *Without Foundations*, 208–211; Fairlamb, "Adam Smith's Other Hand", and John Elliott's discussion of "wealth power" in "Adam Smith's Conceptualization of Power", 430–433. Eric Schliesser's discussion of natural price is very helpful, although he interprets it differently ("Some Principles of Adam

is vividly articulated in Smith's discussion of factors affecting the recompense of labor. Wages are determined by a contract made between the laborer and the employer. However, employers and employees are not Smith's butchers and bakers. It is not only that the "interests" of the two parties are "by no means the same", as "[t]he workmen desire to get as much, the masters to give as little as possible" (*WN*, I.viii.11), but that the two parties possess unequal abilities to "force the other into compliance with their terms" (*WN*, I.viii.12).

> The masters, being fewer in number, can combine much more easily; and the law, besides, authorizes, or at least does not prohibit their combinations, while it prohibits those of the workmen. [...] A landlord, a farmer, a master manufacturer, or merchant, though they did not employ a single workman, could generally live a year or two upon the stocks which they have already acquired. Many workmen could not subsist a week, few could subsist a month, and scarce any a year without employment. In the long-run the workman may be as necessary to his master as his master to him; but the necessity is not so immediate. [*WN*, I.viii.12]

Smith further described wages as determined by secret conspiracies and combinations among masters to exploit their laborers, with the assistance of the legal system (*WN*, I.viii.13).[30] Notice that the description here is not simply of a perversion of the standard of moral judgment of the real price but a different standard of judgment altogether. Since accumulations of stock and relationships of wage labor are taken as "natural", there is no recourse to the simple equality presupposed by the former standard. It is therefore clear that for Smith measuring values by natural prices is somewhat analogous to measuring poverty by an official poverty line: although a poverty line is a common and

---

Smith's Newtonian Methods in *The Wealth of Nations*").

30 See also *LJ*, (A).iv.21: "But here when in the manner above mentioned some have great wealth and others nothing, it is necessary that the arm of authority should be continually stretched forth, and permanent laws or regulations made which may ascertain the property of the rich from the inroads of the poor, who would otherwise continually make encroachments upon it, and settle in what the infringements of this property consists and in what cases they will be liable to punishment. Laws and government may be considered in this and indeed in every case as a combination of the rich to oppress the poor, and preserve to themselves the inequality of goods which would otherwise be soon destroyed by the attacks of the poor [...]." A combination of laborers was considered a heinous crime from 1349's Statute of Labourers until 1825, which was the year that the laws against trade unions were repealed (Marx, *Capital*, 738).

conventional measure of poverty, determining what constitutes poverty is the result of uneven political struggle. As an accepted social convention, a poverty line is often spontaneously used to measure poverty, but upon reflection, it becomes clear that there is nothing natural about this measure.

Let us now proceed to the third and final standard of moral judgment that Smith discussed and ended up endorsing: the market price. The "market price", he writes, "often differs considerably" from the natural price "and is regulated by other circumstances" (*LJ*, (A).VI.70).[31]

> When goods are brought to the market we seldom enquire what profits the person will have if he get such or such price. Other circumstances determine what he shall have. These are 1st, the demand or need for it (whether this be real or capricious); 2dly, the abundance of it in proportion to this demand; and 3dly, the wealth of the demand, or demanders. [*LJ*, (A).VI.70]

In short, the standard of moral evaluation based on the market prices prescribes an evaluation based upon the fairness of the process of bargaining against available supply and demand. Smith makes it abundantly clear that supply, demand, and perception of need are context dependent and often socially constructed. Thus, while we might feel it is outrageous to demand "10000 crowns for one cruise of water" or to pay £250000 for the "famous Pits diamond", these prices become intelligible, though not necessarily justifiable, once we understand the conditions of the market in which such transactions took place (*LJ*, (A).VI.71).

Therefore, we can see that the third standard of moral judgment puts the impartial spectator in a weak position. It does not provide tools for morally evaluating the conditions shaping the supply and demand operating within the market in question (akin to the "toil and trouble" encompassed in real prices and average communal standards in natural prices). Thus, even though Smith acknowledged supply and demand to be contingent and often manipulated, impartial spectators habituated to using market prices perceived them as objective, unalterable conditions of the situation. Smith was fully aware that the most quotidian method of morally evaluating the economic activities and relationships captured in the value set on goods, namely their market price, can overlook many forms of injustice.

The fact that economic exchanges are conducted using nominal price (i.e., with money) complicates the reliance on market price for moral evaluations even further. First, there is no agreed upon unit for measuring the monetary, or

---

31 *WN*, I.viii defines market price as "[t]he actual price at which any commodity is sold".

nominal, price of goods. In different societies, different commodities are used as a common unit for measuring value, and even in commercial societies, both gold and silver are used. Furthermore, the value of each of these commonly used measures is not stable because of variations in supply and demand for the metal itself. The issue of conversion poses a problem that is not merely a technical one. Without a stable and agreed upon measure of value, the process of conversion itself becomes a site of manipulation. The second problem arises out of the use of legal tender as a substitute for the actual use of metals. This lends itself to the practice of "rubbing and wearing" coins to diminish the amount of metal in them (*WN*, I.v.41). Through this practice, "the princes and sovereign states" were able "to pay their debts and to fulfill their engagements with a smaller quantity of silver". This, however, was "in appearance only", for in reality the creditors were "defrauded of a part of what was due to them" (*WN*, I.iv.10).[32]

JURISPRUDENCE AND THE ETHICS OF GROWTH

The "natural system of perfect liberty" endorsed by Smith is one that naturalizes market prices. In this system, the duties of the sovereign are limited to the establishment of external security, domestic justice, and "the duty of erecting and maintaining certain public works and certain public institutions" (*WN*, IV.vii.c.44; ix.51). It is based on a clear distinction between perfect and imperfect rights. The sovereign need only establish a legal system sufficient to protect perfect rights. In this system, values are determined by the market price based on supply and demand. Even though Smith does not say so explicitly, the thrust of the argument is that market exchanges within such a system can be viewed as just in the ongoing and ordinary "habitual reflections" of society's members.

His primary line of defense for this system, constituting one of the main theses of *The Wealth of Nations*, posits the natural price as "the central price" toward which market prices "are continually gravitating" (*WN*, I.vii.15). Thus, the system of perfect liberty should not, in principle and over the long run, produce a distribution of goods different from what would have been produced under a system based on natural price. Market prices can be kept systematically higher than natural prices only thanks to unnecessary "regulations of police" (*WN*, I.vii.20). Smith integrated historical and critical jurisprudence to explain how the feudal laws still paramount in the "policy of Europe" had become fetters to the accumulation of wealth in commercial societies (*WN*, I.x.c.2).[33] His argument is well-known; indeed it is the very foundation of classical economic

---

32 It is interesting to note that in writing on jurisprudence, the only time Smith deals directly with details of commercial contracts regards the effect on debts of debasement of coins (*LJ*, (A).ii.80–84). Smith's point is that a civil law that requires paying the debt with debased coin is contrary to "justice and equity".
33 See discussion in *WN*, III.

liberalism, so there is no need to discuss it any further here.

Nonetheless, Smith's argument does not address the difference between natural price and real value, the latter being the universal and just standard of moral judgment. Istvan Hont and Michael Ignatieff provide the relevant context for dealing with this omission. They affirm that "*The Wealth of Nations* was centrally concerned with the issue of justice, with finding a market mechanism capable of reconciling inequality of property with adequate provisions for the excluded" (*Wealth and Virtue*, 2). The "policing" of grain, which determined practices for its distribution in times of famine, was a main concern of mercantilist policies and an issue with a long history in Europe. Accepted doctrine held that the distribution of grain in times of need could only be made by central authorities (*Wealth and Virtue*, 13). Theorists of natural law dealt extensively with the problem of justifying limitations of property rights. In their view, property rights emerged from a social contract dividing originally common land. One provision of the social contract allowed rights to property to be overridden in times of severe need. Smith, according to Hont and Ignatieff, offered a different approach to this problem:

> he transposed the question from the terrain of jurisprudence and political theory to the terrain of political economy, using natural modeling to demonstrate that by raising the productivity of agriculture, commercial society could provide adequately for the needs of the wage-earner without having to resort to any form of redistributive meddling in the property rights of individuals. Growth in conditions of 'natural liberty' would explode the whole antinomy between needs and rights. [*Wealth and Virtue*, 25]

Smith's "ethics of growth" offered, then, a macro level explanation as to why market price ought to undergird the legal system at the expense of real price. In a "progressive state" free of unnecessary regulations, demand for labor brings higher wages and makes the conditions of the "labouring poor" "the happiest and the most comfortable", at least as compared to other policy options (*WN*, I.viii.43). Notoriously, Smith does not elaborate on the likelihood of infinite growth, and the few remarks he makes are inconsistent.[34] Nonetheless, much of the burden of Smith's defense of the system of natural liberty clearly rests on the claim that it is conducive to economic progress and thus conducive to more liberal rewards for labor.

It is not my intention to evaluate the merits of Smith's "ethics of growth". We now know that the system of natural liberty does not tip the balance of

---

34 Robert E. Prasch, "The Ethics of Growth in Adam Smith's *Wealth of Nations*". I borrow the term "ethics of growth" from Prasch.

power in favor of labor, and that, even were infinite progress possible, economic progress has costs that need to be balanced against other social values. Rather, I want to examine Smith's move from micro level evaluation of the fairness of each individual economic exchange to macro level evaluation of the entire economic system in the context of his own theory of jurisprudence.

As I stated earlier, Smith's meta-theory of jurisprudence articulated in *The Theory of Moral Sentiments* provided (among other things) philosophical foundations for the fundamental distinction of modern natural law—the distinction between perfect and imperfect rights. His analysis of the moral sentiments explains why breaches of justice differ categorically from other moral failings and why only the former lend themselves to legislation. The crux of the argument is that cases of injustice that entail injury uniquely provoke a strong feeling of resentment. This feeling emerges spontaneously, almost instinctively, only in cases of injustice because they are indisputable. In turn, the sentiment of resentment explains both the motivation to punish and the severity of punishment (*TMS*, II.i. and II.ii). The core of the argument can be illustrated by the following contrast. Determining whether someone acted with appropriate generosity in a certain situation requires background information and an intricate analysis of social conventions. However, when someone violently grabs the purse of an old and helpless person and runs away, questions of moral epistemology vanish and the theft is immediately recognized as unjust. In the first case, even a complex system of rules cannot sufficiently determine appropriate generosity. In the latter case, laws are redundant; the situation can be morally judged without them. The distinction between perfect and imperfect rights is therefore intrinsic to the way our moral sentiments operate. As a result, no social contract is necessary either to justify the distinction itself or to specify the content of the perfect rights.

But we can now see the contradictory character of Smith's view. To see this, we need to reconstruct the expected reasoning of an impartial spectator in market societies. Smith clearly wanted economic transactions that *appear* fair and voluntary (without overt coercion or manipulation) to be spontaneously approved. Laborers are only expected to evaluate the fairness of their wages in terms of supply and demand in the job market, not based on comparative evaluations of the long-term performance of different institutional arrangements. Commercial societies cannot function if the institution of commerce itself is constantly being morally questioned. Thus, commerce can neither generate the sentiment of resentment that underlies the evaluation of injury and injustice, nor call forth the complex and intricate moral evaluation needed for evaluating generosity. Nevertheless, if we follow Smith's own reasoning, then we must conclude that the appearance of fairness in commerce is misleading and that the natural feeling of approval for commercial transactions is socially constructed.

Going back to Bittermann's assertion with which I opened the discussion, perhaps the reason that the impartial spectator "puts no appearance" in *The Wealth of Nations* is that Smith thought commercial society could not be hospitable to impartial moral spectatorship. Smith used the impartial spectator as an analytic device to explain the historical emergence of the system of natural liberty. However, once the system is established, spontaneous evaluations of what constitutes injustice become much more difficult. The economic market, the main regulatory mechanism in such a system, defies simple characterization of injury. As the weight of the moral justification for the system of natural liberty shifted away from micro level evaluation of the fairness of individual transactions toward an aggregate macro level comparison of the performance of different systems of political economy, the impartial spectator had no place and therefore was forced to leave the building.

CONCLUSIONS

Libertarians make economic exchange between free individuals the prototype of justice since the value of the goods being exchanged must be equal. Smith never thought this could be the case because he conceived commercial activity as a political realm characterized by manipulation and coercion. His foray into political economy was in part motivated by an interest in better understanding the deceptive nature of the sense of fairness in commercial activity and its implication for the moral and legal regulations of commerce. He ended up endorsing an ideological construction resembling that of libertarians only superficially, a whitewashing of the best available alternative required to bridge the gap between the potentially deceptive appearance of fairness imposed by the system of natural liberty and the real "political" character of commercial activity.[35]

---

35 For their helpful comments on earlier drafts of this article, I would like to thank James Farr, Ryan Jill Hudson, Jeffrey Lomonaco, the participants in the University of Michigan's Political Theory Workshop, the participants in the conference on Adam Smith's *The Theory of Moral Sentiments* held at Rochester Institute of Technology in May 2006, and the anonymous reviewers of *EJPT*.

SELECT BIBLIOGRAPHY

Ashcraft, Richard. "Locke's Political Philosophy". In *The Cambridge Companion to Locke*. Edited by Vere Chappell. Cambridge: Cambridge University Press, 1994, 226–251.

Bittermann, Henry J. "Adam Smith's Empiricism and the Law of Nature: I". *The Journal of Political Economy* 48 (1940): 487–520.

Blaug, Mark. *Economic Theory in Retrospect*, 4th ed. Cambridge: Cambridge University Press, 1985.

Buckle, Stephen. *Natural Law and the Theory of Property: Grotius to Hume*. Oxford: Clarendon Press, 1991.

Campbell, T. D. *Adam Smith's Science of Morals*. London: George Allen & Unwin, Ltd., 1971.

Cohen, E. S. "Justice and Political Economy in Commercial Society: Adam Smith's 'Science of a Legislator'". *The Journal of Politics* 51 (1989): 50–72.

Darwall, Stephen. "Sympathetic Liberalism: Recent Work on Adam Smith". *Philosophy and Public Affairs* 28, no. 2 (1999): 139–164.

Elliott, John E. "Adam Smith's Conceptualization of Power, Markets, and Politics". *Review of Social Economy* 58 (2000): 429–454.

Fairlamb, Horace L. "Adam Smith's Other Hand: A Capitalist Theory of Exploitation". *Social Theory and Social Practice* 22 (1996): 193–223.

Fitzgibbons, Athol. *Adam Smith's System of Liberty, Wealth, and Virtue: The Moral and Political Foundations of* The Wealth of Nations. Oxford: Clarendon Press, 1995.

Fleischacker, Samuel. *On Adam Smith's* Wealth of Nations. Princeton: Princeton University Press, 2004.

Force, Pierre. *Self-Interest before Adam Smith: A Genealogy of Economic Science*. Cambridge: Cambridge University Press, 2003.

Gordley, James. *The Philosophical Origins of Modern Contract Doctrine.* Oxford: Clarendon Press, 1991.

Haakonssen, Knud. *Natural Law and Moral Philosophy: From Grotius to the Scottish Enlightenment.* Cambridge: Cambridge University Press, 1996.

———. *The Science of a Legislator: The Natural Jurisprudence of David Hume and Adam Smith.* Cambridge: Cambridge University Press, 1981.

Herzog, Don. *Without Foundations: Justification in Political Theory.* Ithaca: Cornell University Press, 1985.

Hochstrasser, T. J. *Natural Law Theories in the Early Enlightenment.* Cambridge: Cambridge University Press, 2000.

Hollander, Samuel. "The Historical Dimension of *The Wealth of Nations*". *Transactions of the Royal Society of Canada,* Series IV, 14 (1976): 277–292.

Hont, Istvan, and Michael Ignatieff. "Needs and Justice in *The Wealth of Nations*: An Introductory Essay". In *Wealth and Virtue,* edited by Istvan Hont and Michael Ignatieff. Cambridge: Cambridge University Press, 1983, 1–44.

Hont, Istvan, and Michael Ignatieff, eds. *Wealth and Virtue: The Shaping of Political Economy in the Scottish Enlightenment.* Cambridge: Cambridge University Press, 1983.

Khalil, Elias L. "An Anatomy of Authority: Adam Smith as Political Theorist". *Cambridge Journal of Economics* 29 (2005): 57–71.

Marx, Karl, *Capital.* Vol. 1. Translated by Ben Fowkes. London: Penguin Books, 1976.

Meek, Ronald L. *Social Science and the Ignoble Savage.* Cambridge: Cambridge University Press, 1976.

Montes, Leonidas. *Adam Smith in Context: A Critical Reassessment of Some Central Components of His Thought.* New York: Palgrave Macmillan, 2004.

Otteson, James R. *Adam Smith's Marketplace of Life.* Cambridge: Cambridge University Press, 2002.

Pack, Spencer J., and Eric Schliesser. "Smith's Humean Criticism of Hume's Account of the Origin of Justice". *Journal of the History of Philosophy* 44 (2006): 47–63.

Peil, Jan. *Adam Smith and Economic Science: A Methodological Reinterpretation.* Cheltenham, UK: Edward Elgar, 1999.

Prasch, Robert E. "The Ethics of Growth in Adam Smith's *Wealth of Nations*". *History of Political Economy* 23, no. 2 (1991): 337–351.

Ron, Amit. "The 'Market' and the 'Forum' in Hobbes's Political Philosophy". *Polity* 38 (2006): 235–253.

Rothschild, Emma. *Economic Sentiments: Adam Smith, Condorcet, and the Enlightenment.* Cambridge, MA: Harvard University Press, 2001.

Schliesser, Eric. "Adam Smith's Benevolent and Self-Interested Conception of Philosophy". In *New Voices on Adam Smith*, edited by Leonidas Montes and Eric Schliesser. New York: Routledge, 2006, 328–357.

———. "Some Principles of Adam Smith's Newtonian Methods in *The Wealth of Nations*". *Research in the History of Economic Thought and Methodology* 23-A (2005): 33–74.

Smith, Adam. *Essays on Philosophical Subjects.* Oxford: Clarendon Press, 1980.

———. *An Inquiry into the Nature and Causes of the Wealth of Nations.* Edited by R. H. Campbell, A. S. Skinner, and W. B. Todd. Indianapolis: Liberty Fund, 1981.

———. *Lectures on Jurisprudence.* Edited by R. L. Meek, D. D. Raphael, and P. G. Stein. Indianapolis: Liberty Fund, 1982.

———. *The Theory of Moral Sentiments.* Edited by D. D. Raphael and A. L. Macfie. Indianapolis: Liberty Fund, 1984.

Teichgraeber, Richard F. *"Free Trade" and Moral Philosophy: Rethinking the Sources of Adam Smith's* Wealth of Nations. Durham, NC: Duke University Press, 1986.

Tribe, Keith. "Adam Smith: Critical Theorist?" *Journal of Economic Literature* 37 (1999): 609–632.

Tuck, Richard. *Natural Rights Theories: Their Origin and Development.* Cambridge: Cambridge University Press, 1977.

Winch, Donald. *Adam Smith's Politics: An Essay in Historiographic Revision.* Cambridge: Cambridge University Press, 1978.

Young, Jeffrey T. *Economics as a Moral Science: The Political Economy of Adam Smith.* Cheltenham, UK: Edward Elgar, 1997.

REVISITING SENTIMENTALISM: A SMITHIAN NORMATIVE MORAL THEORY

Monica Gerreck

I. INTRODUCTION

Recently philosophers have found a renewed interest in the sentiments. Robert Solomon, perhaps their biggest advocate, declares that "when being 'reasonable' means repressing, ignoring, or denigrating feeling, then philosophy has gone too far and, so far as most people are concerned, rendered itself irrelevant" (*In Defense of Sentimentality*, vii[1]). Ethically, support comes from the likes of Alvin Goldman, who claims, "moral theory needs to be sensitive to the phenomenon of empathy" ("Empathy, Mind, and Morals", 36); Simon Blackburn, who asserts that "[t]o moralize [...] is to insist on emotional responses" (*Ruling Passions*, 20); Michael Slote, who states, "[m]oral sentimentalism offers virtue ethics some splendid opportunities it has previously, to a large extent, neglected" (*Morals from Motives*, vii–ix); and Mary Midgley, who argues, "[f]eeling and action *are* essential elements in morality [...] Hume was right to stress them. And today there is yet strong ground for doing so" (*Heart & Mind*, 12, original emphasis). More to the purpose of this paper, Stephen Darwall explains:

> Contemporary writers on ethics who are attracted to ethics of virtue or impressed by the role of sympathy, emotion, and feeling in the moral life have generally looked to Hume for inspiration. The remarkable resources of Hume's ethics notwithstanding, however, there are [...] reasons for taking a serious interest in Smith. First, Smith's theory of sympathy and its role in our emotional lives is richer, more sophisticated, and, arguably, more suggestive for a wider range of issues in experimental psychology, philosophy of mind and moral psychology than is Hume's. [...] Second, Smith's theory of moral sentiments deploys this more sophisticated theory of sympathy in a way that is interesting in itself and provides an important sentimentalist alternative to Hume. ["Sympathetic Liberalism", 140–141]

Darwall also maintains that Smith's "distinctive form of sentimentalism [... is

---

[1] Bibliographic information for all references can be found in the Select Bibliography at the end of this essay.

...] probably the most interesting version ever developed" (140).[2]

I agree with the praise bestowed upon sentimentalism, and Adam Smith's version in particular, and think a normative ethic based on Smith's sentimentalism is long overdue. The purpose of this paper is to introduce such an ethic. The moral principle to be derived and supported is "An act is wrong if an impartial spectator cannot sympathize with it and an act is right if an impartial spectator can sympathize with it". In order to do this, I will give a descriptive account of the role of sympathy and the sentiments in making moral judgments, and in doing so explain how a normative ethic can be developed from this account. Then I will give several reasons why this is the moral theory to which we ought to appeal. Finally, I will show how this normative moral theory responds to both non-controversial and controversial cases while also showing how it does not suffer from the problems of the other major normative moral theories.

II. SYMPATHY

In general, sympathy, for Smith, is what occurs when we put ourselves in the shoes of others and feel what they are feeling given their circumstances (*TMS*, I.i.1.5).[3] Today, we consider this to be empathy, a "feeling-with" others, whereas sympathy is thought to be a "feeling-for" others (Goldman, "Empathy, Mind, and Morals", 29; Goldman, "Ethics and Cognitive Science", 351; Slote, "Moral Sentimentalism", 299–300; Slote, "Autonomy and Empathy", 5–6). We can probably attribute the difference in terminology to the fact that the term "empathy" did not arise until the early 20th century (Slote, "Moral Sentimentalism", 297; Slote, "Autonomy and Empathy", 5; Richmond, "Being in Others", 245). Although I think a good argument can be made for using the term "empathy" instead of the term "sympathy" when discussing Smith's theory, in order to remain true to the text, I will continue to use the term "sympathy".

Now, Smith uses the term "sympathy" in several different ways to describe similar, yet slightly different, acts of imagination that all seem to be

---

2   Non-ethical support of sentimentalism is found in Robert Gordon's works on simulation theory in philosophy of mind (e.g., "Folk Psychology as Simulation", "The Simulation Theory", "Simulation Without Introspection", "Sympathy, Simulation, and the Impartial Spectator", "Simulation and the Explanation of Action").

3   Although I will go in to a bit more detail regarding the way an affect match actually occurs between a spectator and the person or people principally concerned, Smith's explanation of it is much more detailed and complicated than the one I am giving here. The one I have provided is enough to serve our purposes, however. All references to Adam Smith's *Theory of Moral Sentiments* will be noted as *TMS* followed by the part number, section number, chapter number (where applicable), and paragraph number.

empathic in nature.[4] For the purposes of this paper, we need only be familiar with his basic definition of sympathy: it is "our fellow-feeling with any passion whatever" (*TMS*, I.i.1.5). However, sympathy does not occur if by coincidence two people are feeling the same passion.[5] Rather, it occurs when one person, the spectator, puts herself in the shoes of another, e.g., the agent, and feels the passion(s) the agent is feeling.

> [I]t is by the imagination only that we can form any conception of what are his sensations. Neither can that faculty help us to this any other way, than by representing to us what would be our own, if we were in his case. [...] By the imagination we place ourselves in his situation, we conceive ourselves enduring all the same torments, we enter as it were into his body, and become in some measure the same person with him, and thence form some idea of his sensations, and even feel something which, though weaker in degree, is not altogether unlike them. [*TMS*, I.i.1.2]

Sympathy enables us to get inside the experience of others by imagining ourselves in their situation; it joins us to their world, their motivations, and to the circumstances to which they are responding. In this strictest sense of the term, sympathy occurs when an affect match between the person principally concerned and the spectator occurs. So, if you are feeling anger and I put myself in your shoes (that is to say, I imagine myself in your situation) and feel anger as

---

4   For Smith, sympathy is an act of the imagination, although not all acts of the imagination are sympathy. See also Goldman, "Empathy, Mind, and Morals", 29: "Central cases of empathy [...] may arise from simulation [...] from imaginatively adopting the perspective of another"; Goldman, "Ethics and Cognitive Science", 351: "Paradigm cases of empathy [...] consist first of taking the perspective of another person, that is, imaginatively assuming one or more of the other person's mental states"; Slote, "Moral Sentimentalism", 300: "Empathy involves seeing or feeling things from the standpoint of others; in some sense [...] empathy involves identifying to some extent with another person"; and Hoffman, *Empathy and Moral Development*, 4: "empathy [is] defined as an affective response more appropriate to another's situation than one's own". Psychological experiments not only support the belief that we are capable of empathy (and that it is a deliberate act of the imagination), but also that such acts produce a greater response in the observer than just watching does, e.g., Hoffman, *Empathy and Moral Development* and Goldman, "Empathy, Mind, and Morals" and "Ethics and Cognitive Science".

5   Admittedly, I am using the term "same" here rather loosely. Smith acknowledges that two people can never feel identical passions, but it is possible for two people to feel passions similar enough that we can call them the same.

well, then I can be said to be sympathizing with you.

III. THE IMPARTIAL SPECTATOR AND MORAL JUDGMENTS

According to Smith, it is an impartial spectator who determines the propriety and merit of passions and actions. The *raison d'être* for the impartial spectator is because those involved in a particular situation are often overcome with too much of a passion or with the wrong passion and thus are not always predisposed to act appropriately. For example, Smith says:

> The insolence and brutality of anger, in the same manner, when we indulge its fury without check or restraint, is, of all objects, the most detestable. But we admire that noble and generous resentment which governs its pursuit of the greatest injuries, not by the rage which they are apt to excite in the breast of the sufferer, but by the indignation which they naturally call forth in that of the impartial spectator; which allows no word, no gesture, to escape it beyond what this more equitable sentiment would dictate; which never, even in thought, attempts any greater vengeance, nor desires to inflict any greater punishment, than what every indifferent person would rejoice to see executed.[6] [*TMS*, I.i.5.4]

The impartial spectator is also crucial to the success of this sentimentalist ethic because, as Slote and Goldman point out, there will be some, e.g., psychopaths and the autistic, who are not only incapable of sympathy, but who are often not able to feel and act appropriately (Slote, "Autonomy and Empathy" and Goldman, "Empathy, Mind, and Morals" and "Ethics and Cognitive Science"). Moreover, the impartial spectator keeps our biases in check. That is, we naturally sympathize with those who are familiar more than with those who are strangers, with those who are similar more than with those who are dissimilar, and with those who are at hand rather than with those who are not (*TMS*, I.i.4.9 and VI.ii.1.1–6). The impartial spectator allows for the consideration of these biases without allowing them to unduly affect our actions and judgments.[7] Therefore, it is the impartial spectator who is the final judge and court when it comes to determining the propriety and meritoriousness of an act.[8]

---

6   This is why motives and actions are judged to be improper or unmeritorious, as we will see shortly. See also Hoffman, *Empathy and Moral Development*, Chapter 8.

7   Again, the impartial spectator has the relevant facts that may include knowledge of the relationship the agent has with the recipient.

8   We are here concerned only with the propriety of actions, although judgments of merit are briefly discussed below.

The impartial spectator represents the viewpoint of the ordinary person when she is in the position of a non-involved spectator. So, although she does not possess those traits specific to the person (or people) principally involved, she does possess all the normal feelings characteristic of human nature. In addition, she is well-informed as she knows the relevant facts of the situation (and she has no trouble determining whether or not she has all the relevant facts because they are those that would be important to her were she actually the agent or the recipient), and she does not make judgments in matters of which she has inadequate knowledge. Yet, the impartial spectator is not omniscient and so is not the perfect moral judge in this sense of the term "perfect". She is perfect, however, in that she is capable of sympathetic accuracy and in the sense that her reactions to particular acts are perfectly indicative of their moral quality.

For those familiar with ideal observer theories, I want to make clear that although the impartial spectator and the ideal observer do have some traits in common (viz., they both have and judge from an impartial point of view), there are significant differences between them. As noted above, the impartial spectator, unlike most ideal observers, does not necessarily possess *all* the facts.[9] She does not possess "superhuman powers of thought, superhuman knowledge and no human weakness" as R. M. Hare's ideal observer does (*Moral Thinking*, 44). Furthermore, as was noted, she is not "incapable of experiencing any emotions at all" as is Roderick Firth's ideal observer ("Ethical Absolutism and the Ideal Observer", 340). In criticism of ideal observer theories, Roger Brandt specifically points out that (unlike the impartial spectator) the ideal observer's lack of emotional responses (or, rather, her inability to emotionally respond) makes it difficult for us not only to trust her judgments, but to consider them as definitive of morality (Brandt, "The Definition of an 'Ideal Observer' Theory in Ethics", 226–228). In addition, the more we build into the definition of the ideal observer, the less useful it becomes as a heuristic device (Walker, "Partial Consideration", 766–768). The impartial spectator does not fall prey to these problems because she is ultimately more human-like than not.

When making moral judgments, the impartial spectator judges the motive (passion), and thus action, of the agent (judgments of propriety), as well as the consequences (viz., the emotional responses of the recipients) of the agent's action (judgments of merit) (*TMS*, I.i.3.1, I.i.3.6, and II.i.Intro).[10] With respect to judgments of propriety, Smith says:

---

9   Roderick Firth argues the ideal observer is omniscient (with respect to non-ethical facts) as well as omnipercipient, disinterested (which means that she is entirely lacking in particular interests), dispassionate, and consistent ("Ethical Absolutism and the Ideal Observer").

10 Smith says that judgments of propriety arise from direct sympathy (sympathy with the agent), while judgments of merit arise from indirect sympathy (sympathy with the recipient) (*TMS*, II.i.5.1).

> When the original passions of the person principally concerned are in perfect accord with the sympathetic emotions of the spectator, they necessarily appear to this last just and proper, and suitable to their objects; and, on the contrary, when, upon bringing the case home to himself, he finds that they do not coincide with what he feels, they necessarily appear to him unjust and improper, and unsuitable to the causes which excite them. [*TMS*, I.i.3.1]

> [A]ll the [...] passions of human nature, seem proper and are approved of, when the heart of every impartial spectator entirely sympathizes with them, when every indifferent bystander entirely enters into, and goes along with them. [*TMS*, II.i.2.1]

> If upon placing ourselves in his situation, we thoroughly enter into all the passions and motives which influenced it, we approve of it, by sympathy with the approbation of this supposed equitable judge. If otherwise, we enter into his disapprobation and condemn it. [*TMS*, III.1.3]

So, if there is an affect match between the spectator and agent, then the motive, and thus the act, is said to be proper. If there is no affect match between the two, then the motive, and thus act, is said to be improper.

Judgments of merit, on the other hand, are determined by "the beneficial or hurtful nature of the effects which the affection aims at, or tends to produce", and these are "the qualities by which it is entitled to reward, or is deserving of punishment" (*TMS*, I.i.3.7). Neither Smith nor I are ultimately consequentialists, but we are concerned about more than just the motive of the agent. Thus, if an act should cause gratitude (as determined by an impartial spectator), then the act is meritorious and should be rewarded. If an act should cause resentment (as determined by an impartial spectator), then the act is lacking merit and should be punished. According to Smith, to be the proper object of gratitude or resentment one must be the cause of the pleasure or pain, must be capable of feeling pleasure or pain, and must not only have produced the relevant sensation, but must have produced it from design (*TMS*, II.iii.1.3).[11] That is, if a person acts so as to produce pleasure, but instead produces pain, she is not to be punished (as resentment toward her is not appropriate) and if she acts so as to produce pain, but instead produces pleasure, she is not to be

---

11 So, inanimate objects and most animals are not proper objects of resentment, although we often do feel resentment toward them.

rewarded (as gratitude toward her is not appropriate).

In sum, if the impartial spectator sympathizes with the agent's motive (if there is an affect match between the impartial spectator and the agent), then the motive, and thus the action, is judged to be proper. If the impartial spectator does not sympathize with the agent in such a way (if there is no affect match between the two), then the motive, and thus the action, is judged to be improper. If the impartial spectator sympathizes with the gratitude of the recipient (if there is an affect match between the two), then the action is meritorious (rewardable). If the impartial spectator does not sympathize with the feeling of gratitude of the recipient, if gratitude is not the appropriate sentimental response to the action (if there is no affect match between the two), then the action is not rewardable. If the impartial spectator sympathizes with the resentment of the recipient (if there is an affect match between the two), then the action is punishable. If the impartial spectator does not sympathize with the feeling of resentment of the recipient (if there is no affect match between the two), then the action is not punishable.

This is not just the case when the impartial spectator is acting as a judge of someone else's actions. Smith thinks that we each have an internal impartial spectator that acts as our conscience: "the tribunal of their own consciences, to that of the supposed impartial and well-informed spectator, to that of the man within the breast, the great judge and arbiter of their conduct" (*TMS*, III.2.32; see also III.3.1). When a person judges her own behavior, she compares the sentiments she actually feels with those she would feel were she a spectator judging her own behavior and feelings.

> The principle by which we naturally either approve or disapprove of our own conduct, seems to be altogether the same with that by which we exercise the like judgments concerning the conduct of other people. We either approve or disapprove of the conduct of another man according as we feel that, when we bring his case home to ourselves, we either can or cannot entirely sympathize with the sentiments and motives which directed it. And, in the same manner, we either approve or disapprove of our own conduct, according as we feel that, when we place ourselves in the situation of another man, and view it, as it were, with his eyes and from his station, we either can or cannot entirely enter into and sympathize with the sentiments and motives which influenced it. We can never survey our own sentiments and motives, we can never form any judgment concerning them; unless we remove ourselves, as it were, from our own natural station, and endeavour to view them as at a certain distance from us. But we can do this in no other way than

by endeavouring to view them with the eyes of other people, or as other people are likely to view them. [*TMS*, III.1.2; see also III.1.6 and III.4.2]

Judgments of propriety and merit are not the only two ways the impartial spectator makes judgments. In fact, there are four sources from which sentiments of approbation arise (and thus four from which sentiments of disapprobation arise). As stated, the first two are approving of the motives of the agent and entering into the gratitude of the recipient. The third occurs when the spectator "observe[s] that [the agent's] conduct has been agreeable to the general rules by which those two sympathies generally act" (*TMS*, VII.iii.3.16).[12] The fourth transpires "when [the spectator] consider[s] such actions as making a part of a system of behavior which tends to promote the happiness either of the individual or of the society, they appear to derive a beauty from this utility, not unlike that which we ascribe to any well-contrived machine" (*TMS*, VII.iii.3.16). The third and fourth sources are not primary sources, however. As T. D. Campbell points out, the third source is derived from the first two, and the last source is an afterthought rather than a part of the origin of moral judgments (Campbell, *Adam Smith's Science of Morals*, 108).[13] Yet, they are not to be ignored either. In fact, given our reliance on general rules (see below), the third source plays a more significant role than Smith seems to imply at this point.

Because we are often in fact so biased and moved by such strong passions, we do not always invoke the impartial spectator when we should (Slote, "Moral Sentimentalism", 296–297; Goldman, "Empathy, Mind, and Morals", 22; Goldman, "Ethics and Cognitive Science", 357–359; Hoffman, *Empathy and Moral Development*, 13–14 and Chapter 8). In fact, Smith says at one point that a person might be, for example, so overcome with resentment toward another who has only slightly provoked him that he feels the death of the provocateur is little compensation for the wrong and that "the fury of his own temper may be such, that had this been the first time in which he considered such an action, he would undoubtedly have determined it to be quite just and proper, and what every impartial spectator would approve of" (*TMS*, III.4.12). However, he has learned through his observations of others how hideous such revenges appear and has therefore set a rule to abstain from acting as such. It is his reverence for the rule that helps him correct his passions.[14] So, according to Smith, in order to avoid

---

12 I discuss Smith's notion of general rules in greater detail below.

13 The fourth source is taken to be an afterthought because, again, although Smith thinks the utility of a system of behavior is important, it is certainly not the basis of his system (*TMS*, IV.2.3).

14 Note that Smith goes on here to explain that a person may still violate a rule, that the passion may just be too strong, but that the person is fully aware of the fact that he is violating the rule and that after "his passion [… is …] gratified and

moral corruption due to these imperfections we develop general moral rules to guide our conduct: "[w]hen these general rules [...] have been formed [...] we frequently appeal to them as to the standards of judgment" (*TMS*, III.4.11). They so often stand in for the impartial spectator that most of us regulate our behavior by them. That is, instead of relying on our conscience or determining what an impartial spectator would feel or do in a certain situation, we look to the moral rules as our guide. He says, "[t]hose general rules of conduct, when they have been fixed in our mind by habitual reflection are of great use" (*TMS*, III.4.12).[15]

The rules are formed by experience of what motives and acts are approved of and what motives and acts are disapproved of, unlike, say, Kantian deontology, which determines which motives and acts are appropriate based on whether they adhere to the rules. With a Smithian-based sentimentalism we do not look to general rules and then determine whether a particular action is proper or meritorious. We look to the motives and actions that are (or are not) proper or meritorious and develop our moral rules from them.

> We do not originally approve or condemn particular actions; because, upon examination, they appear to be agreeable or inconsistent with a certain general rule. The general rule, on the contrary, is formed, by finding from experience, that all actions of a certain kind, or circumstanced in a certain manner, are approved or disapproved of. [*TMS*, III.4.8; see also III.4.7 and III.4.9][16]

---

palled, he begins to view what he has done in the light in which others are apt to view it: and actually feels, what he had only foreseen imperfectly before, the stings of remorse and repentance begin to agitate and torment him" (*TMS*, III.4.12).

15 Smith argues at one point that "those important rules of morality are the commands and laws of the Deity" (*TMS*, III.5.2). What exactly he means by this and the arguments for it need to be explored, but we need not worry about the outcome of such an exploration for the purpose of this paper as what is being argued for here is an ethic based on Smith's sentimentalism. Thus, we need not be entirely true to Smith's own ideas.

16 Smith addresses the question of what actions should be done from duty alone (or solely from a regard for the general rules) and which should arise from a sentiment. He says that such a determination is not easily made and that it depends "first upon the natural agreeableness or deformity of the sentiment or affection which would prompt us to any action independent of all regard to general rules; and secondly, upon the precision and exactness, or looseness and inaccuracy, of the general rules themselves" (*TMS*, III.6.2). He also says that we do not want people always acting solely out of duty and foresees one of the to deontology: that there are times when acting from duty just does not seem to

These rules are not indisputable, however. They are, in fact, open to revision. (Again, it is the impartial spectator that is the ultimate judge and court of appeal to the soundness of the rules.) They are adjusted in light of experience and applicability and there will be differences in societal rules based on the differences in societies (and their economic circumstances, customs, etc.) (*TMS*, V.2.7).[17] This is not to say, however, that this sentimentalist ethic plunges us into full-fledged relativism. According to relativism, any action or practice is acceptable as long as it is accepted by its society or culture. However, there are certain motives and acts that will be deemed morally wrong by an impartial spectator no matter what culture one is in. For example, funerary practices differ between cultures, societies, and religions. Respecting a culture's practices would be deemed morally appropriate by any impartial spectator. On the other hand, not respecting these practices, e.g., complete and utter desecration of corpses, would be deemed morally unacceptable by any impartial spectator as an impartial spectator will not be able to sympathize with the motive of such an action. Random cruel acts, rape, unjustifiable homicide, and complete disregard for another's property are other examples of the types of actions that will be judged morally unacceptable by any impartial spectator in any society or culture due to the inability of the impartial spectator to sympathize with the motives behind such actions.

Now, recall the principle I set out to derive, "An act is wrong if an impartial spectator cannot sympathize with it and an act is right if an impartial spectator can sympathize with it". I have shown that the impartial spectator will approve of an act when there is an affect match between herself and the agent, and thus such an act is morally right. When there is no affect match between the impartial spectator and the agent then the act is morally wrong.[18] Over time we develop moral rules based on these judgments which guide our behavior and we often appeal to them instead of invoking the impartial spectator because we are imperfect and are guided by our passions which can be too strong or biased.

IV. DEFENSE OF THE ETHIC

Thus far the argument presented here has been descriptive in nature. None of it has been prescriptive in that it has not defended the notion that we

---

be enough. For example, Smith imagines the distress of a husband who finds his wife's actions motivated solely by a sense of duty (*TMS*, III.5.1).

17 Likewise, there will be differences in impartial spectators from different countries or cultures.

18 I have also shown, of course, that if an impartial spectator sympathizes with the passions of the recipient of an act, then the act is meritorious. If she does not sympathize, either the recipient is not feeling the proper passion, or the act is not meritorious. Although important to the overall theory, this aspect is not central to the argument being presented here.

should rely on our sentiments to judge moral acts or that we should invoke a sympathetic impartial spectator to make moral decisions or judgments. However, there are plenty of reasons for doing so.[19] For starters, as noted, sympathizing is something we do naturally. Given that we sympathize with others naturally, it seems a small leap to invoke an impartial spectator who sympathizes (or not) to make moral judgments. This theory also satisfies Owen Flanagan's Principle of Minimal Psychological Realism: "make sure when constructing a moral theory or projecting a moral ideal that the character, decision processing, and behavior prescribed are possible [...] for creatures like us" (Flanagan, *Varieties of Moral Personality*, 32).[20] Moreover, whether certain moral theorists want to admit it or not, we also seem to rely on the sentiments and sympathy in making immediate moral decisions and judgments. (Not to mention the fact that many moral theorists hold that sentimentalism is the basis of at least some of the so-called reason-based moral theories, e.g., utilitarianism.)

Next, it is relatively easy. Each of us needs not become an impartial spectator in every situation (or perhaps even at all), and it is not necessary to invoke the impartial spectator in every situation. Again, according to Smith, we develop rules based on what an impartial spectator would say given a particular situation. These rules make day-to-day moral decision-making easy while not imposing on us a strict adherence to rules that are immutable. And, because the rules that are formulated are mutable, they can be reformulated or discarded as changes in society occur. So, as science and technology develop and as our ways of inhabiting the world and interacting with each other change, for example, and we come to have knowledge and abilities we did not previously have, we can invoke the impartial spectator and decide whether an action is morally acceptable or not. Also, it accommodates our intuitions regarding partiality and impartiality. It recognizes our natural biases while not allowing them, due to the impartial spectator, to overwhelm our moral decisions and judgments. Further, it permits a certain degree of relativism while, again via the impartial spectator, not permitting any and every social custom. In addition, it accommodates our inclinations to judge actions based on both the motives (character) behind the action (judgments of propriety) and the consequences (judgments of merit) that are a result of the action. Moreover, it easily includes both moral agents and moral patients in the moral community. Finally, it finds a balance between the use of sentiments in making moral decisions and judgments and the use of

---

19 All of the reasons that follow are pragmatic in nature. Also, I am not saying that any one of these is a necessary or sufficient reason for employing this ethic, and there might be other good reasons for utilizing this ethic that have not been mentioned.

20 A defense of this was presented in both sections II and III above. These are things at which Kantian deontology and utilitarianism fail.

reason in doing so. (Although judgments of propriety and merit are based on whether or not the impartial spectator has an affect match with the agent and recipient, the impartial spectator must also be aware of all the relevant facts, thus she must understand the situation of both the agent and the recipient.)[21]

V. PRACTICAL APPLICATION

Not only do the reasons mentioned above support the use of the sentimentalist ethic presented here, but the fact that it works in a wide range of cases, both uncontroversial and controversial, gives us further reason for employing it. Let us first consider a relatively uncontroversial case, murder.

I am not aware of a major moral theory that does not condemn at least some murderous acts. For the sake of time and simplicity, we will consider a case of unjustifiable homicide, a random drive-by shooting.[22] Clearly, deontologists will condemn such actions as they hold that killing is wrong. Utilitarians would also judge such an action to be morally wrong, as randomly killing a person in such a way certainly does not maximize the good. Social contract theorists would morally disapprove of such an action based on the fact that they agree to restrict their freedoms, in this case the freedom to kill at will, to allow the most liberty for everyone. The sentimentalist ethic presented here is no different from these other moral theories in the fact that it also condemns murder of this kind. First of all, an impartial spectator would not be able to sympathize with the sentiments of the murderer. The act of murder would therefore be judged to be improper (as would the feelings that motivated the act). Secondly, according to Smith, murder "excites the highest degree of resentment in those who are immediately connected with the slain" (*TMS*, II.ii.2.2 and see also III.4.8). Given that resentment is appropriate in such circumstances, the impartial spectator would also judge the act to be punishable.

Let us now consider a more controversial example, infanticide. I consider the morality of infanticide to be controversial because in every day and age some cultures have permitted it while simultaneously other cultures have condemned it. Moreover, the question of the morality of infanticide is a question that is currently being debated in Western philosophy. Kantian deontologists might quickly respond by saying that infanticide is wrong (as taking a human life is wrong). However, it is not clear that Kantians can hold this in every situation. Take for example a situation where one must kill a single infant in order to keep

---

21 Slote gives a nice explanation (and defense) of the role sentimentalism can play in deontology ("Sentimentalist Virtue and Moral Judgement"). Furthermore, there are other aspects of this theory that make it palatable. For example, it does not fall victim to the problems of divine command theory or natural law theory. However, I have chosen to list those aspects that I think are of greatest interest.

22 Some acts of murder might be thought to be justifiable and so might be more controversial, e.g., murder committed for the sake of self-defense.

five others (infants or otherwise) from being killed by someone else. Given that killing is wrong, it seems paradoxical to permit the killing of more rather than fewer. Kantians will generally accept this paradox rather than modify their theory to account for it, but that does not solve the problem. Furthermore, if killing is wrong, then killing one to save many is wrong, and we are forced to morally condemn the one who kills a single infant to save five others, and this is seriously counterintuitive to some, viz., utilitarians.

Now, according to utilitarians, if committing infanticide brings about the most good, one is permitted (required) to commit it. However, there is often great difficulty in determining whether killing an innocent child will actually bring about the greatest good in any particular situation and, in contrast to what act utilitarians may say, rule utilitarians might hold that infanticide in general does not maximize the good and call for a rule declaring it morally wrong. So, not only will utilitarians have difficulty in determining the morality of infanticide, but act utilitarians and rule utilitarians may disagree about whether it is morally acceptable or not.

It is also not entirely clear what the social contract theorist would say about infanticide. As noted above, people agree to give up their freedoms so as to allow the most liberties for everyone. However, the only beings directly covered by the social contract are those who are able to enter into it, who in turn are those who are able to understand it, who in turn are those who are rational. Infants, of course, are not rational and so are not directly covered by the contract. Yet, some contractualists have argued that infants are covered by being potential rational agents or are covered indirectly by being connected to those who are rational agents or are covered so as to avoid any possibility of a slippery slope. Nevertheless, the bottom line is that social contract theory does not give us any clear-cut way to determine the morality of infanticide.

Smith himself actually addresses the issue of infanticide (*TMS*, V.2.15–16). Given that some will inevitably disagree with my interpretation of what Smith says here, I want to spend some time presenting my interpretation of this section of *TMS* before I apply the sentimentalist ethic to this particular action.

The discussion of infanticide appears in Part V of *TMS* which is titled "Of the Influence of Custom and Fashion upon the Sentiments of Moral Approbation and Disapprobation". Smith thinks, of course, that custom is no excuse for morally inappropriate behavior, although we seem to be guided by custom quite often.

> There are other principles besides those already enumerated, which have a considerable influence upon the moral sentiments of mankind, and are the chief causes of the many irregular and discordant opinions which prevail in different ages and nations concerning what is blamable or praise-worthy. These principles are custom and fashion,

principles which extend their dominion over our judgments concerning beauty of every kind. [*TMS*, V.1.1]

It is important to note, however, that "the sentiments of moral approbation and disapprobation, are founded on the strongest and most vigorous passions of human nature; and though they may be somewhat warpt, cannot be entirely perverted" (*TMS*, V.2.1). For example, Smith claims that there is no custom that will ever convince us that the likes of Nero and Claudius (and Hitler for that matter) were anything but vile human beings.[23] So, although custom may influence our sentiments and may temporarily distort them, "the influence of custom and fashion upon the moral sentiments, is not altogether so great" (*TMS*, V.2.2).

Smith introduces the practice of infanticide as follows:

> Can there be a greater barbarity, for example, than to hurt an infant? Its helplessness, its innocence, its amiableness, call forth the compassion, even of an enemy, and not to spare that tender age is regarded as the most furious effort of an enraged and cruel conqueror. What then should we imagine must be the heart of a parent who could injure that weakness which even a furious enemy is afraid to violate? [*TMS*, V.2.15]

He continues on, reminding us that this practice was acceptable in Greece "whenever the circumstances of the parent rendered it inconvenient to bring up the child" (*TMS*, V.2.15) and argues that the practice had probably begun "in times of most savage barbarity" (*TMS*, V.2.15) and that "the uniform continuance of the custom had hindered them afterwards from perceiving its enormity" (*TMS*, V.2.15). Smith acknowledges that it continues today in savage nations but that "in that rudest and lowest state of society it is undoubtedly more pardonable than in any other" (*TMS*, V.2.15).[24]

As the discussion of infanticide unfolds, Smith explains that in certain situations, in particular that in which one is running from an enemy with a child in one's arms, the practice of infanticide would be morally acceptable because unless one lets the child go, both are certain to die. From this it seems to follow that he would also think infanticide in times of tremendous poverty would be morally acceptable: the chances that an infant will survive are slim, the suffering

---

23 As with the discussion of the process of achieving sympathy, Smith's ideas regarding custom are a bit more complicated than I have presented here. Nonetheless, this brief sketch is all that is needed for our purposes.

24 I find this statement of Smith's very interesting. It seems to me that he is, at the very least, open to moral judgments being made on a scale or being based on degrees of rightness or wrongness.

she will incur if not killed is great, and her existence can be an unbearable burden on the other members of the family. In these situations one is moved by the appropriate passions, and the impartial spectator would judge this action to be proper as there will be an affect match between herself and the agent. However, in times of economic prosperity, such an action is condemnable as there is no affect match between the impartial spectator and the agent. During prosperous times, the infant is likely to survive (and can thrive), the likelihood of it suffering significantly is minimal, and family members will generally not be unduly burdened. So, whereas the other prominent moral theories considered above fail to give us a determination regarding the morality of infanticide, this version of sentimentalism provides us with the moral prescription(s) we are looking for.[25]

One might object to my interpretation of Smith with respect to infanticide by citing the following and claiming that he clearly condemns it and thinks it to be an act against humanity:

> When custom can give sanction to so dreadful a violation of humanity, we may well imagine that there is scarce any particular practice so gross which it cannot authorize. Such a thing, we hear men every day saying, is commonly done, and they seem to think this is a sufficient apology for what, in itself, is the most unjust and unreasonable conduct.
>
> There is an obvious reason why custom should never pervert our sentiments with regard to the general style and character of conduct and behaviour, in the same degree as with regard to the propriety or unlawfulness of particular usages. There never can be any such custom. No society could subsist a moment, in which the usual strain of men's conduct and

---

25 Someone might argue that the balancing of considerations here is the same type of process in which a utilitarian might engage. However, there is at least one major difference between the two. The utilitarian is solely concerned with whether the outcome ultimately maximizes the good, happiness, etc. The view presented here allows for the fact that the outcome of an act may not maximize the good, happiness, etc., and yet it can still be morally proper. So, if a parent finds herself in the dire circumstances noted above and decides it is best to kill her infant, but then shortly after becomes financially comfortable through chance circumstances, we can still sympathize with her having killed her infant given the circumstances she was in at the time. On the other hand, utilitarians might say that what she did turns out to be morally wrong. My thanks to Ben Eggleston for bringing to my attention the fact that I needed to explain this difference and for other helpful comments on the paper.

behaviour was of a piece with the horrible practice I have now just mentioned. [*TMS*, V.2.16][26]

I think a superficial reading of this passage may certainly lead someone to object to my interpretation of Smith's position on infanticide. However, upon a closer reading, I believe my interpretation will stand. Although he does call infanticide "a dreadful violation of humanity", I think he is referring to the general practice of it as being accepted by society without taking into account the circumstances of that particular society. That is, he is here condemning the acceptance of infanticide by the ancient Greeks when infants were tossed aside for convenience and not because of dire circumstances. Immediately preceding the cited passage above, in which Smith is addressing the propriety of infanticide in the situation of a parent fleeing from an enemy, he states:

> That in this state of society [...] a parent should be allowed to judge whether he can bring up his child, ought not to surprise us greatly. In the latter ages of Greece, however, the same thing was permitted from views of remote interest or conveniency, which could by no means excuse it. Uninterrupted custom had by this time so thoroughly authorized the practice, that not only the loose maxims of the world tolerated this barbarous prerogative, but even the doctrine of philosophers, which ought to have been more just and accurate, was led away by established custom, and upon this, as upon many other occasions, instead of censuring, supported the horrible abuse, by far-fetched considerations of public utility. [*TMS*, V.2.15]

It is my position that Smith is here arguing against infanticide when certain conditions are met. Accordingly, he will find it permissible when certain other conditions are met.

In the quotation above (*TMS*, V.2.15), we see that Smith again refers to infanticide as barbarous. But, given Smith's sentimentalism, something might be barbarous without being morally unacceptable. Smith thinks, and I think all will agree, that in any circumstance, killing a child is barbarous. It is a terrible thing to do. But, that is not to say that it is always the *wrong* thing to do. Further, one may argue that Smith finds that committing infanticide in conditions in which it is "more pardonable" would be a barbarous thing for a parent to have to do. Moreover, one can also hold that by "barbarous prerogative" Smith means that the prerogative to commit infanticide had become barbarous as it became

---

26 My thanks to Eric Schliesser for bringing to my attention the fact that I needed to address this concern.

a custom that was unnecessary due to the improved conditions in society (as he goes on to condemn Aristotle and Plato for finding it acceptable). Finally, to think that Smith would condemn infanticide in every situation is to ignore his directive that we take the circumstances germane to the act into consideration when making moral judgments.

This version of sentimentalism, I believe, can help us with regard to other current moral concerns as well.[27] Of particular interest to me is what it will have to say regarding our treatment of animals. In fact, I hope to show in the future that this version of sentimentalism not only condemns factory farms and most research on animals as other animal ethics do, but that it goes even further and condemns the exploitation of animals, thus perhaps rendering zoos, circuses, using animals as entertainment, and the like morally objectionable.

One final note: although the theory presented here is based on Smith's sentimentalism, it is not necessarily the case that it has to remain true to it in every way. At the very least, Smith gives us good tools and a good foundation upon which to build a normative sentimentalist theory. As I continue to develop the ethic, its strengths and weaknesses will become more apparent. The good news is that the weaknesses can be addressed in light of all that we have learned since Smith wrote *The Theory of Moral Sentiments*, and yet we can still take advantage of the strengths of his theory.

SELECT BIBLIOGRAPHY

Blackburn, Simon. *Ruling Passions: A Theory of Practical Reasoning*. Oxford: Oxford University Press, 2001.

Brandt, R. B. "The Definition of an 'Ideal Observer' Theory in Ethics". *Philosophy and Phenomenological Research* 15, no. 3 (1955): 407–413.

Campbell, T. D. *Adam Smith's Science of Morals*. Totowa, NJ: Rowman and Littlefield, 1971.

Darwall, Stephen. "Sympathetic Liberalism: Recent Work on Adam Smith". *Philosophy and Public Affairs* 28, no. 2 (1999): 139–164.

Firth, Roderick. "Ethical Absolutism and the Ideal Observer". *Philosophy and Phenomenological Research* 12, no. 3 (1952): 317–345.

---

27 Patrick Frierson has already begun to develop an environmental ethic based on Smith's sentimentalism. See Frierson, *Applying Adam Smith*, and "Adam Smith and the Possibility of Sympathy with Nature".

Flanagan, Owen. *Varieties of Moral Personality: Ethics and Psychological Realism.* Cambridge, MA: Harvard University Press, 1991.

Frierson, Patrick. "Adam Smith and the Possibility of Sympathy with Nature". *Pacific Philosophical Quarterly* 87, no. 4 (2006): 442–480.

———. "Applying Adam Smith: From Adam Smith to Environmental Virtue Ethics". In *New Voices on Adam Smith,* edited by Leonidas Montes and Eric Schliesser. Abingdon: Routledge, 2006, 236–276.

Goldman, Alvin I. "Empathy, Mind, and Morals". *Proceedings and Addresses of the American Philosophical Association* 66, no. 3 (1992): 17–41.

———. "Ethics and Cognitive Science". *Ethics* 103, no. 2 (1993): 337–360.

Gordon, Robert M. "Folk Psychology as Simulation". *Mind & Language* 1, no. 2 (1986): 159–171.

———. "Simulation and the Explanation of Action". In *Empathy and Agency,* edited by Hans Herbert Kogler and Karsten R. Stueber. Boulder: Westview Press, 2000, 62–82.

———. "The Simulation Theory: Objections and Misconceptions". *Mind & Language* 7, nos. 1 & 2 (1992): 11–33.

———. "Simulation without Introspection or Inference from Me to You". In *Mental Simulation,* edited by Martin Davies and Tony Stone. Oxford: Blackwell Publishers Ltd., 1995, 53–67.

———. "Sympathy, Simulation, and the Impartial Spectator". *Ethics* 105, no. 4 (1995): 727–742.

Hare, R. M. *Moral Thinking.* Oxford: Oxford University Press, 1981.

Hoffman, Martin L. *Empathy and Moral Development: Implications for Caring and Justice.* New York: Cambridge University Press, 2000.

Midgley, Mary. *Heart & Mind: The Varieties of Moral Experience.* New York: St. Martin's Press, 1981.

Richmond, Sarah. "Being in Others: Empathy from a Psychoanalytical Perspective". *European Journal of Philosophy* 12, no. 2 (2004): 244–264.

Slote, Michael. "Autonomy and Empathy". *Social Philosophy & Policy* 21, no. 1 (2004): 293–309.

———. "Moral Sentimentalism". *Ethical Theory and Moral Practice* 7 (2004): 3–14.

———. *Morals from Motives*. New York, New York: Oxford University Press, 2003.

———. "Sentimentalist Virtue and Moral Judgement: Outline of a Project". *Metaphilosophy* 34, nos. 1/2 (2003): 131–143.

Smith, Adam. *The Theory of Moral Sentiments*. Edited by D.D. Raphael and A.L. Macfie. Oxford: Oxford University Press, 1976.

Solomon, Robert C. *In Defense of Sentimentality*. New York: Oxford University Press, 2004.

Walker, Margaret U. "Partial Consideration". *Ethics* 101, no. 4 (1991): 758–774.

THE THEORY OF MORAL SENTIMENTS AND SMITH'S ACCOUNT OF SYMPATHY

Tony Pitson

I. INTRODUCTION

The philosophical importance of Adam Smith's appeal to the notion of sympathy in his *Theory of Moral Sentiments* (*TMS*) is widely recognised. It has, indeed, been suggested that sympathy provides the central unifying theme or foundation of Smith's book (Campbell, *Adam Smith's Science of Morals*, 89; Griswold, *Adam Smith and the Virtues of Enlightenment*, 81[1]). Sympathy is clearly central to Smith's moral psychology and it may even provide the basis for the economic theory of his *Wealth of Nations* (Darwall, "Sympathetic Liberalism", 146–147). One of the issues arising from this concerns the part played by sympathy in the moral theory that Smith develops in *TMS* and the comparison, in this respect, with Book 3 of Hume's *Treatise*. But there is also the question of the nature of Smith's account of sympathy itself, which, once again, invites comparison with Hume. It is the latter on which I shall focus. While it is true that Smith employs the notion of sympathy in a variety of ways in *TMS*, it is possible to identify central features of his understanding of this notion: ones that give rise to a number of important philosophical issues. I thus begin with a brief survey of Smith's remarks about sympathy in the opening chapters of *TMS*, and I note some of the questions that come to mind in considering them. After exploring certain of these questions in more detail I say something about the relevance of Smith on sympathy to the "simulation" view of what is involved in our understanding of each other. I conclude with remarks in defense of the role of sympathy in Smith and Hume and an assessment of the distinctive features of Smith's account of this notion.

I. SMITH'S NOTION OF SYMPATHY

Smith introduces the notion of sympathy in relation to pity and compassion as "original passions of human nature" that we feel for the misery of others. It seems clear that sympathy is not to be identified with such passions. Rather, sympathy is essentially a matter of "fellow-feeling"—for example, sharing the other person's state of distress—so that as a result we come to feel pity or compassion for that person.[2] In other words, we feel sorry *for* someone because

---

1   Complete bibliographic information for references can be found in the Select Bibliography at the end of this essay.

2   This notion of sympathy—which is in any case implicit in the etymology of the word—does not of course originate with Smith. Samuel Johnson, in his *Dictionary*

we feel distress *with* them (Campbell, *Adam Smith's Science of Morals*, 94; see also Snow, "Empathy", 66). Sympathy as fellow-feeling is achieved, according to Smith, by changing places in imagination with the sufferer. Smith goes on to suggest that whatever the passion experienced by the original subject, an analogous emotion will be aroused in any "attentive spectator" who reflects on the other person's situation. Thus "sympathy" is used here "to denote our fellow-feeling with any passion whatever" (*TMS*, 9–10).[3]

We should note an important complication in this account of sympathy. It seems evident that we must be able to recognize the passions of others in order for something analogous to occur in us as spectators. But if, as Smith says, "we have no immediate experience of what other men feel", there arises a question as to how recognition of their feelings is possible. This is where Smith again appeals to sympathy: by placing ourselves in the other person's situation and imagining what we should then feel, we are able to form some idea of that person's feelings, and, as a result, to be so affected that we experience some degree of the same emotion. In other words, sympathy has an epistemological dimension (in so far as it explains how we are able to conceive what other people are feeling) as well as an affective one, even if Smith himself does not always clearly distinguish them. On this account, then, sympathy is essentially a two-stage process in which fellow-feeling depends on our ability to form an idea of what the other person feels by putting ourselves in his place; this, in turn, provides the basis for feelings such as pity and compassion.

II. QUESTIONS ABOUT SMITH'S ACCOUNT OF SYMPATHY

Already various questions come to mind in considering this account of sympathy. The above suggests that we may distinguish between *imagining* what the other person feels, on the basis of imagining what we would feel in that person's situation, and actually *having* something analogous to the feelings ascribed to that person. But in order for me to feel pity or compassion for

---

of the English Language (1755), defines "Sympathy" as "Fellow feeling; mutual sensibility; the quality of being affected by the affection of another"; and he provides illustrative quotations from both Shakespeare and Milton. It is a mark of Smith's interest in language that he wrote a review of Johnson's Dictionary in the year of its publication (contributed originally to the *Edinburgh Review*; reprinted in Smith, *Essays*, 232–241).

3 Although Smith may not make this point explicitly, it is obvious that the kind of fellow-feeling with which he is concerned amounts to more than my feeling something that is similar to what you are feeling. It must also be true that what I feel is *dependent* upon what you are feeling; and normally, at least, I will be *aware* of the correspondence between our feelings. Otherwise we have only what might be described as a "community of feeling". For a discussion of some of the issues that arise in this context, see Snow, "Empathy", esp. 65–70.

someone is it really necessary that my sympathy for them should involve actually sharing their feelings as opposed to merely imagining what they might be? We might indeed wonder whether such altruistic emotions *do* normally involve feeling what the other person feels. It seems common enough that we feel sorry for someone who is evidently suffering without our experiencing any actual pain or distress on that person's behalf. Is there, in any case, an essential connection between sympathy as fellow-feeling and feelings of pity or compassion? Even supposing that your state of suffering gives rise in me to feelings of distress, why should this in turn lead me to feel any sympathetic concern for you?[4]

Another important question raised by Smith's account of sympathy is whether fellow-feeling should be made to depend on the imaginary change of place to which this account refers. The objection originally raised by Kames, and subsequently endorsed by Reid, is that there are many examples of individuals (dull people and "illiterate rustics" as well as children) who are able to share the feelings of others in spite of the fact that they may be incapable of the effort of imagination required by Smith's account of sympathy (Kames, *Essays*, 71–72). Apart from this, it is arguable that the grief felt on the death of a friend, for example, is more plausibly construed as the *cause* of any doleful imagining in which one engages than as the *effect* of this operation of the imagination (Reid, *Inquiry*, in Norton and Robertson "Thomas Reid", 397). Doubts about the relation between sympathy and the imagination may also arise when this relation is considered from the reverse perspective. As we have seen already, imagining that I am suffering what the other person appears to be suffering does not seem to guarantee any fellow-feeling with that person.

There is also a question about the *scope* of the process of sympathy by which we are supposed to form an idea of what others are feeling. If we have no immediate experience of what others feel, the same must presumably be true of what they think or believe. So should we infer that we ascribe cognitive states like beliefs to others by imagining what we would believe in their situation?[5]

---

4   It seems that even if feelings of pity *are* aroused, they need not be associated with any concern for the other's plight (Mercer, *Sympathy and Ethics*, 12). Note here the remark from Rousseau's *Emile* (cited by Kames, *Essays*, 79), "Pity is sweet [...] because in putting ourselves in place of the person who suffers, we feel the pleasure of not suffering as he does". Hume's references to the principle of comparison in the *Treatise* suggest a similar idea. "[A]ccording as we observe a greater or less share of happiness or misery in others, we must make an estimate of our own, and feel a consequent pain or pleasure. The misery of another gives us a more lively idea of our happiness, and his happiness of our misery" (2.2.8.8). As Hume goes on to observe, this makes it necessary to identify the rules that determine which of these two principles—sympathy or comparison—will prevail in our responses to the happiness or misery of others (3.3.2.5).

5   It is worth noting here Smith's remark that "Every faculty in one man is the

And what of the nature of the sympathetic process itself? The notion that sympathy enables us to form an idea of what others feel might suggest that the process involved is essentially an inferential one: roughly, by imagining that I would feel so-and-so in that person's situation I thus conclude that this is what that person feels. As such, this would appear to be a variation on the familiar argument from analogy for other minds.[6] While the latter tends to emphasize the importance of behavior as the basis for the ascription of mental states to others, this must obviously take account of the situation in which the behavior occurs. At the same time, Smith's reference to the other person's situation as the source of the idea we form of their feelings would presumably have to include the way in which that person is behaving. If this reading of Smith is correct, then this aspect of his account of sympathy would leave him open to at least some of the criticisms familiarly associated with the argument from analogy. In any case, we should consider in rather more detail how Smith's view of sympathy as the source of our awareness of the mental states of others might bear on the epistemological issues associated with other minds.

III. SYMPATHY AND THE FEELINGS OF OTHERS

While Smith's account of sympathy is not offered as a solution to the "other minds problem" with which the argument from analogy is concerned (Griswold, *Adam Smith*, 105; Griswold, "Imagination", 36–38), some remarks in *TMS* appear to endorse the view that we can form an idea of the sentiments of others only by reference to their effects in observable bodily appearance and behavior.

> There is no other way of marking or distinguishing them [the invisible features of all the different modifications of passion as they show themselves within] from one another, but by describing the effects they produce without, the alterations which they occasion in the countenance, in the air and external behaviour, the resolutions they suggest, the actions they prompt to. [*TMS*, 328–329]

On the other hand, some of the examples Smith provides of sympathy appear not to fit the inferential model (i.e., where fellow-feeling depends

---

  measure by which he judges of the like faculty in another"—where this is illustrated not only by feelings such as resentment and love, but also by both perception and reason (*TMS*, 19).

6 On this understanding of Smith's position he may be seen to anticipate Nozick's view of *verstehen*, or empathic understanding, as a special form of reasoning by analogy, which involves putting oneself imaginatively in the other person's place and seeing him as like oneself (Nozick, *Philosophical Explanations*, 636–637).

on imagining what we should feel in the other person's situation given their appearance and behavior considered as the effects of "invisible" feelings, and thereby forming an idea of those feelings). The idea of "changing places in fancy with the sufferer" is illustrated by the example in which we see a stroke ready to fall on the arm or leg of another person and in response "we naturally shrink and draw back our own leg or our own arm" (*TMS*, 10). If, as Smith goes on to claim, we feel the stroke in some measure when it does fall, then this does not appear to be the result of first imagining what we would feel in the other person's situation. In this kind of case, the sympathetic reaction seems to be spontaneous and unreflective. Smith goes on to describe the reactions of spectators to the movements of a dancer on a "slack-rope"—namely, the way in which they "naturally writhe and twist and balance their own bodies, as they see him do, *and as they feel that they themselves must do in his situation*" (emphasis mine). These are examples of what would now be called "motor mimicry" (Hoffman, *Empathy*, 37).[7] This is understood by psychologists as a process involving two steps, one immediately following the other, in which the automatic imitative movements of the observer trigger feedback that produces feelings matching those of the other person. It is clear that—in contrast to Smith—this is not envisaged as a process in which our sympathetically experienced feelings are a result of imagining what we would feel in the situation of the person who is writhing and twisting; rather, it is one in which our feelings are the product of an automatic motor response.[8]

Smith gives another kind of example, which appears to be at odds with

---

7   We should note that Reid's critical discussion of Smith appeals to the idea that sympathy is an original principle of human nature, rather than something that requires an imaginary change of place, on the basis that our tendency to imitate or mimic the actions and gestures of others is itself an original principle (in Norton and Robertson, "Thomas Reid", 397). This, in turn, should be seen against the background of Reid's notion of a natural language consisting in signs that give expression to our thoughts, namely, modulations of the voice, gestures and facial features (Reid, *Inquiry*, 51–52). Writing about these natural signs, Reid says that nature has not only established a real connection between them and the thoughts and dispositions that they signify, it has also "taught us the interpretation of these signs; so that, previous to experience, the sign suggests the thing signified, and creates the belief of it" (ibid., 190). Arguably, Smith also regards mimicry as something that is natural for us: see De Marchi "Smith on Ingenuity", 144–146.

8   It might then be objected to Smith that he has essentially misconstrued the nature of sympathy. While we may sometimes be roused from a state of indifference by putting ourselves in the other person's place, sympathy is in general instantaneous and unreflective—as witnessed by the fact that we are not normally conscious of our sympathetic responses to others being mediated by any imaginative activity. See Reid in Norton and Robertson, "Thomas Reid", 396–397.

the view of sympathy as a process in which the spectator imagines what he or she would feel in the other person's place. This is where, as Smith puts it, the passions "may seem to be transfused from one man to another, instantaneously, and antecedent to any knowledge of what excited them in the person principally concerned" (*TMS*, 11). Smith has in mind strong expressions of emotions such as grief or joy, which seem immediately to affect the spectator with some degree of the same emotion. What distinguishes such cases is that our sympathetic response does not depend on being aware of the causes of the emotions: as Smith indicates, it may be enough for some fellow-feeling, however imperfect, simply to encounter a smiling face or, on the other hand, a sorrowful one. These cases of emotional transfusion appear at odds with the distinction that is normally drawn between sympathy, as understood by Smith, and the kind of sympathetic emotional infection to which both Hume and Hutcheson refer (Campbell, *Adam Smith's Science of Morals*, 95).[9] But according to Smith, sympathy generally arises from our view of the agent's situation and the kind of passion to which it might be expected to give rise—something that is strikingly illustrated by the case of vicarious emotion in which we blush for the rudeness of another, for example, though he himself appears unaware of the impropriety of his behavior (*TMS*, 12). An even more striking case is that of sympathy with the dead, where, according to Smith, by an "illusion of the imagination" we put our living selves in the "inanimated" bodies of the dead and imagine what our emotions would be in such circumstances (*TMS*, 12–13).[10]

With the possible exception of those cases referred to above in which "sympathy may seem to arise merely from the view of a certain emotion in another person", Smith's discussion of these various examples of sympathy reflects the principle that sympathy is founded on an "imaginary change of

---

9 Sympathy as understood by Smith would involve sharing your sadness, for example, in the sense of feeling sad about whatever it is that is making you sad. We may contrast this with feeling sad for you, although this would be a natural accompaniment of the sympathetic feeling involved in the former case. See Snow, "Empathy", 66. This, incidentally, illustrates the ambiguous nature of the notion of fellow-feeling.

10 It is debatable whether any misery we experience in contemplating the situation of the dead person can be explained in these terms bearing in mind the difficulty of ignoring the "illusion" involved in attempting to imagine ourselves in that situation. A similar point perhaps applies to another of Smith's examples: the anguish that is felt at the sight of someone who suffers a "loss of reason" but is altogether insensible to the change that has occurred (*TMS*, 12). As Smith says, the anguish that is felt in this case cannot be a reflection of any sentiment of the sufferer. The compassion of the spectator must somehow arise from considering how he would feel in this situation given ("what perhaps is impossible") that he would also be "able to regard it with his present reason and judgement".

situation" (*TMS*, 21). To this extent he is committed to the view that fellow-feeling depends on imagining what we would feel in the other person's situation; while this, in turn, may require us to treat the other's appearance and behavior as the effects of feelings that lie beyond our direct experience. Unlike Hume, Smith does not develop his account of sympathy against a background theory of mind which would explain the correspondence between the feelings of agent and spectator (Otteson, *Adam Smith's Marketplace of Life*, 21). This is one reason for being cautious about the comparison between his position and the classical argument from analogy; for the latter is based on a Cartesian view of the relation between mental states and behavior to which Smith may not be committed (though the passage cited above from *TMS*, 328–329 is certainly in the spirit of that view).[11] In any case, while the argument from analogy is directed towards an epistemological problem about other minds, this is clearly not the motivation for Smith's account of sympathy. Nevertheless, Smith does appear committed to the view that we ascribe mental states to others on the basis of imagining what we would feel in their place and so assigning the same feelings to them.[12]

IV. SYMPATHY AS FELLOW-FEELING

As we have seen, questions arise about what might be described as the second stage of the process involved in sympathy—i.e., the fellow-feeling that is supposed to occur when we recognize the feelings of others. How far is Smith committed to thinking that this process results in having the same feelings as those ascribed to the other person? It is obviously not intended to follow from the fact that sympathetic feelings are an outcome of an operation of the imagination that the feelings themselves are merely imaginary ones.[13] On the other hand, whether we experience a feeling that may be compared with that of the original subject appears to depend in part, at least, on the nature of the feeling in question.

---

11 Another reason for caution is Smith's emphasis on the role of imagination in providing the basis for our recognition of the feelings of others (Griswold, *Adam Smith*, 116; Griswold, "Imagination", esp. 25–45). This indeed is part of the point of the comparison of Smith's position with the simulation theory that I make in section 6 below.

12 Apart from the points mentioned above, Smith's position here encounters the fundamental objection that if the torments of the man on the rack are not obvious to us from his behavior, then it is difficult to see what is to be gained from imagining ourselves in his place. As Kames says in his discussion of this example (*Essays*, 71), it seems that this act of the imagination can have some effect only if we already know that the person on the rack is suffering violently, in which case bringing the case home to ourselves will naturally tend to inflame our sympathy.

13 But see *TMS*, 21: the fact that the change of situation from which the sympathetic feeling arises is imaginary makes this feeling significantly different from that of the sufferer.

Smith observes, for example, that "in its most proper and primitive signification" the word "sympathy" denotes our fellow-feeling with the sufferings, rather than the enjoyments, of others (*TMS*, 43). Thus, we tend to have some fellow-feeling with sorrow even when it might be considered excessive, while an intemperate expression of joy is received with contempt and indignation. Smith also points out that we may attempt with some difficulty to suppress our sympathy with the sufferings of others, but we have no such reluctance to indulge any propensity to sympathize with (temperately expressed) joy. Again, while we would often wish to be rid of sympathetic feelings of sorrow, there are many cases in which we would welcome sympathetic feelings of joy where they fail to occur (*TMS*, 44).

It might therefore appear that our propensity to sympathize with sorrow is stronger than our inclination to sympathize with joy. According to Smith, however, to the contrary: our fellow-feeling with joy is closer in vivacity to the feelings of those concerned than in the case of painful feelings like sorrow (*TMS*, 45). This reflects what Smith refers to as "the natural and ordinary state of mankind", i.e., that of the person who is healthy, solvent, and with a clear conscience. So little need be added to this to give rise to feelings of joy that we can readily sympathize with such feelings, while the discrepancy with the circumstances in which misery and sorrow arise makes it more difficult for the spectator to sympathize with this relatively unnatural state.

Leaving aside feelings like grief and joy, Smith is clear that there are other kinds of feeling or sentiment that are not so clearly the objects of fellow-feeling. Smith has in mind, in particular, various kinds of bodily feeling or sensation. In the case of hunger, for example, while we may sympathize with the distress of the sufferer and feel some degree of the fear and consternation that they must be experiencing, we do not feel hunger itself and cannot therefore be said, strictly speaking, to sympathize with it (*TMS*, 28). Somewhat similarly, we may sympathize with the fear of someone who is in danger, but we do not sympathize in the same way with any pain they may be suffering (*TMS*, 30). In general, bodily feelings either excite no sympathy at all or only a relatively slight degree of it (as in the case where I see someone who has been struck a painful blow). As Smith also observes, we cannot really sympathize with our own pain once it is gone, though by contrast we may continue to fret over a remark by which we have been hurt.[14] Smith also lays down a general rule to the effect

---

14 These remarks should be set alongside Smith's observation that since pain is a "more pungent sensation" than pleasure, our sympathy with pain, however far short it may fall from what is felt by the sufferer, is generally a livelier perception than our sympathy with pleasure, even if the latter often approaches more closely to the vivacity of the original feeling (*TMS*, 44, 121). There is, in other words, a distinction to be drawn between the comparative liveliness of a sympathetically experienced sensation and the degree to which it corresponds in liveliness to the original.

that the passions the spectator is most disposed to sympathize with are those of which "the immediate feeling or sensation is more or less agreeable", whereas the passions the spectator is least disposed to sympathize with are those of which "the immediate feeling or sensation is more or less disagreeable, or even painful" (*TMS*, 243). It is difficult to evaluate these various remarks about sympathy; but we should bear in mind that the last of them must be seen in the context of the connection that Smith makes between sympathy and our judgments of propriety and impropriety (where these judgments are supposed to reflect our disposition to sympathize, or fail to sympathize, with passions depending on how agreeable they are).

V. SYMPATHY AS A SOURCE OF PLEASURE

An important and distinctive feature of Smith's account of sympathy is his claim that "nothing pleases us more than to observe in other men a fellow-feeling with all the emotions of our own breast; nor are we ever so much shocked as by the appearance of the contrary" (*TMS*, 13); or, again, "this correspondence of the sentiments of others with our own appears to be a cause of pleasure, and the want of it a cause of pain" (*TMS*, 14). In other words, mutual sympathy is itself a source of pleasure and its absence a source of pain.[15] This is relevant to a crucial question about sympathy as fellow-feeling: namely, our *motivation* for engaging in an imaginary change of situation with others in order to discern their feelings and to share these feelings with them (Campbell, *Adam Smith's Science of Morals*, 103–104; Broadie, "Sympathy", 171).[16] For it appears that our willingness to respond to others in this way is explained by the pleasure we

---

15 When Smith refers to the pleasure of mutual sympathy he evidently has in mind the pleasure both of the spectator and also the agent or sufferer. Thus the sympathy that others express with *our* joy gives us pleasure by enlivening that joy; and *our* grief is alleviated by the sympathy felt for it by others (*TMS*, 14). Conversely, when we cordially congratulate our friends, *their* joy becomes our own, though we tend to have but a "dull sensibility" to their afflictions (*TMS*, 47). As Smith indicates in the former passage, there will be many cases in which the sympathetic interaction between ourselves and others serves to enhance the pleasure felt on both sides. Smith's reference to society providing each of us with a mirror or looking-glass in the countenance and behavior of others which indicates the extent to which they enter into our sentiments (*TMS*, 110, 112) reminds us of Hume's observation about the minds of men being "mirrors to one another" so that thoughts and feelings "may be often reverberated" (*Treatise*, 2.2.6.21).

16 While Smith criticizes the view of Epicurus that bodily pleasure and pain provide the primary objects of desire and aversion (*TMS*, 295–299), there seems no reason to suppose that he would call into question the relation of pleasure in general to desire (and, hence, motivation).

derive from the fellow-feeling resulting from this exercise of imagination.[17]

It is necessary also to bear in mind here the part played by sympathy in the moral theory of *TMS*. In short, Smith seeks to account for the moral sentiments of approval and disapproval by their relation to our fellow-feeling, or lack of it, with the feelings of the other person. As Smith puts it: "To approve of the passions of another [...] as suitable to their objects, is the same thing as to observe that we entirely sympathize with them; and not to approve of them as such, is the same thing as to observe that we do not entirely sympathize with them" (*TMS*, 16). Smith sees this as providing the context for Hume's objection to his position as voiced in a letter to Smith in which Hume refers to a proposed new edition of *TMS*. Hume writes here as follows: "I wish you had more particularly and fully prov'd, that all kinds of Sympathy are necessarily Agreeable. This is the Hinge of your System [...]. Now it would appear that there is a disagreeable Sympathy, as well as an agreeable" (*TMS*, 46, n. 2).[18] In discussing this objection in the second edition of *TMS* Smith represents it in the following way: "It has been objected to me that as I found the sentiment of approbation, which is always agreeable, upon sympathy, it is inconsistent with my system to admit any disagreeable sympathy" (*TMS*, 46, n. b).[19] Smith responds to this objection

---

17   Smith does mention the case of family members with whom we are habituated to sympathize: a parent's sympathy with his children, for example, and the affections founded on it, approach nearer to what he feels for himself than any other sympathetically experienced feelings (*TMS*, 219). We presumably do not need any further motive in this case, at least, for sympathetic engagement. The existence of benevolence as a feature of human nature might also be thought enough in some cases to account for our sympathetic engagement with others, though Smith himself refers to benevolence as a "feeble spark" that is incapable of counteracting the strongest impulses of self-love (*TMS*, 137).

18   In the letter to which Smith refers, Hume adds the following explanation: "And indeed, as the Sympathetic Passion is a reflex image of the principal, it must partake of its Qualities, & be painful where that is so. Indeed, *when we converse with a man with whom we can entirely sympathize*, that is, where there is a warm & intimate Friendship, the cordial openness of such a Commerce overpowers the Pain of a Disagreeable Sympathy, and renders the whole Movement agreeable. But in ordinary Cases, this cannot have place" (*The Letters of David Hume*, 313; Hume's emphasis).

19   It should be noted that Hume himself does not mention the sentiment of approval or approbation in this context; and while this sentiment is, for Hume, an agreeable one (*Treatise*, 3.1.2.3–5), Smith's own references to it in *TMS* amount to a somewhat ambiguous endorsement of this view. It is true that in his discussion of Hume's objection Smith does accept that the sentiment of approbation is always an agreeable one (and he may in any case be committed to doing so); but his subsequent discussion of the moral sentiments appears to be at odds with

by distinguishing with regard to the sentiment of approbation between "the sympathetic passion of the spectator; and the emotion which arises from his observing the perfect coincidence between this sympathetic passion in himself, and the original passion in the person principally concerned" (ibid.). It is the latter, Smith claims, in which the sentiment of approbation properly consists, and it is always agreeable and delightful. As for the former, that may be either agreeable or disagreeable depending on the nature of the original passion.

While Smith himself evidently regards this as an adequate response to Hume,[20] problems still remain. For one thing, even if Smith is justified in claiming that the occurrence of sympathetic feelings is a source of pleasure, it is another matter whether that would be a sufficient motive for engaging in the imaginative change of place required for sympathy (Heath, "The Commerce of Sympathy", 448, 457–480). In any case, why should we accept that recognition of a coincidence between our own sympathetically experienced feelings and those of the original subject *is* in itself a source of pleasure to us, especially when these feelings are disagreeable ones? (Raynor, "Hume's Abstract", 58; Blackburn, *Ruling Passions*, 203, n. 6) Apparent counter-examples to Smith's claim come readily to mind. We may surely be dismayed to find ourselves being infected by unreasonable feelings of fear and anger when they are manifested by those around us. We may also, it seems, be discomfited to find ourselves caught up in feelings of joy or happiness where these are excessive or unwarranted. Smith may be right that there are situations in which the fact that we sympathize with someone's passions may more than compensate for the painfulness with which his situation affects us (*TMS*, 16); but, as Hume observes, this does not appear to be true in general, and if the recognition of sympathy *were* always agreeable then, Hume suggests, "An Hospital would be a more entertaining Place than a Ball" (*Letters*, 313). As Hume also observes here, the dampening effect of an "ill-humord Fellow" on those around him may be accounted for by sympathy, and yet this will surely be disagreeable to us. Hume also seems right that the difficulty he has identified for Smith's account of sympathy does concern a "hinge" of his system, for what is at stake is the extent to which this account can explain the moral sentiments of approval and disapproval. If, as it seems, sympathy is *not* always a source of pleasure (even when the original feelings are themselves pleasant or agreeable ones), then Smith would apparently have to concede that there is not, after all, any direct connection (either logical or psychological) between sympathy as fellow-feeling and approval (Heath, "The

---

this in so far as it suggests that there is really no such thing as *the* sentiment of approbation (or of disapprobation)—rather, there are different forms of these sentiments depending on the context in which they occur and with no common features between them (*TMS*, 324–326).

20 As indicated by his claim to have "entirely discomfitted" Hume in a letter to Gilbert Elliot of 10 Oct. 1759.

Commerce of Sympathy", 453).

Clearly a great deal more might be said both for and against Smith's crucial claim about the pleasure of mutual sympathy. It does appear to be true, for example, that any *dissonance* between our feelings and those of the other person is liable to be a source of discomfort (*TMS*, 14, 16; Sugden, "Beyond Sympathy and Empathy", 72–73). It is also true that the pleasure of fellow-feeling is an important feature of many of the activities in which we choose to engage with each other—and that it may well account in these cases for our preferring to do things together rather than individually (Sugden, "Beyond Sympathy and Empathy", 80).[21] But even taking into account the valuable psychological insights provided by Smith's emphasis on the pleasure of mutual sympathy, it still seems to be another matter whether fellow-feeling is *always* a source of pleasure as Smith's position in *TMS* apparently requires. Not the least of the difficulties in attempting to resolve this issue is the apparent lack of consistency in the way that Smith depicts the relation between sympathy and approval (or disapproval). Initially he says of approbation that it is "ultimately *founded* upon a sympathy or correspondence of this kind" (i.e., of sentiments: *TMS*, 17; emphasis mine). Subsequently Smith writes of "complete sympathy" or "that perfect harmony or correspondence of sentiments which *constitutes* approbation" (*TMS*, 44; emphasis mine). His considered view appears to be represented by what he says about the sentiment of approbation in his response to Hume, viz. that it incorporates both "the sympathetic passion of the spectator" and also "the emotion which arises from observing the perfect coincidence between this sympathetic passion in himself, and the original passion in the person principally concerned" (*TMS*, 46, n. b). In other words, approval or approbation essentially consists in the sentiment that arises when we recognize the coincidence between our own sympathetically experienced feelings and those of the other person. If the sentiment of approval is, by its nature, a pleasurable one, then this reflects the pleasurable character of the sentiment associated with the recognition of fellow-feeling.

There is, however, a problem with trying to defend Smith's claim about the pleasure of sympathy by reference to the connection between the sentiments associated with fellow-feeling and approval. The kinds of cases I have mentioned above indicate that sympathy and approval may more easily come apart than Smith's view of their relation would suggest. It seems that I can find myself sharing the feelings of others while at the same time feeling uncomfortable about doing so precisely because they would not gain my approval (in so far

---

21 As an illustration, the experience of watching a film as a member of a cinema audience is often a very different one from watching the same film alone in the privacy of one's own home—and for many of us the shared experience is also a more enjoyable one.

as I am aware that they are at least disproportionate to their cause).[22] It may, perhaps, be true that sympathetically sharing the feelings of others often does amount to an endorsement or confirmation of those feelings;[23] but there is no invariable connection of a kind that would help to vindicate Smith's claim about the pleasures of sympathy. We should also take into account the fact that the pleasure associated with mutual sympathy will not be the same for spectator and agent (bearing in mind, for example, the nature of the agent's engagement in his situation as compared with the imaginary involvement of the sympathetic spectator—Griswold, *Adam Smith*, 121). This kind of asymmetry may help to explain why Smith's claim about the pleasurable nature of sympathy seems especially implausible where fellow-feeling relates to the correspondence between our sympathetically experienced feelings as spectators and the feelings of those observed. For the very fact of the spectator's more detached involvement in the agent's situation allows for the possibility of a negative response to the shared feelings arising from the former's view of that situation. Smith's thesis may, however, have greater plausibility where sympathy is a matter of the fellow-feeling of others with our own emotions as agents, as in the cases to which he refers when introducing the idea of sympathy, bearing in mind our natural desire for the feelings on which we act to be endorsed by those around us.

VI. SYMPATHY AND SELFISHNESS

One of the most familiar objections to Smith's account of sympathy is that it is really no more than "a refinement of the selfish system", as Reid puts it (Norton and Robertson, "Thomas Reid", 383), in spite of Smith's own criticisms of the systems of Mandeville and Hobbes and his explicit denial that sympathy itself is a selfish principle (*TMS*, 317). We have already encountered some reasons for accepting that what Smith has to say about sympathy distinguishes his position from that of the selfish theory. For example, the fact that pity and compassion are "original passions" indicates that we are not exclusively selfish; and the fact that we often derive sorrow from the sorrow of others provides another reason for accepting this conclusion. Nevertheless, Smith evidently takes the objection sufficiently seriously to provide what is evidently intended as a clarification of his account of sympathy, although it might easily be seen as an important revision to that account.

> When I sympathize with your sorrow or your indignation, it may be pretended, indeed, that my emotion is founded in self-love, because it arises from bringing your case home to

---

22 There is in any case the general point that sympathy and approval cannot be identified given the more or less indiscriminate nature of sympathy in so far as we are able to sympathize with almost any passion (Griswold, *Adam Smith*, 85).

23 Darwall, "Empathy, Sympathy, Care", 269.

myself, from putting myself in your situation, and thence conceiving what I should feel in the like circumstances. But though sympathy is very properly said to arise from an imaginary change of situations with the person principally concerned, yet *this imaginary change is not supposed to happen to me in my own person and character, but in that of the person with whom I sympathize*. When I condole with you for the loss of your only son, in order to enter into your grief I do not consider what I, a person of such a character and profession, should suffer, if I had a son, and if that son was unfortunately to die: but *I consider what I should suffer if I was really you, and I not only change circumstances with you, but I change persons and characters*. My grief, therefore, is entirely upon your account, and not in the least upon my own. It is not, therefore, in the least selfish. [*TMS*, 317; emphasis mine]

A couple of things are surprising about this passage. One is that Smith should apparently concede the premise of the objection (i.e., that any feelings that arise from putting myself in your place will be an expression of self-love) without demur; and the other is that the explanation now given of what is meant by the notion of sympathy as involving an imaginary change of situation with the other person is not anticipated at any earlier stage in Smith's discussion.[24] So far as the former point is concerned, it seems possible that Smith is influenced here by a passage in Butler's sermon "Upon Compassion", where he discusses an argument on behalf of the view that we are motivated solely by self-love: namely, that when we apparently substitute the interests of others for our own, we are really concerned only for ourselves. Butler has in mind here positions like that of Hobbes, who represents pity as the "imagination or fiction of future calamity to ourselves, proceeding from the sense of another man's calamity" (Butler, *Fifteen Sermons*, 84 n. 1). What, in any case, should we make of the notion that sympathy, understood as imagining how we would feel in the other person's place, is a manifestation of self-love?[25] It might be thought that, on the

---

24 It is true that when introducing the notion of sympathy Smith says that this is a matter of placing ourselves in the other person's situation so that we "become in some measure the same person as him" (*TMS*, 9). But the context suggests that Smith means no more by this than that by changing places in imagination with the other person we are then able to conceive what *we* would feel were we in his situation. Note, incidentally, that the passage just quoted occurs in the first edition of *TMS*. (Appendix I, page 376, in *TMS* lists minor variants in the sixth-edition version of this passage as compared with earlier editions.)

25 We should bear in mind here that there are contexts in which both Butler and

contrary, being prepared to put ourselves in the place of the other person, even if it does not extend beyond imagining how we would feel in their situation, is in itself counter-evidence to the selfish theory. If we are concerned exclusively with our own interests, and not at all with those of others, why would we bother to look at the world from any perspective but our own (except, of course, in those cases in which there is an obviously self-interested reason for doing so)? And if, as a result of imagining how we would feel in the other person's situation, we are then concerned for him, it seems even more obvious that the selfish theory must be rejected.[26]

But leaving this point aside, there is also the striking reference to sympathy as involving not merely a change of situation, but also a change of person and character.[27] It is this notion of sympathy that leads Smith to suggest that the selfish theory has arisen from a "confused misapprehension of the system of sympathy" (*TMS*, 317). Once more, Smith may have Butler in mind, though Smith doesn't refer to him in this context. In the sermon mentioned above Butler counters Hobbes's view that compassion amounts only to fear for ourselves by suggesting that mutual sympathy or a fellow-feeling among mankind is an example of substituting ourselves for others rather than substituting others for ourselves (Butler, *Fifteen Sermons*, 67). Smith presents his own version of this distinction without further comment or elaboration, but the distinction itself is surely not without its problems. What Smith has in mind might be described as the *identification* of oneself with the other person.[28] It

---

Smith would distinguish self-love from selfishness. Thus Butler declares that self-love "does in general perfectly coincide with virtue" (*Fifteen Sermons*, 67), and in his discussion of Mandeville Smith accepts that "self-love may frequently be a virtuous motive to action" (*TMS*, 309). But elsewhere both of them mention the principle of self-love in referring to the reductionist account of human nature provided by the selfish theory.

26 "I esteem the man, whose self-love, *by whatever means*, is so directed as to give him a concern for others, and render him serviceable to society: As I hate or despise him, who has no regard to anything beyond his own gratifications and enjoyments" (Hume, *Enquiry*, App. 2.4; emphasis mine). (References to *Enquiry* in this and subsequent footnotes are to section and paragraph numbers.)

27 It might be thought especially implausible to suppose that our sympathetic responses to others always involve an imaginative exercise of *this* kind. Hume, in his account of sympathy, appears to reject the very possibility of an imaginary change of person or character: "No force of imagination can convert us into another person" (Hume, *Enquiry*, 6.3).

28 It may be suggested that even in the case of Smith's earlier examples of sympathy there is a sense in which the spectator identifies himself with the other person. It is clear, however, that in these cases the identification—if that is the right word—is only partial. Indeed, the connection that Smith goes on to draw between sympathy

seems clear that where something of this kind is said to occur there need be no connection with sympathy as fellow-feeling. For example, an actor may think in terms of identifying himself with the character whose part he is playing; but someone who in this way immerses himself in a role such as that of Othello does not thereby *share* feelings of jealousy with anyone. But what of the kind of case with which Smith is concerned? The point of his example is that he, as an unmarried man who has never known what it is like to be a parent, can enter into the grief of the bereaved father only by imagining how that man, as a father, must be suffering. What is it to engage in a piece of imagining of this kind?

It would be helpful here to consider an account of the way in which we understand and predict each other's actions, which appeals to the idea of *simulation*: i.e., that our ability to respond to each other in this way depends on being able to simulate being in the other person's situation, not only by simulating being in that situation ourselves, with our own psychological propensities, but also by simulating *being the other person* in that situation with their own particular psychological traits.[29] The distinction being drawn here obviously corresponds quite closely with the distinction implicit in Smith's remarks about sympathy in the passage from *TMS* quoted above. So how are we meant to understand the claim that we are able to understand the other person by simulating *being* that person? This is a question to which different simulation theorists might well give different answers. One possible view of what it is to simulate being the other person is that this is to simulate *oneself* as the person engaged in the simulation, in that situation, albeit with the psychological traits

---

and approval seems to require that the identification should be only partial, in so far as the spectator is concerned with the question of how far his sentiments would correspond to those of the other person in that person's situation (Sugden, "Beyond Sympathy and Empathy", 74). It has been argued that this is true even of Smith's example of sympathy as involving a change of person and character (ibid., 75); but this seems to downplay the significance of the distinction between the different kinds of imaginative project to which Smith's notion of sympathy refers. Griswold also claims that there is no case of sympathy in which we can be said to identify with the other (*Adam Smith*, 28), if only because, as Smith himself indicates, the spectator remains aware of the fact that he or she is engaged in an imaginary change of situation (*TMS*, 22). Nevertheless there is a point in referring to identification in this context, as we shall see shortly.

29 This, at least, is how the idea of simulation has been presented in a number of papers by Robert Gordon (for example, "The Simulation Theory"). Other proponents of the simulation approach may have something less than this notion of "total projection" in mind. We should note, incidentally, that the word "simulation" is evidently being employed by these theorists in a somewhat technical sense—as it is, for example, in the very different context of computing—with no implication of any form of deceit being involved.

of the other person. There is, however, an air of paradox, at least, about this view. For it appears that one is somehow identifying oneself with the other person while yet retaining one's own identity as the person who is performing this imaginative identification. Apart from the difficulty of making sense of this, it seems evident that it is against the spirit of the type of simulation involved, where one's own psychology forms no part of what is being simulated. (A similar point might be made about the non-egocentric form of sympathy to which Smith refers.) But what, then, is going on in the case where one is supposed to simulate being another person? Is there any alternative to thinking of this as a matter of imagining an identity between oneself and this other person? One possibility is that when I consider what I should be suffering if I was really you, as in Smith's example, the word "I" (as in "I have lost my only son") does not refer to me as the person doing the imagining (or simulating) but rather to the person with whom I have changed places in imagination (Gordon, "The Simulation Theory", 118–119). This may involve a controversial view of the reference of personal pronouns like "I", but it indicates the kind of philosophical moves that might be necessary in trying to make sense of Smith's revised account of sympathy.

CONCLUSION

While I have been mainly concerned with exploring Smith's account of sympathy in *TMS*, I should acknowledge the skepticism that has been expressed about the notion of sympathy as it is employed by Smith (and, for that matter, Hume).[30] This is obviously not the place to attempt a detailed response to such skepticism, but it is worth noting that sympathy, in something like the sense(s) employed by Smith, provides the basis for a flourishing research program in social cognitive neuroscience (stimulated by the discovery of mirror neurons);[31] and that it is also a central theme of 19th-century novels such as George Eliot's *Daniel Deronda*.[32] Certainly, there are aspects of the accounts of sympathy provided by both Hume and Smith that might be questioned. For example, Hume appears to take it for granted that a sensation like pain may be transmitted by the process of sympathy from the sufferer to the spectator (*Treatise*, 2.1.11.2; 3.3.1.7)[33]; but, as Smith's own discussion suggests, it may be doubted whether sympathy with the sufferings of others *does* normally involve experiencing pain on their behalf. (Why does "I feel your pain" almost invariably ring false?) In regard to what Smith himself has to say about sympathy, there are important questions about what exactly is involved in the imaginative projection of

---

30 "'[S]ympathy' as used by Hume and Smith is the name of a philosophical fiction" (MacIntyre, *After Virtue*, 49).
31 For a useful survey of the literature in this area see Blakemore et al., "Social Cognitive Neuroscience".
32 See, for example, Toker, "Vocation and Sympathy", esp. 567–570.
33 References to *Treatise* are to book, part, section, and paragraph numbers.

oneself into another's situation and how we are to make sense of this idea. But it seems hard to deny that both philosophers use "sympathy" to refer to genuine phenomena—such as the transfer of emotion that often occurs between human beings and the empathy or fellow-feeling that appears to underlie emotions such as pity and compassion. To this extent both Hume and Smith may be said to have identified important aspects of our moral psychology that would provide the basis for an ethical theory.

Although I have said little about this, I think it might be considered a virtue of Smith's account of sympathy, in particular, that it represents what is involved as being more than merely the operation of a kind of mental mechanism, and makes due allowance for the role of our imaginative capacities in this context.[34] There are, of course, as we have seen, difficulties with Smith's view of the connection between sympathy and imagination, but that is not to deny the interest and importance of this connection. As we have also seen, Smith's account of sympathy as fellow-feeling is more complex than it might appear to be at first sight, especially given what he says about the indirect character of our awareness of the feelings of others. This, in turn, is related to Smith's view of fellow-feeling as a phenomenon that depends, in almost every case, on imagining what we would feel in the other person's place: a view that we have found reason to question. There is also a difficulty about the supposed relation between sympathy as fellow-feeling and the altruistic emotions, and it seems fair to say that Smith himself says too little about this relation. So far as the claimed relation of sympathy to pleasure is concerned, Smith's response to Hume's objection appears inadequate, especially bearing in mind the crucial part played by sympathy in Smith's account of the moral sentiments. Finally, Smith's response to the objection that his theory of sympathy is nothing more than a refinement of the selfish theory leads to a revised account of sympathy that is of considerable interest in its own right. The parallel to the simulation view that has become prominent in recent philosophy of mind indicates ways in which this account of sympathy might be developed, while also reminding us of some of the problems to be faced by any such account.

---

34   I have in mind here the contrast with Hume's initial account of sympathy as a process in which ideas are converted into impressions and where imagination is involved only in so far as the process depends on certain principles of association (*Treatise*, 2.1.11.1–7). Hume does, however, go on to refer to a kind of "extensive" sympathy, where the observer is more actively engaged in the situation of the other person (see Herdt, *Religion and Faction*, Chapter 2).

SELECT BIBLIOGRAPHY

Blackburn, Simon. *Ruling Passions*. Oxford: Clarendon Press, 2000.

Blakemore, Sarah-Jayne, J. Winston, and U. Frith. "Social Cognitive Neuroscience: Where Are We Heading?" *Trends in Cognitive Neuroscience* 8, no. 5 (2004): 216–222.

Broadie, Alexander. "Sympathy and the Impartial Spectator". In *The Cambridge Companion to Adam Smith*, edited by K. Haakonssen. Cambridge: Cambridge University Press, 2006, 158–188.

Butler, Joseph. *Fifteen Sermons and a Dissertation on the Nature of Virtue*. London: Bell and Sons, 1726, 1958.

Campbell, T. D. *Adam Smith's Science of Morals*. London: Allen and Unwin, 1971.

Darwall, Stephen. "Empathy, Sympathy, Care". *Philosophical Studies* 89, nos. 2–3 (1998): 261–282.

———. "Sympathetic Liberalism: Recent Work on Adam Smith". *Philosophy and Public Affairs* 28, no. 2 (1999): 139–164.

De Marchi, Neil. "Smith on Ingenuity, Pleasure, and the Imitative Arts". In *The Cambridge Companion to Adam Smith*, edited by K. Haakonssen. Cambridge: Cambridge University Press, 2006, 136–157.

Gordon, Robert M. "The Simulation Theory: Objections and Misconceptions". In *Folk Psychology*, edited by M. Davies and T. Stone. Oxford: Blackwell, 1995.

Griswold, Charles L., Jr. *Adam Smith and the Virtues of Enlightenment*. Cambridge: Cambridge University Press, 1999.

———. "Imagination: Morals, Science, and Arts". In *The Cambridge Companion to Adam Smith*, edited by Knud Haakonssen. Cambridge: Cambridge University Press, 2006, 22–56.

Heath, Eugene. "The Commerce of Sympathy: Adam Smith on the Emergence of Morals". *Journal of the History of Philosophy* 33, no. 3 (1995): 447–466.

Herdt, Jennifer A. *Religion and Faction in Hume's Moral Philosophy.* Cambridge: Cambridge University Press, 1997.

Hoffman, Martin L. *Empathy and Moral Development.* Cambridge: Cambridge University Press, 2000.

Hume, David. *An Enquiry Concerning the Principles of Morals.* Edited by Tom L. Beauchamp. Oxford: Oxford University Press, 1751, 1998.

———. *The Letters of David Hume.* Edited by J. Y. T. Greig, 2 vols. Oxford: Oxford University Press, 1932.

———. *A Treatise of Human Nature.* Edited by David Fate Norton and Mary J. Norton. Oxford: Oxford University Press, 1739–1740, 2000.

Johnson, Samuel. *Dictionary of the English Language* (1755).

Kames, Lord (Henry Home). *Essays on the Principles of Morality and Natural Religion.* Edited by Mary Moran. Indianapolis: Liberty Fund, 1779, 2005.

MacIntyre, Alasdair. *After Virtue: A Study in Moral Theory*, 2nd ed. London: Duckworth, 1992.

Mercer, Philip. *Sympathy and Ethics.* Oxford: Clarendon Press, 1972.

Mossner, Ernest C., and I. S. Ross. *The Correspondence of Adam Smith.* Oxford: Clarendon Press, 1977.

Norton, D. F., and S. Robertson. "Thomas Reid on Adam Smith's Theory of Morals". *Journal of the History of Ideas* 41, no. 3 (1980): 381–398.

Nozick, Robert. *Philosophical Explanations.* Cambridge, Massachusetts: Harvard University Press, 1981.

Otteson, James R. *Adam Smith's Marketplace of Life.* Cambridge: Cambridge University Press, 2002.

Raynor, David R. "Hume's Abstract of Adam Smith's *Theory of Moral Sentiments*". *Journal of the History of Philosophy* 22, no. 1 (1984): 51–64.

Reid, Thomas. *An Inquiry into the Human Mind on the Principles of Common Sense*. Edited by Derek R. Brookes. Edinburgh: Edinburgh University Press, 1764, 1997.

Smith, Adam. *Essays on Philosophical Subjects*. Edited by W. P. D. Wightman and J. C. Bryce. Oxford: Clarendon Press, 1980.

———. "Letter to Gilbert Elliot". In E. C. Mossner and I. S. Ross, *The Correspondence of Adam Smith*. Oxford: Clarendon Press, 1977.

———. *The Theory of Moral Sentiments*. 1759. Edited by D. D. Raphael and A. L. Macfie. Oxford: Clarendon Press, 1976.

Snow, N. E. "Empathy". *American Philosophical Quarterly* 37, no. 1 (2000): 65–78.

Sugden, Robert. "Beyond Sympathy and Empathy: Adam Smith's Concept of Fellow-Feeling". *Economics and Philosophy* 18, no. 1 (2002): 63–87.

Toker, Leona. "Vocation and Sympathy in *Daniel Deronda*: The Self and the Larger Whole". *Victorian Literature and Culture* 32, no. 2 (2004): 565–574.

"THE MOST CRUEL MISFORTUNE": SUFFERING INNOCENCE IN *THE THEORY OF MORAL SENTIMENTS*

Vincent Bissonette

I. INTRODUCTION

In *The Theory of Moral Sentiments*[1] (*TMS*), Part III, Chapter 2, Adam Smith describes an "innocent man, brought to the scaffold by the false imputation of an infamous or odious crime". Smith does not equivocate on the significance of this situation. Such a man "suffers the most cruel misfortune which it is possible for innocence to suffer". Smith goes on to enumerate all the feelings that will assault this man, making his demise such a dark and melancholy thing:

> The innocent man [...] over and above the uneasiness which this fear [of death] may occasion, is tormented by his own indignation at the injustice which has been done to him. He is struck with horror at the thoughts of the infamy which the punishment may shed upon his memory, and foresees, with the most exquisite anguish, that he is hereafter to be remembered by his dearest friends and relations, not with regret and affection, but with shame, and even with horror for his supposed disgraceful conduct: and the shades of death appear to close round him with a darker and more melancholy gloom than naturally belongs to them. [*TMS*, III.2.11]

In his discussion, Smith touches on a common philosophical topic, the problem of evil. In general, the problem of evil refers to the universal phenomenon that innocent people often suffer unjustly and how philosophical systems account for this phenomenon, explain, or mitigate it.

Through this particular case, Smith suggests that his "humble philosophy", as he calls it, might be inadequate to address the innocent man's suffering. Religion may be a necessary palliative:

> To persons in such unfortunate circumstances, that humble philosophy which confines its views to this life, can afford, perhaps, but little consolation. Every thing that could render life or death respectable is taken from them. They

---

1   Bibliographic information for all references can be found in the Select Bibliography at the end of this essay.

are condemned to death and to everlasting infamy. Religion can alone afford them any effectual comfort. She alone can tell them, that it is of little importance what man may think of their conduct, while the all-seeing Judge of the world approves of it. She alone can present to them the view of another world; a world of more candour, humanity, and justice, than the present; where their innocence is in due time to be declared, and their virtue to be finally rewarded: and the same great principle which can alone strike terror into triumphant vice, affords the only effectual consolation to disgraced and insulted innocence. [*TMS*, III.2.12]

In writing of "that humble philosophy which confines its views to this life", Smith refers not only to his own philosophy but to an anti-speculative kind of British philosophy, forcefully articulated by his contemporary and friend David Hume in *A Treatise of Human Nature* (*THN*) (1739-1740)[2] and memorably captured in Alexander Pope's couplet from his *Essay on Man* (1733-34): "Know then thyself, presume not God to scan; / The proper study of Mankind is Man" (516).[3] In mentioning a "humble philosophy", Smith alludes to a philosophy that anticipates a social-scientific approach to describing human interaction while eschewing the normative framework provided by religion.

In this context, his recommendation of religion is clearly retrograde, a view that seems to be acknowledged in Smith's prose. In the passage, the insights of philosophy are presented as objective description: "Every thing [...] is taken from them. They are condemned [...]". In contrast, the "consolation" offered by religion is spoken by Religion herself, personified as a woman who comforts the victims. She "afford[s] them [...] comfort", "tell[s] them" that God's judgment is more important than man's, and "present[s] them" with a view of heaven. She gives the innocent sufferers just what they need, but that does not make it true.[4]

---

2   See especially Hume's Introduction and Conclusion to Book I. See also John Biro, "Hume's New Science of the Mind", 33-36.

3   Compare Hume: "Human Nature is the only science of man; and yet has been hitherto the most neglected" (*THN*, 1.4.7, 273).

4   In a pragmatist vein, we might understand Smith to be recommending religion as "effectual" in certain situations where philosophy would be useless. When we try to understand the dynamics of human interaction, we use philosophical ideas. But for the last things—death, heaven, hell, and judgment—we turn to religion. That kind of compartmentalizing can be attractive. It seems to have worked for many deathbed converts (though Hume calmly and notoriously passed without it). However, this compartmentalizing explanation neglects the way Smith's writing implicitly values his "humble philosophy" as pursuing truth, while religion merely offers "comfort" and "consolation".

Thus, Smith seems to offer religion as a necessary supplement to philosophy, providing comfort to those who suffer innocently and a perspective from which they can see themselves as innocent. Is this Smith's wisdom, that in certain cases the truth must be supplemented with fiction? Or is the fiction of religion a supplement that Smith would rather do without?

In what follows, I will consider at length this innocent man's unfortunate fate without the supplement of religion. Smith's "humble philosophy" describes mechanisms of the human constitution that are developed through experience. These mechanisms are themselves functional in everyday life, but perhaps ill-adapted to deal with an event that we must hope is very rare, such as an innocent man being sentenced to death.[5] I wish to consider two of these mechanisms as they bear on the scene at hand, which I will call the causal imagination and the sympathetic imagination. Through an understanding of these mechanisms, Smith's humble philosophy pursues truth. My ultimate question will be: Despite Smith's protestations, might there be some consolation in this truth?

II. THE CAUSAL IMAGINATION

Smith adds the example of the man about to be hanged to the sixth edition of *TMS* (1790) to supplement a discussion of the distinction, made in the first five editions (1759–1781), between being praise-worthy and being praised. That distinction serves the purpose of anticipating the criticism that in Smith's ethics too much emphasis is placed upon the approbation and disapprobation of others (see *TMS*, III.1.2.n.$^{e-e}$). A dependence on the judgment of others can go wrong in a number of ways. These others might be too selfish or too malicious to impartially judge a case of right and wrong. They may lack necessary seriousness, treating someone's actions as if they were the latest fashion. They may lack the necessary facts, or they may mistake the facts, applauding someone for virtues that are lacking, or failing to blame for a crime that has been committed.

All of these potential problems are inherent in an ethics that depends upon the approbation of others and tend towards instability, subjectivism, and/or relativism. Smith recognizes this problem, and his solution is very clearly connected with his understanding of the mechanism by which we think causally, which I am calling the causal imagination. In a passage deleted from the sixth edition, Smith writes:

> The desire of approbation and esteem of those we live with, which is of so much importance to our happiness, cannot be fully and intirely contented but by rendering ourselves the

---

5   Smith shows some anxiousness about the frequency of events like this: "Such fatal accidents, for the tranquility of mankind, it is to be hoped, happen very rarely in any country; but they happen sometimes in all countries, even in those where justice is in general very well administered" (*TMS*, III.2.11).

just and proper objects of those sentiments, and by adjusting our character and conduct according to those measures and rules by which esteem and approbation are naturally bestowed. [*TMS*, III.1.2.n.^{e–e}][6]

We see here a version of the impartial spectator. I am interested in exploring Smith's detailed explanation of the mechanism behind the impartial spectator. In this passage, Smith makes an important distinction between the desire for an obviously factual "approbation and esteem" and the more abstract desire to be the "just and proper objects" of approbation. Although the former may be foremost in our minds, Smith contends that the latter is the more fundamental desire.[7] In order to be fully satisfied, we must not simply be praised; we must deserve praise. However, in the former, I simply have to recognize an empirical fact: I am given "approbation and esteem". In the latter, on the other hand, I must rationally assess myself vis-à-vis the "just and proper objects" of approbation. But before this reasoning can take place, I must know these "just and proper objects" of approbation. How do I gain this knowledge?

Traditional answers to this question have involved God's revealed law, a rational understanding of Nature or the Cosmos, and the use of the God-given faculty we call conscience. These answers depend upon an objective and absolute order. Smith's "humble philosophy" cannot rely on such an order. Thus, he attempts a naturalistic and empirical answer. We know the "just and proper objects" of approbation because we have observed them in experience and have internalized them along the lines that Hume describes in his discussion of causality.

---

6   The import of this passage seems to be reworked for the sixth edition in the following: "Emulation, the anxious desire that we ourselves should excel, is originally founded in our admiration of the excellence of others. Neither can we be satisfied with being merely admired for what other people are admired. We must at least believe ourselves to be admirable for what they are admirable. But, in order to attain this satisfaction, we must become the impartial spectators of our own character and conduct. We must endeavour to view them with the eyes of other people, or as other people are likely to view them. When seen in this light, if they appear to us as we wish, we are happy and contented" (*TMS*, III.2.3). This passage is, I believe, rhetorically superior and thus more compelling than the passage I've quoted from the first edition. However, it also includes little indication of the mechanism I am here exploring.

7   "[S]o far is the love of praise-worthiness from being derived altogether from that of praise; that the love of praise seems, at least in a great measure, to be derived from that of praise-worthiness" (*TMS*, III.2.3). This sentence is found only in the sixth edition.

How Hume Works for Smith

Hume's writings on causality, in their specificities and inconsistencies, are beyond the scope of this essay.[8] I am interested quite narrowly in his account of how one comes to make causal connections, an essentially psychological account that roots these connections in experience, habit, and imagination. In the *Treatise*, Hume describes the "very principles, on which all judgments concerning causes and effects depend":

> Our judgments concerning causes and effects are deriv'd from habit and experience; and when we have been accustom'd to see one object united to another, our imagination passes from the first to the second, by a natural transition, which precedes reflection, and which cannot be prevented by it.[9]

As Hume explains, we repeatedly find that in our experience, certain events ([A] and [B]) are connected, and our minds learn to habitually connect the ideas of these events ([a] and [b]). This habitual connection will then guide our imagination. Thus, when we observe (A) and have the corresponding idea (a), our imagination quickly anticipates the idea (b). This imaginative connection can happen even if we do not actually observe (B), and it happens independent of and sometimes even in spite of reflection. Hume's psychology of causality is more a process of conditioning the imagination than an act of reasoning.

Adam Smith, as I've explained, is trying to balance a love of praise with a love of praise-worthiness. In order to do this, he suggests a causal relation between praise-worthiness and praise. Praise-worthiness acts as a cause, the effect of which is praise. The same general rule applies to blame-worthiness and blame. Smith gives several examples of how this relationship works. A man praised for a virtue he does not possess will be embarrassed. A woman who uses makeup, if praised for her beauty, will simply be reminded of the effect her unmade-up face would have on others. A virtuous man, who is not praised, will imagine the praise that ought to follow from his virtue. And a criminal whose crime goes undetected will be tormented by the imagined blame he knows should follow from his crime. In what follows, I concentrate on the last two of these examples, for it is there that Smith most explicitly uses Hume in explaining the causal imagination.

When writing of the virtuous man who goes unpraised, Smith states: "The man who is conscious to himself that he has exactly observed those measures of conduct which experience informs him are generally agreeable,

---

8 For a rundown of Hume on causation and induction, including references to academic debate on the matter, see pp. 71–77 and the accompanying notes in Alexander Rosenberg, "Hume and the Philosophy of Science".

9 *THN*, 1.3.13, p. 147. See also the *Enquiry Concerning Human Understanding*, 5.1.

reflects with satisfaction on the propriety of his own behaviour" (*TMS* III.2.5). This is possible, "though mankind should never be acquainted with what he had done". He cares less about how others "actually regard him" than with how they "would regard him if they were better informed". The praise is imagined only, but has an effect on the man as if it were real.

> He anticipates the applause and admiration which in this case would be bestowed upon him, and he applauds and admires himself by sympathy with sentiments, which do not indeed actually take place, but which the ignorance of the public alone hinders from taking place, which he knows are the natural and ordinary effects of such conduct, which his imagination strongly connects with it, and which he has acquired a habit of conceiving as something that naturally and in propriety ought to follow from it. [*TMS* III.2.5]

In this passage, the praise-worthy man's self-approbation is supported by sympathetic approval, though, in fact, he anticipates praise that is not actual. The scenario—someone proud of himself imaging how others would praise him, if they only knew—is unremarkable in itself. Smith's explanation, with its recourse to Hume's notions of causality, is remarkable. Smith is clearly drawing on Hume here, and the passage uses several of Hume's key words. The man *anticipates* the praise. His *imagination* connects praise and praise-worthiness because he has formed the *habit* of conceiving the two together. Further, the connection between the two is first known, as Smith has written earlier, because *experience* informs him. It's worth noting here that Smith's logic resides in five consecutive clauses, each beginning with "which" and modifying the sentiments of approbation the man imagines in others:

(1) which do not indeed actually take place, but
(2) which the ignorance of the public alone hinders from taking place,
(3) which he knows are the natural and ordinary effects of such conduct,
(4) which his imagination strongly connects with it, and
(5) which he has acquired a habit of conceiving as something that naturally and in propriety ought to follow from it.

This presentation suggests the layers of actuality and imagination, experience and habit, in intersubjective relations. In its accumulation of these several layers, Smith's "humble philosophy" points to a standard of virtue that emerges out of, but has some independence from, the actual praise and blame others bestow.

As I've already suggested, Smith's "humble philosophy" is essentially a form of naturalism. The role of this naturalism is evident in his description of the guilty man who is thought innocent. This case is the obvious counterpart to the example of the virtuous man who goes without praise. The criminal, though unblamed, imagines and anticipates how others would view him if they knew his crime. The habitual connection made between the crime and the proper and fitting response to it is so great that the imagination makes the connection "though he [the criminal] could be assured that no man was ever to know it, and could even bring himself to believe that there was no God to revenge it" (*TMS*, III.2.9). Recall how Hume writes that reflection cannot prevent the connection from happening. The criminal can assure himself and bring himself to believe whatever he wants. He is still a passive victim of the habitual connections that his imagination makes.

> These natural pangs of an affrighted conscience are the daemons, the avenging furies, which, in this life, haunt the guilty, which allow them neither quiet nor repose, which often drive them to despair and distraction, from which no assurance of secrecy can protect them, from which no principles of irreligion can entirely deliver them, and from which nothing can free them but the vilest and most abject of states, a complete insensibility to honour and infamy, to vice and virtue. [*TMS*, III.2.9]

Smith again accumulates a series of modifying clauses to advance his argument about the role these "daemons" play. I will focus, however, on the main clause, in which he moves from "natural pangs" to "affrighted conscience" to "daemons" and "avenging furies". The daemons and avenging furies are clearly supernatural and, for Smith, superstitious. He uses them figuratively to signify a guilty conscience. Yet conscience itself, theologically an intuitive faculty implanted in the human by God, is naturalized. Much of the thrust of Smith's discussion has been to explain how the socialized individual feels these "natural pangs"—natural because they emerge out of the mechanisms of the human constitution rather than a god-implanted conscience. The individual sees connections in experience between virtue and praise, vice and blame; the ideas are habitually connected; eventually, his imagination begins to anticipate these connections. "Conscience" here is merely an internalization of this habitual linking of ideas as it regards certain ethical choices. Thus, in a nice articulation of Smith's naturalizing humble philosophy, the daemons are an externalization of this internalization.

How Smith Comes to Incorporate Hume's Skepticism

Most of the passages I have been discussing are found in all editions of Smith's work. In the sixth edition, however, this discussion was greatly expanded. The distinction that informs it—between praise and praise-worthiness—is more clearly articulated in the sixth edition than in previous editions, and the relation between the two is more fully examined. Smith considers the relationship between worthiness and praise, considering the four major permutations of the two. In the first editions, Smith discusses praise without praise-worthiness; praise-worthiness without praise; and blame-worthiness without blame. From a schematic point of view, he obviously omits blame without blame-worthiness. The sixth edition rectifies this omission with the example of the innocent man brought to the scaffold.

This example marks a significant moment in Smith's use of Hume. All of the examples in the first five editions of *TMS* can be described by Hume's naturalistic account of causality. In the example of the virtuous man who imagines praise, Smith's use of this mechanism to describe the man's satisfaction is quite explicit. However, in all the examples, this habitual connection of ideas works "correctly". In other words, the upshot of each example is much the same as it would be if he relied on a more traditional concept such as conscience or faith in the just rewards that God metes out. The problem of evil may be raised in actual events, but it seems that the causal imagination (properly conditioned and socialized to connect merit and praise) offers the individual a spontaneous corrective. The naturalistic account of how this works is of academic interest but has little practical consequence. In the first five editions, Smith emphasizes these pragmatic successes of the causal imagination and neglects the skeptical consequences of a causality rooted in experience, habit, and imagination.[10] The example of the innocent man about to be hanged recognizes these consequences, and thus raises the problem of evil.

This innocent man is condemned by all around him. No one knows his innocence. Because of the unanimous blame he receives, all easily imagine that he is blame-worthy. The innocent man knows his own innocence, which might be enough for a Stoic, but according to Smith's philosophy, he must imagine others knowing his innocence. This, it seems, he cannot do. He cannot console himself because he cannot sympathize with his hypothetical sympathizers.

Smith, as I mentioned at the beginning, realizes that his philosophy has no avenue of comfort for such a man as this:

---

10 In the first editions, Smith also considers the possibility that an unworthy man praised will not be bothered by his unworthiness (*TMS*, III.2.4). The praise will, in Humean fashion, actually lead him to believe himself to be worthy in some way. In a move that, I think, shows how invested Smith was at this time in having a properly working "conscience", he dismisses such a case as mere vanity—as if calling it that would make it a negligible case.

> To persons in such unfortunate circumstances, that humble philosophy which confines its views to this life, can afford, perhaps, but little consolation. Every thing that could render either life or death respectable is taken from them. They are condemned to death and to everlasting infamy. Religion alone can afford them any effectual comfort [...]. [*TMS*, III.2.12]

III. THE SYMPATHETIC IMAGINATION

When Smith recommends religion for such cases, he is offering God as the great sympathizer who is not fooled by the unjust praise or blame but recognizes worthiness and rewards or punishes accordingly. The great difficulty faced by this man, I've just claimed, is that he cannot imagine anyone sympathizing with him. But this is not exactly right. His friends are not without sympathy. The problem is that they believe he is guilty; they are sympathizing with a guilty man and therefore feel the shame that a publicly condemned guilty man would feel. If they knew that he was an innocent man unjustly accused of an infamous crime, they would feel the anger and indignation that anyone in that situation would feel. However, like the causal imagination, the sympathetic imagination—a vital mechanism in human life—is not perfect.

For Smith, the sympathetic imagination is an imperfect response to imperfect human nature. Because no two people share the same circumstances, there is always a discrepancy between different individuals' passions. This discrepancy is evident when something *happens* to one person, while others merely *witness* it. It is especially problematic when it involves a misfortune or injury. Smith writes, "My companion does not naturally look upon the misfortune that has befallen me, or the injury that has been done me, from the same point of view in which I consider them. They affect me much more nearly" (*TMS*, I.i.4.5). The discrepancy of feeling may lead to a complete severance of companionship. "We become intolerable to one another. I can neither support your company, nor you mine. You are confounded at my violence and passion, and I am enraged at your cold insensibility and want of feeling" (*TMS*, I.i.4.5).

The sympathetic imagination is part of the natural response to this problem.[11] The spectator of another's misfortune may "endeavour" to sympathize—to put himself in the other's place, imagining all the circumstances that surround that person:

---

11 In addition to the sympathetic imagination, by which the spectator must "endeavour" to feel what the principle person feels, the principle person attempts to "lower [...] his passion to that pitch, in which the spectators are capable of going along with him. He must flatten" his passion (*TMS*, I.i.4.6–7). Ideally, then, they meet in the middle. In reality, they never actually meet but do get close enough for the "harmony of society".

> [T]hat there may be some correspondence of sentiments between the spectator and the person principally concerned, the spectator must, first of all, endeavour, as much as he can, to put himself in the situation of the other, and to bring home to himself every little circumstance of distress which can possibly occur to the sufferer. He must adopt the whole case of his companion with all its minutest incidents; and strive to render as perfect as possible, that imaginary change of situation upon which his sympathy is founded. [*TMS*, I.i.4.6]

This "endeavour", Smith makes clear, is difficult. Sympathy itself is natural and spontaneous, but to fully imagine another's circumstances is not. The spectator must "strive" in what, to some extent, is an ethical act. It is also, potentially, a virtuosic performance, possible only to the man of taste. Smith suggests this point in emphasizing the importance of "every little circumstance" and the "minutest incidents". These are the subtleties that many would not even notice; yet they are necessary for a more perfect sympathy.[12]

Still, sympathy is never perfect. The best one may hope for is what Smith calls the "harmony of society":

> What they [the sympathetic spectators] feel, will, indeed, always be, in some respects, different from what he feels, and compassion can never be exactly the same with original sorrow; because the secret consciousness that the change of situations, from which the sympathetic sentiment arises, is but imaginary, not only lowers it in degree, but, in some measure, varies it in kind, and gives it a quite different modification. These two sentiments, however, may, it is evident, have such a correspondence with one another, as is sufficient for the harmony of society. Though they will never be unisons, they may be concords, and this is all that is wanted or required. [*TMS*, I.i.4.7]

Each individual consciousness is, fundamentally, "secret". I can never perfectly imagine another's situation, and even if I could, I still lack the nearness to the situation that brings it home to the "person principally concerned". There

---

[12] There is a parallel here with David Hume's idea of taste. In "On the Standard of Taste" Hume claims that taste is universal but that fineness of taste is not (234–238). Similarly, for Smith sympathy is universal, but the fine perception that appreciates and brings home "every little circumstance" and the "minutest incidents" is rare.

can thus never be "unison" of feeling. But Smith claims that the "concords" and the "harmony of society" are good enough. It is, in fact, "all that is wanted or required".

To sum up Smith's sympathetic imagination, we can note several characteristics. Most importantly, the sympathetic imagination is an imperfect solution to the problem of unshared passions. The feelings of the sympathetic spectator are not only less intense than the feelings of the principle person, they have a different character; they are more distinct. Also, though the urge to sympathize is universal, sympathy itself requires work from the sympathizer and is limited by the sympathizer's fineness of perception. There is a final corollary here that the act of sympathy can make previously hidden details visible. Thus a virtuosic sympathizer can help others to sympathize.

The Friends' Shame

In the case of the innocent man, the sympathetic imagination goes wrong. Consider the kind of sympathy that would be hoped for. This man might imagine his friends remembering him "with regret and affection". He would then sympathize with his own imagining and perhaps be consoled by the tender thought. Such would be a consolation for anyone facing death. Or, if his friends knew that he was unjustly accused, then they would feel pity or share his indignation at the injustice; perhaps, he would even imagine his friends pursuing the revenge that he cannot carry out. To imagine this from his friends and to sympathize with the anger they felt on his behalf would surely console the condemned man and perhaps even give him a feeling of vindication in his death.

But look at what Smith writes:

> He is struck with horror at the thoughts of the infamy which the punishment may shed upon his memory, and foresees, with the most exquisite anguish, that he is hereafter to be remembered by his dearest friends and relations, not with regret and affection, but with shame, and even with horror for his supposed disgraceful conduct [...]. [*TMS*, III.2.11]

Alas, he can imagine only how his friends feel at witnessing the just execution of their sometime friend. He thus imagines them neither regretful nor indignant but shamed. The tragedy that Smith describes has everything to do with the complex layering of the indignation the condemned man does feel, the regret he wishes his friends would feel, and the shame he imagines they must feel. Later Smith will describe the lot of those in such a situation. "Every thing that could render either life or death respectable is taken from them. They are condemned to death and to everlasting infamy." Here he merely refers to it as "horror".

With this horror Smith intimates a particularly modern tragedy. There is no cosmic order in which the man is redeemed. There is no suggestion that truth will out. Rather there are simply sympathetic yet incompatible understandings of the man's death. There is not an absence of sympathy, but the friends' sympathy is in terrible dissonance with the innocent man's self-understanding.

IV. CONCLUSION

In closing, I will turn to a sort of antecedent to the innocent man condemned to the scaffold. Earlier in *The Theory of Moral Sentiments*, Smith writes:

> When an inhuman murderer is brought to the scaffold, though we have some compassion for his misery, we can have no sort of fellow-feeling with his resentment, if he should be so absurd as to express any against either his prosecutor or his judge. The natural tendency of their just indignation against so vile a criminal is indeed the most fatal and ruinous to him. But it is impossible that we should be displeased with the tendency of a sentiment, which, when we bring the case home to ourselves, we feel that we cannot avoid adopting. [*TMS*, II.i.3.3]

If Smith's discussion of the innocent man is consistently focused on that man's consciousness—his indignation at injustice, his anguish to think what his friends must feel and how he will be remembered—then this passage focuses on the spectators' consciousness. Smith attempts to resolve the ambivalence of sympathy, where the spectators (as "we") feel compassion for the murderer, but (as "they") also feel indignation towards him. Compassion seems likely to prevail. Smith identifies, through his use of the first person, with the sympathizers' compassion, while alienating indignation to the third person. In addition, the fact that the spectators' indignation has such dire consequences—it is "most fatal and ruinous" to the criminal—would seem to strengthen compassion. Nonetheless, "when we bring the case home to ourselves", Smith writes, "we feel that we cannot avoid adopting" an indignant stance toward him, nor will we be "displeased" with our indignation. These two negatives that articulate the apparent necessity of the indignant stance and the self-approbation of those who achieve it comprise an apparent triumph of the impartial spectator over the too-compassionate onlooker.

As Smith allows the impartial spectator to emerge out of this ambivalence of sympathy, one thing is certain. "[W]e can have no sort of fellow-feeling with his resentment, if he should be so absurd as to express any against either his prosecutor or his judge" (*TMS*, II.i.3.2). Yet putting this case next to the one of the condemned innocent man might suggest that the obverse of absurdity is horror. To the external spectators, the situation is absurd, yet to the condemned man, the absurdity of his situation is a horror. We see how easily tragedy, in the absence of religion and the presence of certainty, descends to horror and absurdity.

I began this essay by reflecting on the possibility that in order to treat the problem of evil, Smith's philosophy requires religion as a supplement that provides comfort and consolation. My suggestion was that Smith wants to do without the fiction of religion but that this is viable only if the truth of the human holds some consolation. I have examined Smith's understanding of the human by looking at two important mechanisms, the causal imagination and the sympathetic imagination. Without God as the true objective and ideal spectator, Smith's philosophy must imagine a spectator that is not only sympathetic but also within the bounds set by these mechanisms.

In conclusion, it seems to me that Smith's consolation must be in uncertain sympathy. By uncertain, I mean, of course, that Smith's "humble philosophy" cannot claim with certainty that this sympathy will emerge, but also that certainty—such as the certainty with which spectators view the condemned murderer as absurd—must be questioned. Earlier I enumerated the characteristics of the sympathetic imagination. The sympathizing spectator's feelings are not as intense as the feelings of the person principally concerned. The feelings are in fact qualitatively changed, modified in some way. The urge to sympathize is natural, but the act requires work. The work of sympathizing makes visible details of circumstance that might otherwise be overlooked or indistinguishable. All of these characteristics are present in Smith's description of the man about to be hanged. The representation lacks the marks of passionate speech, but this cessation of violence allows for a more clear-eyed view. Smith details the elements that most certain spectators would miss. Rather than focusing on the physical appearance of the man—with whatever markers of passion it might have, perhaps blood in his face to indicate indignation and wide gaping eyes for horror—Smith describes the circumstances as the man might enumerate them if he could look at himself with less passion: the injustice of a false accusation that has brought him here, his anger and impotence at the situation, the general infamy that will henceforth be attached to his name, and the shameful significance of this whole episode for his friends.

As Smith makes clear earlier in *TMS*, sympathy involves work. A "common" spectator might lack a sympathetic appreciation for the innocent man's situation. Smith's representation not only shows his own sympathy for the man. It also, perhaps, opens up the channels of sympathy for others. It is notable that one feature of Smith's description is that no one sympathizes with this man's situation. Most look at him and view his infamy. His friends see him with shame and horror. If this failure of sympathy is certain, then religion is necessary. Smith, however, by taking into account his innocence, is able to understand the mixture of passions having to do with innocence, wrongful accusation, grave injustice, infamy, shame, and horror. No one takes all of this in—not even the man himself is well aware of it—except for Smith and the reader whom one hopes is less certain after his reading.

SELECT BIBLIOGRAPHY

Biro, John. "Hume's New Science of the Mind". In *The Cambridge Companion to Hume*. Edited by David Fate Norton, 33–63. Cambridge: Cambridge University Press, 1993.

Hume, David. *Enquiry Concerning the Human Understanding*. In *Enquiries Concerning the Human Understanding and Concerning the Principles of Morals*, 2nd ed. Edited by L. A. Selby-Bigge. Oxford: Clarendon Press, 1902.

———. "On the Standard of Taste". In *Essays Moral, Political, and Literary*, rev. ed. Edited by Eugene Miller. Indianapolis: Liberty Fund, 1985.

———. *A Treatise of Human Nature*, 2nd ed. Edited by L. A. Selby-Bigge and P. H. Nidditch. Oxford: Clarendon Press, 1978.

Pope, Alexander. *The Poems of Alexander Pope*. Edited by John Butt. New Haven: Yale University Press, 1963.

Rosenberg, Alexander. "Hume and the Philosophy of Science". In *The Cambridge Companion to Hume*. Edited by David Fate Norton, 64–89. Cambridge: Cambridge University Press, 1993.

Smith, Adam. *The Theory of Moral Sentiments*. Edited by D. D. Raphael and A. L. Macfie. Indianapolis: Liberty Fund, 1984.

TAMING RESENTMENT

Michael S. Pritchard

PREFATORY COMMENTS

Eighteenth-century Scotland's three most renowned philosophers, David Hume, Adam Smith, and Thomas Reid, were familiar with and admired the work of their English predecessor Joseph Butler. Smith and Reid made explicit use of Butler's account of resentment in their writings.[1] Hume did not. Why he chose not to is unclear. Reid employed it in his critique of Hume's moral theory—in particular, Hume's handling of the challenge of the sensible knave. Smith, as I will show, could have done this as well; but he did not explicitly do so. However, a careful reading of Smith's account of resentment in his *Theory of Moral Sentiments* (*TMS*) reveals important differences between Smith and Hume, despite their obvious admiration of each other's work. On these points of difference, Smith and Reid can be joined as allies.[2] What follows is an exploration of the role of resentment in Smith and Reid's accounts of morality, both as a point of departure from Hume's account of justice and as providing an important link to Smith's *Wealth of Nations*.

"UNSOCIAL PASSIONS"

The *Theory of Moral Sentiments* opens with the firm assurance that human selfishness is limited. It is a principle of human nature, says Smith, that we care about the fortune of others, as evidenced by the pleasure we often get from witnessing their happiness. Even the "greatest ruffian, the most hardened violator of the laws of society" is not immune to having some degree of pity or compassion for the misery of others. Thus, we have sympathies that express genuine concern about others, not just ourselves.

Given this initial appeal to our compassion for others, we might expect Smith's subsequent account to dwell on the positive. However, Smith quickly turns to our nasty side, to what he calls the "unsocial passions"—most notably, *resentment*. Such passions, he says, "excite no sort of sympathy, but

---

1   Butler's account of resentment is found in *Fifteen Sermons*, originally published in 1730. See, especially, Sermon VIII, "Upon Resentment". Complete bibliographic information for references can be found in the Select Bibliography at the end of this essay.

2   It should be pointed out, however, that Reid's critique of Smith's *TMS* is as trenchant as his critique of Hume. Reid's criticisms of Smith can be found in his "Review of *The Theory of Moral Sentiments*, by Adam Smith".

before we are acquainted with what gave occasion to them, serve rather to disgust and provoke us against them" (*TMS*, 11). Furthermore, resentment is especially morally suspect. Smith warns us, "There is no passion, of which the human mind is capable, concerning whose justice we ought to be so doubtful, concerning whose indulgence we ought so carefully to consult our natural sense of propriety, or so diligently to consider what will be the sentiments of the cool and impartial spectator" (*TMS*, 37). Finally, insofar as it is merely an expression of hatred and anger, resentment is "the greatest poison to the happiness of a good mind" (*TMS*, 37).

Given such an indictment, shouldn't we strive to rid ourselves of this poison? No, says Smith, for resentment "is the safeguard of justice and the security of innocence" (*TMS*, 79). It is a defensive response that "prompts us to beat off the mischief which is attempted to be done to us, and to retaliate that which is already done; that the offender may be made to repent of his injustice, and that others through fear of the like punishment, may be terrified from being guilty of the like offense" (*TMS*, 79).

That is, this is how resentment *ought* to function, at least among moral agents. However, in fact, it does so much more—and worse. It is prone to various excesses; and indeed, one of the tasks of moral education is to teach us to reign in these excesses. This is not a matter of attempting to *eliminate* resentment, rather, the task is to *tame* it. Much of *The Theory of Moral Sentiments* is an account of what this requires and how it might be accomplished. Excessive hatred and resentment, Smith admonishes, "renders a person the object of universal dread and abhorrence, who, like a wild beast, ought, we think, to be hunted out of all civil society" (*TMS*, 40). Nevertheless, Smith believes, our resentment can be tamed in such a way that is fully consistent with our humanity.

Suitably tamed, according to Smith, resentment can be "even generous and noble" (*TMS*, 38). However, the road from our initial, natural defensive impulses to this morally refined response to wrongdoing is difficult and never ending. To see how the poison of resentment might be transformed into something morally acceptable, if not admirable, we must begin with the child.

CHILDREN

Smith's somewhat detailed account of child development begins with the very young child, pointing out the child's extreme dependency on caregivers and peers for acquiring the sort of "self-command" necessary for moral responsibility. Smith says, "A very young child has no self-command; but, whatever are its emotions, whether fear, or grief, or anger, it endeavours always, by the violence of its outcries, to alarm, as much as it can, the attention of its nurse, or of its parents. While it remains under the custody of such partial protectors, its anger is the first and, perhaps, the only passion which it is taught to moderate" (*TMS*, 145). Although young children may learn to moderate their anger to some extent in their home setting, schooling may present them with a rude shock. In the company of peers, the child's self-absorption is unlikely to be well received:

> [The child] naturally wishes to gain their favour, and to avoid their hatred or contempt. Regard even to its own safety teaches it to do so; and it soon finds that it can do so in no other way than by moderating, not only its anger, but all its other passions, to the degree which its play-fellows and companions are likely to be pleased with. It thus enters into the great school of self-command, it studies to be more and more master of itself, and begins to exercise over its own feelings a discipline which the practice of the longest life is very seldom sufficient to bring to complete perfection. [*TMS*, 145]

In line with Butler, Smith characterizes the anger of the very young child as a form of resentment. But it is not just human beings who express this sort of anger. Non-human animals do, too. They, like young children, exhibit "sudden resentment", a defensive posture, that serves to warn others of impending retaliation. Although this is a communicative act, it does not yet involve *moral* judgment. In the case of young children, it is pre-moral, as eventually it will be transformed into moral judgment. But, for this transformation to take place, Smith says, we require the company of others:

> Were it possible that a human creature could grow up to manhood in some solitary place, without any communication with his own species, he could no more think of his own character, of the propriety or demerit of his own sentiments and conduct, of the beauty or deformity of his own mind, than of the beauty and deformity of his own face. All these are objects which he cannot easily see, which naturally he does not look at, and with regard to which he is provided with no mirror which can present them to his view. Bring him into society, and he is immediately provided with the mirror which he wanted before. [*TMS*, 110]

This "mirror" serves as our first critic. Judged by others, we become concerned with how we seem to them. "We begin, upon this account, to examine our own passions and conduct, and to consider how these must appear to them, by considering how they would appear to us if in their situation. We suppose ourselves the spectators of our own behaviour, and endeavour to imagine what effect it would, in this light, produce upon us. This is the only looking-glass by which we can, in some measure, with the eyes of other people, scrutinize the propriety of our own conduct" (*TMS*, 112).

Although we desire the approval of others, Smith says that this is not enough to make us fit for society. We also need to desire "what ought to be approved of" (*TMS*, 114). This second desire can be satisfied only by becoming "impartial spectators of our own character and conduct" (*TMS*, 114). It is from this vantage point that merited self-approval is to be sought. Smith concludes, "This self-approbation, if not the only, is at least the principal object, about which he can or ought to be anxious. The love of it, is the love of virtue" (*TMS*, 117).

MISERY LOVES COMPANY?

How all of this works in the case of resentment is particularly instructive. Smith points out that resentment is as unpleasant for its bearer as it is for its audience. The resentful person wants support from others. Such misery loves company. Given the unpleasantness of resentment, we are more anxious for our friends to "enter into our resentments" than for them to "enter into our gratitude". We "lose all patience if they seem indifferent about the injuries which may have been done to us". Agreeable passions can be borne alone more easily. However, Smith concludes, "The bitter and painful emotions of grief and resentment more strongly require the healing consolation of sympathy" (*TMS*, 12).

However, this poses an immediate problem. As already noted, resentment is among those "unsocial passions" that initially "serve rather to disgust and provoke us against them":

> The furious behaviour of an angry man is more likely to exasperate us against himself than against his enemies. As we are unacquainted with his provocation, we cannot bring his case home to ourselves, nor conceive any thing like the passions which it excites. But we plainly see what is the situation of those with whom he is angry, and to what violence they may be exposed from so enraged an adversary. We readily, therefore, sympathize with their fear of resentment, and are immediately disposed to take part against the man from whom they appear to be in so much danger. [*TMS*, 11]

So, somehow the bearer of resentment needs to determine how to overcome the inclination of others to side with the target of resentment rather than its bearer. Here, says Smith, there is much work to be done: "Nature, it seems, teaches us to be more averse to enter into this passion, and, till informed of its cause, to be disposed rather to take part against it" (*TMS*, 11).

A key to success at this point is the realization that the "compassion of the spectator must arise altogether from the consideration of what he himself would feel if he was reduced to the same unhappy situation, and, what perhaps is impossible, was at the same time able to regard it with his present reason and judgment" (*TMS*, 12). So, sympathy is essential, but it is the sympathy of the spectator. The bearer of resentment must try first to see things as the spectator does.

The important lesson to be learned is that resentment is among the "set of passions, which, though derived from the imagination, yet before we can enter into them, or regard them as graceful or becoming, must always be brought down to a pitch much lower than that to which undisciplined nature would raise them" (*TMS*, 34). Because of our aversion to aggression against others, our initial sympathy is likely to be with those who are the object of aggression. For resentment to be seen as "graceful and agreeable, it must be more humbled and brought down below that pitch to which it would naturally rise, than almost any other passion" (*TMS*, 34).

An essential function of this humbling of resentment is to provide a check on the natural preference we have for ourselves. Smith astutely observes, "Though it may be true, therefore, that every individual, in his own breast, naturally prefers himself to all mankind, yet he dares not look mankind in the face, and avow that he acts according to this principle. He feels that in this preference they can never go along with him, and that how natural soever it may be to him, it must always appear excessive and extravagant to them" (*TMS*, 83). Shifting to a third person perspective has a leveling effect. It is a move in the direction of impartiality: "When he views himself in the light in which he is conscious that others will view him, he sees that to them he is but one of the multitude in no respect better than any other in it. If he would act so that the impartial spectator may enter into the principles of his conduct, which is what of all things he has the greatest desire to do, he must, upon this, as upon all other occasions, humble the arrogance of his self-love, and bring it down to something which other men can go along with" (*TMS*, 83).

The perspective of an impartial spectator does not condemn partiality to oneself as such. It is acceptable for someone to pursue his[3] own happiness more arduously than that of others, but only within the constraints of justice and fair play.

So, others play a crucial role in developing one's sense of justice. The playing field is leveled—I am only one among the multitude, and *each* of us is recognized as legitimately laying claim to not being wronged. It is only by operating within these constraints that one can realistically hope to have one's resentment endorsed by others. What Smith has in mind is a social process, especially when one's resentment is clearly excessive. He concludes, "Society and conversation, therefore, are the most powerful remedies for restoring the

---

3   To be consistent with the passage quoted below, I retain here Smith's use of "his" and "man".

mind to its tranquillity, if at any time, it has unfortunately lost it; as well as the best preservatives of that equal and happy temper which is so necessary to self-satisfaction and enjoyment" (*TMS*, 23).

For Smith, we can speak of the *dignity* of a passion, which, he says, is a matter of the "recollection and self-command" it expresses. Untamed, resentment is excessive and undignified. However, its absence is sometimes a defect, as well. The *propriety* of resentment requires a "certain mediocrity" (*TMS*, 27).

When resentment does match the demands of propriety, it expresses the *indignation* of an impartial spectator, "which allows no word, no gesture, to escape it beyond what this more equitable sentiment would dictate; which never, even in thought, attempts any greater vengeance, nor desires to inflict any greater punishment, than what every indifferent person would rejoice to see executed" (*TMS*, 24). It is only when resentment takes on the form of indignation that it can be said to be properly tamed.

Even so, the effects of passions like resentment "are so disagreeable, that even when they are most justly provoked, there is still something about them which disgusts us". We are not disposed to sympathize with them "before we are informed of the cause which excites them" (*TMS*, 36). "It was, it seems, the intention of Nature, that those rougher and more unamiable emotions, which drive men from one another, should be less easily and more rarely communicated" (*TMS*, 37). Thus, several conditions that must be met before spectators will *thoroughly* sympathize with our resentment (*TMS*, 38):

- The cause must be severe enough that others would regard it as contemptible if one didn't "in some measure" resent it.
- Resentment should be tempered by the seriousness of the offense.
- Our resentment is best experienced as if by another, more from a sense of the propriety of resentment than from a more directly felt passion.
- Our resentment must be borne with dignity (magnanimity).
- Expressions of it must be "plain, open, and direct; determined without positiveness, and elevated without insolence; not only free from petulance and low scurrility, but generous, candid, and full of proper regards, even for the person who has offended us".
- The passion must not appear to have "extinguished our humanity". Revenge must be taken "with reluctance, from necessity, and in consequence of great and repeated provocations".

Smith concludes, "When resentment is guarded and qualified in this manner, it may be admitted to be even generous and noble" (*TMS*, 38).

JUSTICE AND PUBLIC UTILITY

Smith takes great pains to note that our sense of justice (or injustice) is not derived from a direct concern for public utility. Although he does not mention Hume by name, Smith distances his own account of justice from Hume's. Hume claims that the sentiment of justice is derived either from our reflecting on the tendency of justice to promote public utility or from some "simple original instinct, and is not ascertained by any argument or reflection".[4]

Hume includes resentment in his list of "simple original instincts". However, unlike Butler, he apparently did not see resentment as playing a key role in explaining our sense of justice. Rather than picking up on Butler's account of the role of reflection in transforming "sudden resentment" into "deliberate resentment", Hume fixes his attention on property and public utility. In contrast, while acknowledging the public utility of justice, Smith claims, "it is not the view of this utility or hurtfulness which is either the first or principal source of our approbation and disapprobation [...] [I]t will be found, upon examination, that the usefulness of any disposition of mind is seldom the first ground of our approbation; and that the sentiment of approbation always involves in it a sense of propriety quite distinct from the perception of utility" (*TMS*, 188–189).[5]

Furthermore, insofar as it is an expression of our sense of justice, resentment is "a passion which is never properly called forth but by actions which tend to do real and positive hurt to *some particular persons*" (*TMS*, 79, emphasis mine). Regarding either the destruction or loss of a single man, or the loss of a single guinea that is part of a thousand guineas, Smith insists:

> In neither case does our regard for the individuals arise from our regard for the multitude: but in both cases our regard for the multitude is compounded and made up of the particular regards which we feel for the different individuals of which it is composed. As when a small sum is unjustly taken from us, we do not so much prosecute the injury from a regard

---

4 David Hume, *Enquiries Concerning Human Understanding and Concerning the Principles of Morals* (*EPM*), 201.

5 Similarly, Smith says: "But although it commonly requires no great discernment to see the destructive tendency of all licentious practices to the welfare of society, it is seldom this consideration which first animates us against them. All men, even the most stupid and unthinking, abhor fraud, perfidy, and injustice, and delight to see them punished. But few have reflected upon the necessity of justice to the existence of society, how obvious soever that necessity may appear to be" (*TMS*, 89).

to the preservation of our whole fortune, as from a regard to that particular sum which we have lost; so when a single man is injured, or destroyed, we demand the punishment of the wrong that has been done to him, not so much from a concern for the general interest of society, as from a concern for that very individual who has been injured […]. [*TMS*, 89–90]

It might be thought that, since Smith emphasizes the importance of general rules of morality and recognizes that the observance of these rules does, in fact, serve public utility, his account of justice resembles Hume's more closely than I have suggested. However, Smith consistently distinguishes the public utility of justice from our motives to justice. Also, he introduces moral rules as a way of combating self-serving self-deception rather than as a means to public utility. The seriousness of the problem of self-deception for Smith can be seen in the following passage: "This self-deceit, this fatal weakness of mankind, is the source of half the disorders of human life. If we saw ourselves in the light in which others see us, or in which they would see us if they knew all, a reformation would generally be unavoidable. We could not otherwise endure the sight" (*TMS*, 158–159).

The most effective remedy, Smith suggests, is the observance of "certain general rules concerning what is fit and proper either to be done or to be avoided" (*TMS*, 159). These rules express in general form what in particular instances, at least when we are clear-headed, we approve or disapprove. But it is important to realize that our original approval or disapproval of actions falling under these rules is not that a particular action falls under a general rule:

> The general rule, on the contrary, is formed, by finding from experience, that all actions of a certain kind, or circumstanced in a certain manner, are approved or disapproved of […] [One's] detestation of this crime, it is evident, would arise instantaneously and antecedent to his having formed to himself any such general rule. The general rule, on the contrary, which he might afterwards form, would be founded upon the detestation which he felt necessarily arise in his own breast, at the thought of this, and every other particular action of the same kind. [*TMS*, 159–160]

If we acquire habitual respect for these general rules, we can avoid doing what is contrary to what we would otherwise directly see is objectionable if we were not blinded by excessive partiality to ourselves. As for the relationship between general rules and public utility, Smith comments, "The administration of the great system of the universe, however, the care of the universal happiness of all rational and sensible beings, is the business of god and not of man. To man is allotted a much humbler department, but one much more suitable to the weakness of his powers, and to the narrowness of his comprehension; the care of his own happiness, of that of his family, his friends, his country" (*TMS*, 237).

HUME'S SENSIBLE KNAVE

Although familiar with Smith's *The Theory of Moral Sentiments*, Hume did not waver from his view that justice is grounded in considerations of public utility and self-interest. Confident that, even from the standpoint of self-interest, he had successfully shown the superiority of virtue over vice in nearly every instance, Hume raises one last doubt in the Conclusion of his *Enquiry Concerning the Principles of Morals* (*EPM*). In the case of *justice*, he asks what we should say about a sensible knave, who appreciates the advantages rules of justice provide but thinks that further gains may be possible by making himself an exception to the rules. Such a knave, while acknowledging the importance of justice for society (and himself), "may think that an act of iniquity or infidelity will make a considerable addition to his fortune, without causing any considerable breach in the social union and confederacy" (*EPM*, 282).

For such acts of iniquity or infidelity to be successful, deception is required in order to maintain the appearance of being fully supportive of justice. So, it seems we have two features of such acts that contribute to their wrongfulness. First, they are acts of *iniquity*, thereby wronging others. Second, they are acts of *dishonesty*. Hume represents the sensible knave's approach to dishonesty in the following way: "That *honesty is the best policy*, may be a good general rule, but is liable to many exceptions; and he, it may perhaps be thought, conducts himself with most wisdom, who observes the general rule, and takes advantage of all the exceptions" (*EPM*, 283).

Might such a thought also occur to others—those who do not regard themselves to be sensible knaves? Yes, says Hume, but it should not take much for such a person to reject the sensible knave's "wisdom", especially if the heart is allowed to rule:

> If his heart rebel not against such pernicious maxims, if he feel no reluctance to the thoughts of villainy or baseness, he has indeed lost a considerable motive to virtue [...]. But in all ingenuous natures, the antipathy to treachery and roguery is too strong to be counter-balanced by any views of profit or pecuniary advantage. Inward peace of mind, consciousness of integrity, a satisfactory review of our own conduct; these are circumstances very requisite to happiness, and will be cherished and cultivated by every honest man, who feels the importance of them. [*EPM*, 283]

Knaves, it seems, trade their integrity, and even their happiness, for "worthless toys and gewgaws" (*EPM*, 283).

Smith would seemingly agree with these sentiments. However, he may not have seen that a Butlerian account of resentment could be used to challenge Hume's response to the sensible knave. Thomas Reid did.[6] While agreeing with the sentiments Hume attributes to "honest men", Reid wonders how Hume can effectively employ them, given his view of justice and the importance each of us apparently attaches to self-interest. The sensible knave, after all, seems to attend to both justice and self-interest. If convinced that making himself an exception to the rules of justice will harm the public interest, he will refrain. In fact, like others, *publicly* he supports the rules; such a public stance is essential for the system to work. But this does not necessarily require one *privately* to agree. Of course, publicly denouncing what one privately approves for oneself is a form of duplicity. Still, by hypothesis, this is not contrary to the public interest—and it does serve one's self-interest. So, what is *wrong* with it?

The unhappiness Hume attributes to anyone who settles for "toys and gewgaws" is presumably the result of a stricken conscience; one cannot sustain "consciousness of integrity, a satisfactory review of our own conduct". Smith and Reid would undoubtedly agree. But what Reid finds puzzling is how Hume can explain this. Public utility is intact, and private interest is served. What else is there to be concerned about? Reid attempts to supply something else, but with a price for Hume. Hume must either accept what Reid offers and thereby concede that our sentiment of justice is not derived solely from public utility, or he must admit that he has no adequate response to the sensible knave's challenge.

While Hume confines his notion of justice to property in relation to public utility, Reid identifies six "branches" of justice. Reid classifies four branches as *natural*, as distinct from *acquired*, rights: "the right of an innocent man to the safety of his person and family, to his liberty and reputation" (*EAP*, 313). The fifth concerns the making and keeping of promises, while only the sixth concerns property. Reid does not claim that his list is complete. But he does contend that it represents commonly held moral convictions.

It is likely that Smith would agree with much of what Reid says here. In fact, he explicitly remarks, "There is no greater tormentor of the human breast than violent resentment which cannot be gratified. An innocent man, brought to the scaffold by the false imputation of an infamous or odious crime, suffers the most cruel misfortune which it is possible for innocence to suffer [...]. The innocent man, on the contrary, over and above the uneasiness which this fear may occasion, is tormented by his own indignation at the injustice which has been done to him" (*TMS*, 119–120).

Although Reid casts much of his account of justice in terms of rights, more important for our purposes here is his account of the role of resentment.

---

6   Thomas Reid, *Essays on the Active Powers of the Mind* (*EAP*).

Reid says that when we sense that our rights are violated, we feel *injured*. But *injury* and *hurt* are distinct. Humans and animals alike naturally respond to *hurt* with what Butler calls "sudden resentment"—a defensive mechanism that expresses anger toward the purported cause of the hurt. As Reid puts it, "Every action that gives pain or uneasiness produces resentment. This is common to man before the use of reason, and to the more sagacious brutes; and it shews no conception of justice in either" (*EAP*, 309).

However, as human reason develops, the notion that resentment needs a "proper and formal object" also develops. This is Butler's "deliberate resentment", which includes a rational element. Reid continues:

> If we consider, on the other hand, what an injury is which is the object of the natural passion of resentment, every man, capable of reflection, perceives that an injury implies more than being hurt. If I be hurt by a stone falling out of the wall, or by a flash of lightning, or by a convulsive and involuntary motion of another man's arm, no injury is done, no resentment raised in a man who has reason. In this, as in all moral actions, there must be the will and intention of the agent to do the hurt. [*EAP*, 310]

It is important for Reid's account of resentment that, although "deliberate resentment" is not present at birth, its development is "natural" in the sense that "these sentiments spring up in the mind of man as naturally as his body grows to its proper stature" (*EAP*, 313–314). Although the particular forms these sentiments take on may vary somewhat with instruction provided by "parents, priests, philosophers, or politicians", the seeds for their development are present prior to any instruction (*EAP*, 314).

Reid does not mean that our sense of justice develops prior to socialization with others. He concedes to Hume "that men have no conception of the virtue of justice til they have lived some time in society. It is purely a moral conception, and our moral conceptions and moral judgments are not born with us. They grow up by degrees, as our reason does" (*EAP*, 305–306). Furthermore, Reid acknowledges that he does not know exactly when, or in what order, our moral conceptions develop. However, like Smith, what he does claim is that the idea of public utility arises only *after* we already have a rather well-developed sense of justice. So, from a *developmental* point of view, our concept of justice is not derived solely from that of public utility. Reid insists that "every man is conscious of a specific difference between the resentment he feels for an injury done to himself, and his indignation against a wrong done to the public" (*EAP*, 314). It is this distinction that is crucial to Reid's reply to the sensible knave, but which is slighted in Hume's account. A judge, Reid says, can be expected to consider the public good when punishing someone for a private injury, but this "seldom enters into the thought of the injured person" (*EAP*, 314). And this, Reid adds, is reflected in the criminal law, which distinguishes the redress due the victim from redress due the public. Hume might reply, however, that justice does not come into play until the public good is considered. Smith and Reid oppose this, as their accounts of resentment make clear.

While Hume attempts to derive justice from utility, Reid claims the idea of justice is inseparable from the notions of *favor* and *injury* (as distinct from *hurt*): "[A] favour, an act of justice, and an injury, are so related to one another, that he who conceives one must conceive the other two. They lie, as it were, in one line, and resemble the relations of greater, less, and equal [...]. In a like manner, of those actions by which we profit or hurt other men, a favour is more than justice, an injury is less; and that which is neither a favour nor an injury is a just action" (*EAP*, 311). Favor is linked with gratitude, and injury with resentment. Insofar as gratitude and resentment involve understanding and judgment, they embrace the conceptions of justice and injustice. But, since Hume acknowledges that both gratitude and resentment are natural sentiments, Reid concludes, the notion of justice must also be natural.

However, Hume might reply that gratitude and resentment are natural sentiments only insofar as they are not yet *moral* sentiments. Moral sentiments for Hume must meet a test of *generality*, which for him seems to presuppose public utility. Natural gratitude, resentment, and even benevolence are pre-moral, directed as they are at only this or that particular object. Only *enlarged* sentiments are inclusive enough to count as moral. But Hume seems to conceive of the moral enlargement of sentiments in only one way—that of public utility, implying that a sentiment is moral only if it is somehow directed to the good of all. This seems to be the force of his notion that the sentiment of justice is derived solely from public utility.

Reid thinks of the enlargement of sentiments differently. The transition from "sudden resentment" to "deliberate resentment", introduces rational features. As Reid puts it, "The feeling of his heart arises from the judgment of his understanding" (*EAP*, 313). If I am the sufferer of wrongdoing, I will feel resentment in my own behalf. However, it must be added that Reid accepts a notion of universalizability as the most fundamental moral principle of all, as it "comprehends every rule of justice without exception" (*EAP*, 275). "In every case, we ought to act that part towards another, which we would judge to be right in him to act toward us, if we were in his circumstances and he in ours; or more generally—What we approve in others, that we ought to practise in like circumstances, and what we condemn in others we ought not to do" (*EAP*, 274). This is a principle of *impartiality*—not only a requirement of logical consistency, but also a requirement of fairness, or justice.

Acceptance of this principle is, for Reid, a necessary condition for being a moral agent: "If a man is not capable of perceiving this in his cool moments, when he reflects seriously, he is not a moral agent, nor is he capable of being convinced of it by reasoning" (*EAP*, 177). Not only does Reid think that this sort of impartiality is necessary for moral judgment in general, it has special importance for judgments concerning favor, justice, and injury. For someone's resentment at being injured by another to rise to the level of moral judgment, it must be implicitly general. That is, if it is appropriate for me to resent being treated a certain way, it is appropriate for anyone else who suffers similar treatment to feel the same way.

But *I* need not be the one who is wronged in order to feel resentment. Butler calls resentment in behalf of others *indignation*. "The indignation raised by cruelty and injustice, and the desire of having it punished, which persons unconcerned would feel, is by no means malice. No, it is resentment against vice and wickedness: it is one of the common bonds, by which society is held together; a fellow-feeling, which each individual has in behalf of the whole species, as well as of himself" (*Fifteen Sermons*, 129–130). However, it is crucial to notice that this is not merely resentment, or indignation, at someone for acting contrary to public utility (a wrong *to the public*). Rather, as we have noted with Smith, the focus remains on those *individuals* who have been injured and the agents responsible for causing their injury. The generality of the response, then, is that one's resentment can have as its proper object injury to *anyone*. One might also be angered by attacks on public utility as such, but this is distinct from being moved directly by the plight of the specific injured party.

Hume does occasionally make passing reference to private wrongs as distinct from harms to public utility, but he pays remarkably little attention to this when talking about justice. Reid expresses surprise at Hume's restriction of justice to property and the keeping of contracts, noting that Hume simply remains silent on the other branches of justice. However, Reid adds, "He no where says, that it is not naturally criminal to rob an innocent man of his life, of his children, of his liberty, or of his reputation; and I am apt to think he never meant it" (*EAP*, 315). But if Hume were to agree that this was merely an oversight on his part, Reid would press his point all the further: "No man would allow him to be a man of honour, who should plead his interest to justify what he acknowledged to be dishonourable; but to sacrifice interest to honour never costs a blush" (*EAP*, 170). Hume, too, might well want to applaud Reid's assessment. What must be recalled is that Hume's sensible knave is asking us to consider an *act of iniquity or infidelity*. Such "thoughts of villainy or baseness", says Hume, are repulsive to the heart of an honest person. But, to understand this, it is essential that we focus on the *injured party*. That is, this is first and foremost a *private injury* rather than an injury to the public interest.

What sort of private injury is it? Reid maintains that it is an act of *injustice* against the injured party. It violates, as Reid would put it, "the right of an innocent man to the safety of his person and [perhaps to his] family, to his liberty and reputation" (*EAP*, 656). Without acknowledging this, it is not clear how the voice of justice can be fully heard. However, by acknowledging it, Reid insists, Hume must concede that there are at least some branches of justice that are natural—or at least not derived solely from public utility.

So, an important consequence of Reid's insistence that justice is not derived solely from public utility is that space is provided for a more satisfying response to the sensible knave. A "feeling of the heart" can, indeed, arise "from the judgment of [one's] understanding"—one's understanding that one who acts as the sensible knave proposes is causing private injury to specific persons, whether oneself or others. This warrants resentment, or indignation. Of course, if the number of sensible knaves were to grow large enough, this could cause a "considerable breach in the social union and confederacy"; but that would be an *additional* injury to those already caused by the individual acts of "iniquity or infidelity" the sensible knave proposes. A sensible knave may not be moved by this, but for Reid's "man of honour" or Hume's "ingenuous natures", "the antipathy to treachery and roguery is too strong to be counterbalanced by any views of profit or pecuniary advantage"—or, if Reid is right, perhaps even by views of public utility. As Reid and Smith (as well as Butler) acknowledge, justice can serve public utility, but it serves other moral ends as well.

In fact, Reid is willing to acknowledge an obligation to support justice that is based on its tendency to support public utility. However, he adds, "To perceive that justice tends to the good of mankind, would lay no moral obligation upon us to be just, unless we be conscious of a moral obligation to do what tends to the good of mankind. If such a moral obligation be admitted, *why may we not admit a stronger obligation to do injury to no man*? The last obligation is as easily conceived as the first, and there is as clear evidence of its existence in human nature" (*EAP*, 326).

For both Reid and Smith it is important to distinguish the *consequences* of one's resentment from its *object*. As Smith puts it, "What chiefly enrages us against the man who injures or insults us, is the little account which he seems to make of us, the unreasonable preference which he gives to himself above us, and that absurd self-love, by which he seems to imagine, that other people may be sacrificed at any time, to his conveniency or his humour" (*TMS*, 96). Although the sensible knave may take care not to harm the public good or his own self-interest, he cannot escape this criticism. Furthermore, this criticism is grounded in resentment insofar as it is constrained by the inner voice of the impartial spectator.

For Smith, it is understandable that one will be partial to oneself. As already noted, the perspective of the impartial spectator does not oppose this partiality as such. It only insists that it be constrained by considerations of justice:

> There can be no proper motive for hurting our neighbour, there can be no incitement to do evil to another, which mankind will go along with, except just indignation for evil

which that other has done to us. To disturb his happiness merely because it stands in the way of our own, to take from him what is of real use to him merely because it may be of equal or of more use to us, or to indulge, in this manner, at the expence of other people, the natural preference which every man has for his own happiness above that of other people, is what no impartial spectator can go along with. [*TMS*, 82]

In contrast, Smith says, those of us with a robust sense of justice "endeavour to examine our own conduct as we imagine any other fair and impartial spectator would examine it. If, upon placing ourselves in his situation, we thoroughly enter into all the passions and motives which influenced it, we approve of it, by sympathy with the approbation of this supposed equitable judge. If otherwise, we enter into his disapprobation and condemn it" (*TMS*, 110).

For Smith, the sensible knave will not be well received by those with the self-command of an impartial spectator. This is because, even though the sensible knave will try to avoid undermining the public good, he is prepared to commit acts of iniquity at the expense of others when it seems to be to his advantage. In contrast, someone with the virtue of firm self-command "does not merely affect the sentiments of the impartial spectator. He really adopts them. He almost identifies himself with, he almost becomes himself that impartial spectator, and scarce even feels but as that great arbiter of his conduct directs him to feel" (*TMS*, 147). The indignation that the knave's acts of iniquity and dishonesty give rise to is an expression of the integrity of those with self-command. As Smith says, "One individual must never prefer himself so much even to any other individual, as to hurt or injure that other, in order to benefit himself, though the benefit to the one should be much greater than the hurt or injury to the other" (*TMS*, 138). The sensible knave is quite prepared to ignore this when he is convinced he can get away with making himself an exception to the rule.

BUTCHERS, BAKERS, AND BREWERS

So, for Smith, the fact that the sensible knave's actions might not seriously harm the public good is no defense; an individual has been wronged. Still, there may be a puzzle about how Smith can avoid playing into the hands of the sensible knave after all. In his *Wealth of Nations* (*WN*), Smith is noted for claiming that the public good may actually be best served by aiming at private rather than public interest. Merchants and manufacturers might better aim at profitable exchanges, transactions between themselves and others that are undertaken for mutual gain rather than in order to promote the general good of society. If they do this well, the good of society will benefit as if by an "invisible hand".

It is in this context that Smith makes his famous statement about the butcher, baker, and brewer: "[I]t is not from the benevolence of the butcher, the brewer, or the baker, that we expect our dinner, but from their regard to their own interest. We address ourselves, not to their humanity but to their self-love, and never talk to them of our own necessities but of their advantages" (*WN*, 26–27). The central point of this example is that we should not expect others to provide us with our needs simply from their good will (benevolence). Appealing to their self-interest gives them a different, more reliable, reason to provide their services: "A man must always live by his work, and his wages must at least be sufficient to maintain him. They must even upon most occasions be somewhat more; otherwise it would be impossible for him to bring up a family, and the race of such workmen could not last beyond the first generation" (*WN*, 67–68).

Smith's comment about the butcher, baker, and brewer may invite an oversimplified understanding of exchange. Yes, they work in exchange for "advantages", but an essential function they perform is to *provide for others*. For butchering, baking, or brewing to be successful, the services provided must be longstanding. So, it is a mistake to think only of one exchange, say, the baker selling a loaf of bread to a customer on a specific occasion. The baker has the *occupation* of baking, and presumably hopes to continue in this capacity for some time. So, the "advantages" sought by the baker are not exhausted in any single exchange with a particular customer.

There are other complications. The baker may never see the customer, or the customer's money. The baker may work for an employer who pays a weekly, monthly, or annual wage for these services. The actual exchange of money for bread may be between the customer and clerk (who also does not keep the money). So, the baker's formal exchange here is best understood as an agreement with an employer to bake for a wage. The customer makes an exchange of money for bread with the seller. Nevertheless, it is clear that no one who plays a role in providing the customer with bread is expected to act from benevolence alone, if at all.

As Smith points out, the "great manufactures" are much more difficult to observe in action than the local, self-employed baker. Much goes on behind the scenes that those who depend on the goods and services must simply assume is conducive to their reliability. Furthermore, much that goes on behind the scenes in ultimately bringing goods to the market depends on the cooperative activities of those who are in no position to closely monitor one another's work. Here *trust* is needed. But is it warranted, or deserved? As Martin Hollis notes, "[T]rusting people to act in their self-interest is one thing and trusting them to live up to their obligations another. The former does not capture the bond of society, since the bond relies on trusting people not to exploit trust" (*Trust within Reason*, 13). This worry about whether people can be trusted not to exploit trust warrants careful examination. In the end, *this* trust seems to require more than relying simply on appeals to the self-interest of those who enter into exchanges with one another.

What must be borne in mind is that, in discussing the vital role exchange plays in the division of labor, Smith emphasizes the importance of *both* cooperation and self-interest. An appeal to self-interest may be necessary to initiate exchanges, but a commitment to cooperation is equally necessary if such exchanges are to be sustained; and with such commitment comes obligation. It might be thought that appeals to self-interest alone are sufficient to provide the sort of stability needed for cooperative ventures. After all, when we have the sorts of exchanges Smith has in mind, presumably there are "advantages" for all parties. However, without the parties having a sense of obligation to keep their end of the exchange, Hollis's problem of trust remains unresolved.

Smith can distance himself somewhat from the sensible knave by distinguishing *aims* from *constraints*. I may intend only my own gain but still be constrained by considerations of justice. It is not that I *intend* justice—but I can still care about it. I stand in line with the intention of getting a ticket to the movies. But, I will not cut in line in order to get what I intend—nor will I deliberately shortchange the vendor. If someone greets me and asks what I am doing here, I won't say: "I'm here to refrain from injustice". Rather, quite simply, "I'm here to get a ticket to the movies". If it is suggested that I will fulfill my intention more quickly if I cut in front of someone ahead of me in line who is not looking, I may object that this would not be appropriate. From this, however, it would not follow that not cutting in line is another one of my intentions. I have no intention of cutting in line, pushing others out of my way, or using any other unfair means of obtaining the ticket. But this does not mean that I *have* the intention of not cutting in line, and so on.

Of course, the intention of obtaining a ticket need make no reference to serving others. I may want the ticket only for myself. In contrast, the butcher, baker, and brewer are in the business of providing for others. So, however much they may be concerned to promote their own advantage, it is also presumably a part of their intention to provide for others. What we want to know is whether *that* part of their intention is going to hold up well enough to warrant our placing trust in them to provide us with the services we expect from them.

There are two important parts to Smith's statement about the butcher, baker, and brewer. The first is a denial—a denial that we should expect them to provide us with a free dinner. This would be benevolence; and we should not expect such good-heartedness as a matter of course. Not only do we not have any entitlement to a free meal (at least not from them), they may not be able to stay in business if they do this on a regular basis. They are in the *business* of providing food; this is how they make their living.

We might ask: What is the difference between the butcher who has a large supply of meat prepared and the ordinary person who has an extra portion of meat in his or her home? Neither can be expected simply to offer a portion of meat to another from benevolence—at least not without there being some special circumstance. However, suppose we have someone in special need of a meal, but without any means of purchasing it. Does the butcher have a reason for providing that meal that is different from the ordinary person who has an extra portion available? Should we expect greater benevolence from the butcher than the ordinary person? It is not at all clear why we should say yes. Presumably, the butcher always prepares more meat than he or she will consume. However, the reason for this is that this is the butcher's means of livelihood. Why, Smith might ask, should we expect a butcher simply to provide others with produce from benevolence alone?

This leads to the second important part of the passage. Ordinarily we do not ask for a handout (by appealing to one's humanity). We *make an offer* for the services of the butcher, baker, or brewer. We offer them "advantages"—something in return for the services provided. This is quite different from simply expecting them to respond to our perceived needs. If I were impoverished and lying hungry on their doorstep, they might well come to my aid (benevolence). But this is not how I present myself to them in the butcher shop, bakery, or brewery. I am there to *trade*—in this case, money for food. In this context, the language of advantage is at home. However, while an advantage is a gain, the gains here are mutual—the provider gets money, and the customer gets a meal. There need be no suggestion that the provider gains an advantage *over*, or *at the expense of*, the customer. Subject to the constraints of justice, however, the butcher will be interested in a fair price for services rendered—not a "free ride" for the customer. Just as the customer should not expect a free meal, the butcher should not expect a "benevolent" customer who offers money for nothing, or virtually nothing, in return. In fact, the continued success of the butcher depends on both parties being more-or-less satisfied that they are getting what they want and are not being treated unfairly.

This requires some clarity regarding the terms of the agreement between provider and customer. The customer does not expect a free meal. In a direct exchange between butcher and customer, an offer of money is made for, say, a pound of hamburger. The butcher says, or implies, that money will be accepted in exchange for hamburger. The two parties understand each other and each accepts the terms of the other. So, what are the "advantages" the customer brings to the attention of the butcher? It is that, *in return for services*, the customer will provide remuneration—and there may be the suggestion that, assuming the services are satisfactory, there will be more business.

This should be welcome news for the butcher. How does the butcher understand this arrangement? Is it "buyer beware"? Does the butcher think that the customer would not mind if horseburger were substituted for hamburger? Of course, it is possible that the customer would not mind—if asked. However, for the butcher to do this in hopes that the customer will never find out is another matter. The customer does not think they are playing a game: "I'll give you money for hamburger. You give me what you think you can get away with.

If I find that it's not hamburger, I'll tell you and demand a refund—I may even take my business elsewhere. However, if I don't find this out, you win; and that's okay". In short, the customer expects a certain level of honesty in the transaction and integrity in the provision of services.

It is worth noting that the butcher expects a certain level of honesty from the customer, too. Counterfeit money is unacceptable. Wadding up the bills to make it look like more than is actually there is unacceptable. Writing a check that the customer knows will bounce, with the customer planning to leave town before this is discovered, is unacceptable. In short the butcher expects the customers to live up to their end of the bargain, too.

The fact that neither party would enter the bargain unless they thought they would get something they want (or need) explains why the customer will address the butcher's "advantages" and "self-love". However, typically it is assumed that there is no need explicitly to address the moral terms of the situation. If the customer were to add, "And I expect you to be honest with me, not substitute horseburger for hamburger, or the like", this would be an expression of *distrust*. Such matters will not routinely come up in the relationship. Rather, it is assumed that certain moral norms will not be violated by either party—and, most especially, by the butcher. *These* terms are not subject to the negotiation; they are not up for bargaining. (Imagine the customer saying: "Look, I want an honest butcher. Promise me you won't try to disguise horseburger as hamburger.") So, the moral terms will not be part of what the customer addresses to the butcher. Somehow, the butcher must have conveyed to the customer that he or she can be trusted.

However, what if the butcher reasons this way? "I need somehow to convey to the customer that I am worthy of being trusted. But, I always reserve to myself the privilege of taking advantage of the trust extended to me. Should an opportunity to gain an advantage over the customer arise, I will take it—even if it involves 'cheating' the customer." This is an attitude that needs to be kept to oneself. This is what a sensible knave would do. Does having such an attitude mean that the butcher *will*, in fact, cheat the customer? No, it means only that he or she is *ready* to do so—at the appropriate moment. But we can be assured that what he or she regards to be the appropriate moment will not be so regarded by the customer—who thinks such a attitude (and the preparedness that goes with it) has no appropriate place in the relationship.

There is no reason to think that Smith would approve of butchers, bakers, and brewers operating as Hume's sensible knave would. Seeking one's "advantage" by providing services to others is quite compatible with striving to be fully trustworthy in that capacity. Always being ready to make oneself the exception to the rule is not. This is contrary to being seriously committed to justice, the cornerstone of Smith's view of morality in both *The Theory of Moral Sentiments* and *The Wealth of Nations*. Both books credit our sense of justice with the greatest potential for morally constraining sensible knavery and other excesses of self-love. The following passage from *The Theory of Moral Sentiments* is quite consistent with the tenor of *The Wealth of Nations*:

> It is not the soft power of humanity, it is not that feeble spark of benevolence which Nature has lighted up in the human heart, that is thus capable of counteracting the strongest impulses of self-love [...]. It is not the love of our neighbour, it is not the love of mankind, which upon many occasions prompts us to the practice of those divine virtues. It is a stronger love, a more powerful affection, which generally takes place upon such occasions; the love of what is honourable and noble, of the grandeur, and dignity, and superiority of our own characters. [*TMS*, 137]

There is no reason to assume that Smith meant to exempt the butcher, baker, and brewer from these promptings.

Finally, there is no need to transform the "advantage" the butcher seeks into some sort of "maximization of value". It is in the butcher's self-interest to make a decent living. Is it in the butcher's self-interest to take advantage of all opportunities to make more money (even if by somewhat nefarious means)? It isn't clear that it is. The fact that a sensible knave might crave more doesn't necessarily mean that those without knavish tendencies do—or that they would perceive passing up an opportunity to gain something through dishonesty as somehow being less than fully rational.

The baker, let us say, puts up a sign, "Bakery", displays goods in the shop window, places advertisements in the newspaper, smiles at customers who enter the shop, and says, "May I help you?" At some point, the customer will ask what the price of bread is, whether this or that product has certain qualities, whether it will meet certain needs or interests, and so on. It is in the interest of the baker to succeed in these exchanges—but succeeding doesn't mean "winning", "vanquishing", "triumphing", or the like. Succeeding is making the trade—and keeping one's customers satisfied.

But *at what* is the baker succeeding? At making a living *as a baker*. Will one have succeeded as a baker by exercising the sensible knave's option of cheating the customer when the opportunity arises? If the baker refuses to take advantage of opportunities to make more money by cheating, is this acting contrary to self-interest? Certainly not if the price of not refusing is, as Hume suggests, trading one's integrity for gee-gaws—and, Smith might add, for the warranted resentment of others.

There is another aspect of being a butcher, baker, or brewer that warrants some discussion. What if the baker aspires to be recognized as the *best* baker in town—not in order to make more money, but as a matter of competitive pride? What if the baker enjoys serving others, putting his or her talents to good use *for others*? This need not be construed as aiming at promoting the "public good"—as distinct from the good of those he or she directly serves. So, insofar as customers make clear to the baker that they like his or her baked goods (or, better, prefers them to those of competitors), they could be said to be addressing the baker's self-interest—not in the narrow sense of contributing to profits, but in the sense of contributing to the regard that others have of him or her *as a baker*.

As already noted, in *The Theory of Moral Sentiments*, Smith insists that we desire, not simply to win the approval of others, but to be *worthy* of that approval. Suppose the baker has a solid reputation of being a terrific baker but has been deliberately shortchanging customers. Whatever praise is received will be unmerited. This does not enhance self-love. It might well induce shame.

So, there is no reason why Smith's famous passage about the butcher, baker, and brewer has to be construed narrowly in terms of financial gain. But even if one did, there could be moral constraints on how one proceeds. The following passage from *The Theory of Moral Sentiments* could just as well have been included in *The Wealth of Nations*: "In the race for wealth, and honours, and preferments, [a person] may run as hard as he can, and strain every nerve and every muscle, in order to outstrip all his competitors. But if he should justle, or throw down any of them, the indulgence of the spectators is entirely at an end. It is a violation of fair play, which they cannot admit of" (*TMS*, 83). In competitive sports one can have "winning" as one's sole *aim*, but be *constrained* by considerations that define, in part, what is to count as "winning". Violators of these constraints of fair play can expect to be met with resentment from others.

So, we return to the importance of taming resentment. Insofar as those evincing resentment at being victimized by others appear simply hostile and aggressive, or themselves out to gain advantage over others, they may find that they are the ones perceived to be engaging in unjustified behavior. However, insofar as they seem themselves to be playing fairly but are being unfairly taken advantage of by others, their resentment will seem reasonable.

For Smith, regardless of the context, each moral agent is to strive to satisfy the demands of an impartial spectator. That is, the moral claims one advances should be acceptable from the third-person perspective of someone with no personal stake in the outcome. This implies considerable constraint in the pursuit of self-interest, and it is quite compatible with being moved by sympathy with customers in regard to treating them fairly and caring about their specific needs. In the context of a business arrangement, direct concern for the public good in general may be as likely to deflect the merchant's attention away from the entitlements of the customer as from the self-interest of the merchant. Sympathizing with the *customer* is quite different from benevolent regard for the *public* good. Also, there is little reason to believe that the customer is looking for a handout from the merchant; the customer expects a fair deal, which means paying for goods received. None of this is incompatible with the merchant caring about the well-being of the customer, as well as his own advantage. The butcher, baker, brewer, or merchant need not be a sensible knave in order to seek his own advantage in his dealings with others.

SELECT BIBLIOGRAPHY

Butler, Joseph. *Butler's Fifteen Sermons*. Edited by T. A. Roberts. London: Society for Promoting Christian Knowledge, 1970.

Hollis, Martin. *Trust within Reason*. New York: Cambridge University Press, 1998.

Hume, David. *Enquiries Concerning Human Understanding and Concerning the Principles of Morals*. 3rd ed. Reprinted from the 1777 edition with introduction and analytical index by L. A. Selby-Bigge. With text revised and notes by P. H. Nidditch. Oxford: Clarendon Press, 1975.

Reid, Thomas. *Essays on the Active Powers of the Mind*. Edited by Knud Haakonssen and James A. Harris. Edinburgh: Edinburgh University Press, 2010.

———. "Review of *The Theory of Moral Sentiments*, by Adam Smith". In *On Moral Sentiments: Contemporary Responses to Adam Smith*, edited by John Reeder. Bristol: Thoemmes Press, 1997, 69–88.

Smith, Adam. *An Inquiry into the Nature and Causes of the Wealth of Nations*. Edited by R. H. Campbell and A. S. Skinner. New York: Oxford University Press, 1976.

———. *The Theory of Moral Sentiments*. Edited by D. D. Raphael and A. L. Macfie. Indianapolis: Liberty Fund, 1984. The original sixth edition was published in 1790.

SKEPTICISM AND IMAGINATION: SMITH'S RESPONSE TO HUME'S *DIALOGUES*

Ryan Patrick Hanley

The otherwise unblemished friendship of David Hume and Adam Smith was marred by one significant incident. Prior to his death in 1776, Hume named Smith his literary executor and requested that he see to press his *Dialogues Concerning Natural Religion*. But this Smith consistently refused to do.[1] As previous commentators have noted, Smith's reticence is striking, given his commitments. Not only was he committed to be generous to the dying—having once claimed that "we naturally find a pleasure in remembering the last words of a friend and in executing his last injunctions"[2]—but Smith was clearly committed to Hume, as evident in his notorious praises of Hume's death-bed magnanimity.[3] Nevertheless, Smith begged their mutual publisher "that his life and those dialogues may not be published together; as I am resolved, for many reasons, to have no concern in the publication of those dialogues".[4] This prompts an obvious question: why?

Several explanations have been proposed. One concerns Smith's solicitude for Hume's reputation, and perhaps his own as well; on this view, his reticence can be partly attributed to a calculating "cold prudence".[5] A second suggestion concerns the substance of the critique of natural religion and the argument from design set forth in the *Dialogues*. Smith, it has been conjectured, may not have wished to align himself with Hume's public attack on religion.[6] On related grounds it has also been suggested that Smith's reticence may be attributable to his grasp of the implications of Hume's assaults on the design argument for his own political thought; Smith, that is, perhaps "had not or could not come to grips with their content", since a successful attack on teleology might

---

1 For accounts of the incident, see John Rae, *Life of Adam Smith*, 295–314; and Ian S. Ross, *The Life of Adam Smith*, 289–304, 338–342. Bibliographic information for all references can be found in the Select Bibliography at the end of this essay.

2 Smith, *Lectures on Jurisprudence*, report dated 1766 [report B], 165.

3 For the relevant texts and commentary, see esp. Eric Schliesser, "The Obituary of a Vain Philosopher".

4 Smith to William Strahan, 5 September 1776, in *Correspondence of Adam Smith*, 211.

5 See T. D. Campbell and I. S. Ross, "The Theory and Practice of the Wise and Virtuous Man", 68, 71; cf. Ross, *Life of Adam Smith*, 341; and Rae, *Life of Adam Smith*, 296.

6 See Ernest C. Mossner, "Hume and the Legacy of the *Dialogues*", 16.

compromise his defense of the superiority of spontaneous orders governed by an invisible hand.[7] All of these suggestions are plausible, and the aim of the present essay is not to question them but to supplement them by proposing one important but overlooked reason for Smith's stance—a reason that is neither personal nor political nor theological, but philosophical.

Thus the claim that I wish to put forth: Smith recognized that the effect of Hume's critique of natural religion in the *Dialogues* was not merely an assault on its stated object—namely the capacity of the argument from design to provide us with reliable knowledge of God's existence or nature—but also an assault on the very possibility of productive philosophical inquiry. Put differently, Smith recognized that an essential epistemological claim of the *Dialogues*—its claim that all speculation or inference beyond the limits of experience is illegitimate—would be fatal not only to the sort of theological speculation that Hume wished to restrain but also to the sort of philosophical theorizing and scientific inquiry that Smith wished to encourage. The evidence for this claim lies in Smith's "History of Astronomy". By setting the two pieces against each other, we can see that for all their similarities, the understanding of philosophical inquiry defended in the "History of Astronomy" depends upon encouraging precisely the sort of imaginative speculation beyond experience that the *Dialogues* are intended to contain.

This fact is important for two reasons. First, it helps to illuminate a key difference between Smith and Hume. Smith's central contributions to both ethics and economics are often regarded as commensurate with Hume's positions. Yet as I hope to show, for all its borrowings from Hume, Smith's understanding of the epistemic and psychological foundations of scientific inquiry is not simply derivative of Hume's.[8] This in turn suggests a second reason why

---

7 See Ross, *Life of Adam Smith*, 340; and Campbell and Ross, "Theory and Practice", 70.

8 These differences remain largely uncharted waters, but a helpful recent discussion can be found in Eric Schliesser, "Wonder in the Face of Scientific Revolutions"; cf. the treatment of the differences in Hume's and Smith's conceptions of moral psychology (especially envy and resentment) and political theory (especially justice and property rights) in Spencer J. Pack and Eric Schliesser, "Smith's Humean Criticism of Hume's Account of Justice"; and my comparison of Smith and Hume on natural belief in "Skepticism and Naturalism in Adam Smith". Recent studies of Smith's theological commitments have likewise called attention to differences with Hume's; see A. M. C. Waterman, "Economics as Theology"; Lisa Hill, "The Hidden Theology of Adam Smith"; James E. Alvey, "The Secret, Natural Theological Foundation of Adam Smith's Work"; Alvey, "The Hidden Theology of Adam Smith: A Belated Reply to Hill"; and Alvey, "The Role of Teleology in Adam Smith's *Wealth of Nations*: A Belated Reply to Kleer". For a concise overview of the recent debate, see Jerry Evensky, *Adam Smith's Moral Philosophy*, 23–25.

such a comparison deserves attention, namely because it serves to clarify the challenges to speculative inquiry in the wake of Hume's critique of metaphysics. Hume, it is well known, in both the *Dialogues* and the *Enquiries*, sought to steer a course for philosophy between dogmatic theology and dogmatic skepticism; similarly, the Philo of the *Dialogues* (and particularly the Philo of *Dialogues* XII) is generally considered an embodiment of the "mitigated skepticism" that Hume defined in the *Treatise* and the first *Enquiry*.[9] Yet it is this very conception of philosophy that the "History of Astronomy" challenges. Smith's argument there suggests that the mitigated skepticism that confines itself to experience deprives philosophical inquiry of the possibility of genuine progress; skepticism limited to experience, that is to say, must inevitably culminate in a philosophical quietism. Yet at the same time, Smith is himself enough of a skeptic to be reticent to embrace that which Hume warns against: both philosophical and theological dogmatism are as thoroughly rejected by Smith as by Hume. Seen thusly, Smith's challenge is to steer a new middle course, one that preserves open the possibility of philosophical inquiry while also remaining authentically skeptical; mitigated skepticism, that is, must give way to zetetic skepticism. Herein lies, I believe, a crucial, but overlooked, reason why Smith may have divorced himself from the *Dialogues*: namely his concern to define a path for the continued persistence of a philosophical inquiry free of both the dogmatism that the two friends each decried, and the unproductive, or strictly critical, skepticism that Hume's Philo defended.

I

Hume's *Dialogues* were written to expose the weaknesses of the argument from design as a reliable means of achieving certain knowledge concerning the existence or nature of God. To this end, the *Dialogues* are built around a conversation among three interlocutors: Demea, a believer with mystic tendencies who defends the argument a priori; Cleanthes, a rationalistic believer who argues that human reason is sufficient for knowledge of the divine and thus defends the argument a posteriori; and Philo, a skeptic who aims to refute both positions, and who has generally—though not uncontroversially—been taken to speak for Hume.[10] The main story of the work is Philo's refutation of the design argument as set forth by Cleanthes. Cleanthes's position is clear: observation of the world, he claims, reveals it to be merely a machine subdivided into multiple smaller machines, and attention to these subordinate machines, in

---

9 See, for example, Stanley Tweyman, *Scepticism and Belief in Hume's* Dialogues, esp. ix, 24, 42, 120–122; and Claudia Schmidt, *David Hume*, 354–355.

10 See Kemp Smith's Introduction to his edition of the *Dialogues*, 59. Donald Livingston endorses this claim while emphasizing Philo's and Hume's "true" or "philosophical" theism over their skepticism; see his *Philosophical Melancholy and Delirium*, 53–79.

turn, is said to reveal that "the curious adapting of means to ends, throughout all nature, resembles exactly, though it much exceeds, the productions of human contrivance; of human design, thought, wisdom, and intelligence". Cleanthes on these grounds concludes that "since therefore the effects resemble each other, we are led to infer, by all the rules of analogy, that the causes also resemble, and that the Author of Nature is somewhat similar to the mind of man, though possessed of much larger faculties, proportioned to the grandeur of the work which he has executed" (*Dialogues*, 15). Philo's refutation of this claim centers on exposing the illegitimacy of its analogy from like causes to like effects: in this case, that the creations that are the product of human design (machines) are analogous to creations that are the product of divine design (universes). By so doing, Philo aims to demonstrate that the argument from design is incapable of providing accurate knowledge about the nature of God, and that its continued hold on our minds owes less to its reasonableness than its appeal to our desire for order. The effect of this critique is to weaken the claims set forth by Cleanthes to a point at which they can be rendered acceptable even to so great a skeptic as Philo, who, in a seeming reversal at the end of the *Dialogues*, appears to embrace a weak form of the argument from design (*Dialogues*, 77). Examined closely, however, this apparent concession does little but enable Philo to better achieve his original intention. That is, by showing that belief in the design argument rests on a sentimental preference for order rather than on reason, the argument can itself be exposed as arbitrary and thus unreliable as a means of achieving certain knowledge, and hence illegitimate as a foundation for any further theological or moral inference. Philo's reversal thus seems to represent something more than Hume's ironic attempt to preserve reputation in an age of religious persecution.[11] Hume's intention for Philo in Part XII rather seems to be to corral or "attenuate" religious speculation and belief so that they can be rendered inconsequent for further moral or political inference,[12] itself a victory for Hume's dual projects to minimize the threats posed by organized religion to political order and the threats posed by theology to moral philosophy.

These largely well-known features of the *Dialogues* must now be supplemented by critical analysis of the consequences and implications of its argument. For what has been less emphasized in the commentary on the *Dialogues* is that the method of Philo's challenge to natural religion compels him to reject not only theology, but also the legitimacy of imaginative inquiry in other speculative fields, and particularly in natural philosophy. In so doing,

---

11 For this view, see Mossner, "Hume and the Legacy", 2; and J. C. A. Gaskin, "Hume on Religion", 320–321.

12 For this view, see Terence Penelhum, "Hume's Skepticism and the *Dialogues*", 273–276; Tweyman, *Scepticism and Belief*, 7–10, 121–122; David Fate Norton, "Of the Academical or Sceptical Philosophy", 390–391; and Gaskin, *Hume's Philosophy of Religion*, 219–229.

the *Dialogues* go considerably further than even the most radical claims of the *Treatise* and the first *Enquiry*, even though all three share a similar departure point. In all three works the departure point is the weakness of human reason and the possible remedies that might be offered to mitigate the effects of its abuse. In the *Dialogues* Philo introduces this claim in his apparent agreement with Demea. "Let us become thoroughly sensible of the weakness, blindness, and narrow limits of human reason", Philo insists, for having done so, "who can retain such confidence in this frail faculty of reason as to pay any regard to its determinations in points so sublime, so abstruse, so remote from common life and experience?" (*Dialogues*, 4). On these grounds Philo in fact develops the central argument of the *Dialogues*: namely that reason should be restricted to analysis of common life and experience alone, as all suppositions that would carry us beyond experience are necessarily arbitrary.

Philo's critique then questions the legitimacy of all forms of inquiry that fail to take our direct experience as their starting point. The consequence of such an attack is to draw an unbreachable line of demarcation between two types of philosophical inquiry. Philo presents this distinction in the first dialogue. "So long as we confine our speculations to trade, or morals, or politics, or criticism", he claims, "we make appeals, every moment, to common sense and experience, which strengthen our philosophical conclusions and remove (at least in part) the suspicion, which we so justly entertain with regard to every reasoning, that is very subtle and refined". On the other hand, "when we look beyond human affairs and the properties of the surrounding bodies" and speculate on either cosmogony or the nature of God, "we must be far removed from the smallest tendency to skepticism not to be apprehensive that we have here got quite beyond the reach of our faculties" (*Dialogues*, 7). This distinction is important for at least three reasons. First, Philo here reveals himself to be something other than a dogmatic or thoroughgoing skeptic. Far from insisting that all sorts of inquiry are necessarily vitiated, Philo instead claims that imaginative inquiry with regard to the human sciences is wholly legitimate. The second aspect of the claim's importance then lies in the nature of the standard that Philo uses to distinguish legitimate from illegitimate types of inquiry. As Philo makes clear, what makes inquiry into ethics, politics, commerce, and criticism legitimate is the fact that their phenomena are part and parcel of ordinary life and hence their conclusions are easily confirmed by the experience of the inquirer. But it is precisely this test that does not hold in the forms of inquiry that Philo wishes to restrain. This leads Philo to reject theology in what immediately follows, on the grounds that the nature of theological phenomena are such that in the course of its researches "we have not this advantage" of appealing to common sense and experience. Later he explicitly applies this same test to cosmogony, which concludes with his insistence that "we have no *data* to establish any system" of such: "Our experience, so imperfect in itself and so limited both in extent and duration, can afford us no probable conjecture concerning the whole of things"

(*Dialogues*, 45). This observation, in turn, raises a question that suggests a third reason why Philo's distinction is important. The bifurcation of philosophy into the (legitimate) human sciences and the (illegitimate) theoretical sciences naturally leads one to wonder into which sphere natural philosophy is to be placed.

Without answering this third question explicitly, Philo goes on to present the main dangers endemic to the pursuit of inquiry beyond experience. His presentation of these comes in the course of his exposure of the dangers of reasoning from one's experience of a specific effect back to infer a cause of which we have no direct experience, itself a key element of Cleanthes's argument from observable design. In response to his interlocutor's argument, Philo argues that as one moves beyond experience, "the utmost you can here pretend to is a guess, a conjecture, a presumption concerning a similar cause", insisting that if a man were to "abstract from everything which he knows or has seen", he would essentially be set adrift, as "every chimera of his fancy would be upon an equal footing", rendering him unable to "assign any just reason why he adheres to any one idea or system, and rejects the others which are equally possible". Arbitrariness is the inevitable consequence:

> Again, after he opens his eyes and contemplates the world as it really is, it would be impossible for him at first to assign the cause of any one event, much less the whole of things, or of the universe. He might set his fancy a rambling, and she might bring him in an infinite variety of reports and representations. These would all be possible; but, being all equally possible, he would never of himself give a satisfactory account for his preferring one of them to the rest. Experience alone can point out to him the true cause of any phenomenon. [*Dialogues*, 16–17]

Imagination is not wholly useless insofar as it enables us to conjecture potentially accurate explanations. But in the absence of the final arbitration that the test of experience provides, the representations of the imagination tend to produce more confusion than clarity, and given their arbitrariness, "can never be foundations for any inference" (*Dialogues*, 69). Philo reiterates this conclusion in insisting to Cleanthes that "a man who follows your hypothesis is able, perhaps, to assert or conjecture that the universe sometime arose from something like design: But beyond that position he cannot ascertain one single circumstance, and is left afterwards to fix every point of his theology by the utmost license of fancy and hypothesis" (*Dialogues*, 37). This is Philo's consistent stance throughout the *Dialogues*: not that design is simply false, but rather that there are no good reasons for believing it to be any more true than any other proposition. Philo's defense of his skepticism draws heavily on this position.

Given the arbitrary nature of all conjectures beyond experience, he insists, we have no sufficient standards to judge one better than another, and hence we do best to suspend judgment, for "we know so little beyond common life, or even of common life, that, with regard to the economy of a universe, there is no conjecture, however wild, which may not be just; nor any one, however plausible, which may not be erroneous. All that belongs to human understanding, in this deep ignorance and obscurity, is to be skeptical or at least cautious, and not to admit of any hypothesis whatever, much less of any which is supported by no appearance of probability" (*Dialogues*, 69).

Now, in making such a claim the *Dialogues* develop an aspect of the critique of the argument from design that Hume initially set forth in Part XI of the first *Enquiry*: namely that conjectures beyond experience, as well as reasonings from effects to causes, are "entirely imaginary", and as they are imaginary, are also "arbitrary" (*Enquiry*, XI.12, 15, 26). Indeed Philo's main claim in the *Dialogues* is wholly faithful to the objection that Hume puts in the mouth of the Epicurean of the first *Enquiry*: those who infer from effects to causes have "aided the ascent of reason by the wings of imagination" (*Enquiry*, XI.16). Imagination thus requires restraint, and the best antidote to the false philosophies driven by imagination is fidelity to common life; hence Philo's claim that true philosophy "is nothing essentially different from reasoning on common life" (*Dialogues*, 7). Here Philo is merely repeating Hume's claim in the first *Enquiry* that "philosophical decisions are nothing but the reflections of common life, methodized and corrected", and his belief that philosophers who appreciate the limits of speculative reason "will never be tempted to go beyond common life" (*Enquiry*, XII.25; cf. XI.27). In both natural theology and metaphysics then, the imagination, which runs "without controul, into the most distant parts of space and time", must be restrained by judgment, which, "avoiding all distant and high enquiries, confines itself to common life, and to such subjects as fall under daily practice and experience" (*Enquiry*, XII.25).

Alongside this resemblance in the treatments of the imagination in the *Dialogues* and the first *Enquiry*, however, a difference between these treatments and the treatment of the imagination in the first book of the *Treatise* must also be noted. In the *Treatise*, Hume clearly envisions a positive role for the imagination even as he warns against the possible abuses of the fancy. The whole of *Treatise* I.i.4 is thus dedicated to demonstrating the role of the imagination as the nexus of the association of ideas via relations of resemblance, contiguity, and cause and effect. Hume considers these imaginative constructs useful in ordinary life as they give rise to our necessary beliefs in causality and the persistence of the external world. But Philo is silent on this aspect of the imagination in the *Dialogues*, emphasizing instead its perils rather than its utility, tending thus to agree with the position of the *Treatise* that in spite of the imagination's utility in common life, its conclusions are unworthy of a "true philosopher", who instead strives to "restrain the intemperate desire" to make imaginative inquiries into causes (*Treatise*, I.i.4.6). The imagination that is a necessity in common life is a liability in philosophy.

The central aim of Hume's critique of imagination to this point has been to expose the arbitrary character of conclusions that are not derived from experience. Yet Hume's critique of imaginative inquiry was made not only on the grounds of its arbitrariness, but also on the grounds of its incapacity to bring satisfaction to the inquirer. The very act of speculation about the origins or operation of natural order, Philo repeatedly insists, is inimical to happiness, as it tends to unsettle the imagination and disturb our tranquility rather than promote it. The tragic note is initially sounded by Pamphilus, the *Dialogues*' narrator, who claims that God's nature and Providence are topics "so interesting that we cannot restrain our restless inquiry with regard to them", even though "nothing but doubt, uncertainty, and contradiction have as yet been the result of our most accurate researches" (*Dialogues*, 2). To speculate about the nature of God and the plan of nature is tragic insofar as it is at once irresistible and yet unproductive, and if the *Dialogues* offer any respite from this bad state of affairs, it lies in their consistent teaching that it is better not to pursue those sorts of inquiry that can bring neither certainty nor tranquility. This point is made most forcefully in Philo's response to Demea. To Demea's suggestion that the cause of natural order is the order of ideas in a divine mind, Philo responds that such an account can lead only to endless speculation about the possible cause of that cause. To engage in a search for first causes is to commit one's self to an unending inquiry:

> How can we satisfy ourselves without going on *in infinitum*? And, after all, what satisfaction is there in that infinite progression? Let us remember the story of the Indian philosopher and his elephant. It was never more applicable than to the present subject. If the material world rests upon a similar ideal world, this ideal world must rest upon some other, and so on without end. It were better, therefore, never to look beyond the present material world. By supposing it to contain the principle of its order within itself, we really assert it to be God; and the sooner we arrive at that Divine Being, so much the better. When you go one step beyond the mundane system, you only excite an inquisitive humor which it is impossible ever to satisfy. [*Dialogues*, 31]

Restricting inquiry to matter known by experience is then necessary not only because of the limited capacities of our reason, but now also for reasons that concern the nature of happiness. Hence Philo's most damning claim against Demea: "what do we gain by your system, in tracing the universe of objects into a similar universe of ideas? The first step which we make leads us on forever. It were, therefore, wise in us to limit all our inquiries to the present world, without looking farther. No satisfaction can ever be attained by these speculations which so far exceed the narrow bounds of human understanding" (*Dialogues*, 31–32). Given the lack of profit to be gained from philosophical inquiry of this sort, it seems better not to pursue it. Philo hints that this conclusion is, to some degree, deflationary: "I am sensible that I must at last be contented to sit down with the same answer which, without further trouble, might have satisfied me from the beginning" (*Dialogues*, 33). But nevertheless the claim remains: given the unproductivity of all theoretical inquiry, philosophical quietism, while it cannot bring satisfaction, at least absolves speculators of unnecessary discomfort.

With this we glimpse the potentially radical consequences of the *Dialogues*, and indeed can see how the skepticism that Philo defends extends further than the mitigated skepticism that Hume had defended in previous works. In these works, skepticism is a ground-clearing exercise; that is to say, the aim of the skeptic is to illustrate the ostensible arbitrariness of metaphysics, and then to commence inquiry into politics and into morals, the practical aspects of life.[13] But in the *Dialogues*, while the critical element is easily seen, no constructive account of philosophy follows, even if Philo occasionally hints that such an account would not conflict with his essential principles. Skepticism, that is to say, seems to be a wholly negative enterprise, for the absurdities of theological disputes merely

> prepare a complete triumph for the skeptic, who tells them that no system ought ever to be embraced with regard to such subjects: For this plain reason, that no absurdity ought ever to be assented to with regard to any subject. A total suspense of judgment is here our only reasonable resource. And if every attack, as is commonly observed, and no defense among theologians is successful, how complete must be *his* victory who remains always, with all mankind, on the offensive, and has himself no fixed station or abiding city which he is ever, on any occasion, obliged to defend? [*Dialogues*, 53]

Even if such skepticism is not Pyrrhonian, the skeptic's "victory" is pyrrhic. Philosophy has been redefined as a merely critical or deconstructive enterprise, one that takes pride in having no fixed position of its own. Indeed, all synthetic ambitions are, on such a definition, violations of genuine philosophy. In turn, false philosophy can itself be exposed by its ambition to make synthetic connections. This is of course the sort of error that Hume uses Philo to expose: "What we see in the parts, we may infer in the whole; at least, that is the method

---

13   I am indebted to conversations with Lauren Brubaker for this formulation.

of reasoning on which you rest your whole theory" (*Dialogues*, 42). But it is precisely this discretion—and even the very identification of discreteness as opposed to synthesis—that separates philosophers from non-philosophers (*Dialogues*, 19).

Philo's position thus represents a distinct challenge to the sort of skepticism that Hume wished to defend in the first *Enquiry*. There "mitigated skepticism" is offered as an alternative to an insupportable Pyrrhonian skepticism; any thinking Pyrrhonian, Hume there claims, knows "that all human life must perish, were his principles universally and steadily to prevail. All discourse, all action would immediately cease; and men remain in a total lethargy, till the necessities of nature, unsatisfied, put an end to their miserable existence" (*Enquiry*, XII.23). Hume is satisfied that nature will not permit such to occur, and will rescue us from the awful fate of total lethargy (*Dialogues*, 5–7). Yet it is difficult to see how Hume's critique of lethargy in the first *Enquiry* can be reconciled with Philo's stance. For even if Philo does not explicitly advocate intellectual lethargy, his position—and particularly his insistence that skepticism ought to be critical and not synthetic—seems inimical to the productive ambitions of enlightened philosophy.

In this respect Philo's claim has more radical implications than Hume's previous position. These radical implications can be seen by evaluating the likely effect of Philo's doctrines on science. Hume himself had to some degree anticipated such effects in the *Treatise*. There he notes that abuses of the imagination might seem to call for it to be dismissed altogether, but Hume also cautions that "this resolution, if steadily executed, would be dangerous, and attended with the most fatal consequences", foremost among them the possibility that one would "cut off entirely all science and philosophy". This leads Hume to propose a remedy that Philo cannot: "We save ourselves from this total skepticism only by means of that singular and seemingly trivial property of the fancy, by which we enter with difficulty into remote visions of things" (*Treatise*, I.iv.7.7).[14] Hume's early explicit recognition of the importance of fancy to "science and philosophy" constitutes a sharp departure from Philo's much more radical position, and itself compels a reconsideration of the degree to which Philo can be said to speak for Hume.

II

Smith's "History of Astronomy" might be read as a response to Philo's critique. As we turn from the *Dialogues* to the astronomy essay we in fact find both contrasts and similarities. On the one hand, the essay's treatment of the role of constant conjunction in causal reasoning is clearly indebted to its embrace

---

14 For a helpful illumination of the significance of this passage, see Gerhard Streminger, "Hume's Theory of Imagination", 103–105.

of Hume's terminology, as has been convincingly demonstrated.[15] Yet Smith's intentions in embracing this language require further attention. Put simply, the question at issue concerns whether Smith's embrace of Hume's language ought to be taken as his endorsement of Hume's skepticism, or whether the subtle difference in their conclusions, in spite of their shared terminology, ought to be taken as evidence of a more fundamental disagreement. Here I argue the latter; my main claim is that even in embracing elements of Hume's skeptical epistemology, Smith breaks with Hume in insisting that imaginative speculation beyond experience can be genuinely useful as a means of achieving truth and as a means of achieving individual tranquility.

The difference in Hume's and Smith's orientations to philosophy is evident even in the departure point for the "History of Astronomy". As is well known, Smith's essay begins as an inquiry into the operations of the intellectual sentiments of wonder, surprise, and admiration. Wonder is the focus of the majority of the piece, and is identified as the psychological or anthropological origin of philosophy. But what is striking in Smith's account is his understanding of what prompts wonder. On Smith's view, what gives rise to wonder, which in turn gives rise to philosophy, is mind's experience of that which is "new and singular".[16] The impetus for speculation is the desire to understand phenomena that lie outside of our previous experience. But this constitutes a significant departure from Hume. For Hume, as noted above, the proper province of philosophy is the realm of common life; true philosophy, insofar as it is merely a "refinement" of common life, stops at the boundary of common experience. But for Smith, philosophy is an attempt to account for phenomena beyond common life. Put differently, philosophy begins for Smith at precisely the point at which it ends for Hume.

Smith's and Hume's disagreements become more pronounced as Smith goes on to account for our natural psychological response to wonder. Herein lies a second principal difference in their conceptions of philosophy. According to Smith, when we confront an object that "stands alone and by itself in the imagination, and refuses to be grouped or confounded with any set of objects whatever", we immediately wonder: "What sort of a thing can that be? What is that like?" Such, Smith insists, "are the questions which upon such an occasion, we are all naturally disposed to ask" ("Astronomy", II.3). Here and elsewhere Smith thus suggests that asking such questions is both natural and necessary.[17] By "natural" Smith seems to mean that such a response is inevitable, and by

---

15   See D. D. Raphael, "'The True Old Humean Philosophy' and Its Influence on Adam Smith", esp. 27–28, 31.

16   Smith, "The Principles Which Lead and Direct Philosophical Enquiries; Illustrated by the History of Astronomy", Intro. 1; II.3.

17   Smith, *Wealth of Nations*, V.i.f.24; cf. Smith, *Lectures on Rhetoric and Belles-Lettres*, ii.v.18.

"necessary" he means that such a response is the only possible route to the restoration of the psychological tranquility so necessary for happiness. Thus he claims that in order to "get rid of that Wonder" induced by apprehension of the new and singular, it is necessary to identify the resemblance of the unfamiliar with phenomena already familiar from experience ("Astronomy", II.4). But this again constitutes a significant break from the epistemology of the *Dialogues*. On Philo's view, philosophy of the speculative sort is necessarily unpleasant; the endless search for causes cannot end in satisfaction. The only available options are intellectual torment or intellectual torpor; the former is the only possible conclusion if inquiry continues, and the latter is the only possible respite once inquiry is abandoned for common life. But for Smith, not only does natural curiosity render Philo's intellectual stasis unsustainable, but philosophy is itself regarded more hopefully, as an enterprise in which a satisfying alleviation of anxiety, however fleeting, remains possible. Put differently, where philosophy is for Hume the cause of anxiety, and thus best abandoned for the study of common life, philosophy is for Smith the only remedy for anxiety, and hence requires the abandonment of common life.

A third disagreement between Smith and Hume emerges in the course of Smith's account of the proper method of restoring psychological tranquility disturbed by wonder. We have seen Philo argue that it is illegitimate to reason on the basis of remote analogy on the grounds that like effects cannot be taken as evidence of like causes. This is the foundation of his critique of the vulgar who too quickly take superficial resemblances for genuine connections—connections that Hume himself reveals to be nothing more than effects of constant conjunction in the mind rather than in nature. Smith too is interested in the propensities of the mind to establish order and connection, yet his attitude towards this process is more optimistic than Hume's. For Hume again, philosophy's goal is the discernment of difference and disconnect and hence the exposure of the errors of vulgar synthesis. But for Smith, this same process takes on a much different cast. A disposition to see connections, so far from vulgar, is both natural and pleasurable; thus his opening claim that "it is evident that the mind takes pleasure in observing the resemblances that are discoverable betwixt different objects" ("Astronomy", II.1). Indeed the entire goal of the philosophical enterprise, according to Smith, is to discern the connecting thread that unites discrete objects into a coherent system: "observe but one single quality that is common to a great variety of otherwise widely different objects, that single circumstance will be sufficient for it to connect them all together, to reduce them to one common class, and to call them by one general name" ("Astronomy", II.1).[18] Herein then lies a third initial difference between Smith's and Hume's

---

18 For helpful discussions of "the importance of reasoning from analogy" in Smith, see Schliesser, "Wonder in Scientific Revolutions", 700–702; and Andrew S. Skinner, "Adam Smith: Science and the Role of the Imagination", 178–179.

conceptions of philosophy. Where Hume insists that the goal of philosophical investigation is to reveal the discrete nature of phenomena and to expose the lack of any substantive connection between them, for Smith the aim of philosophy is to synthesize and unite the formerly discrete into coherent wholes.

With these observations in place, we are better positioned to see the difference in Hume's and Smith's positions even where their terms most agree. Their crucial point of contact comes in their respective accounts of the role of the imagination in causal apprehension. In several of his key discussions of causation, Smith clearly adopts Hume's characterization of constant conjunction, noting that "when two objects, however unlike, have often been observed to follow each other, and have constantly presented themselves to the senses in that order, they come to be so connected together in the fancy, that the idea of the one seems, of its own accord, to call up and introduce that of the other". So far, this is little more than a textbook restatement of Hume's account of the connection of ideas in the imagination in the first book of the *Treatise*. Smith further reinforces this connection when he examines the role of the "habit of the imagination" in this process, explaining how a mind apprehending discrete phenomena may glide "easily along them, without effort and without interruption" ("Astronomy", II.7). Confronted with phenomena that are seemingly disconnected, it is the imagination's job "to find out something which may fill in the gap", something "like a bridge" or "the supposition of a chain of intermediate, though invisible, events, which succeed each other in a train" ("Astronomy", II.8). This too seems in line with the epistemology of the *Treatise*, and particularly its emphasis on the constructive role in common life of a "smooth and uninterrupted passage of the imagination".[19] Yet for all these similarities, a crucial difference separates Hume and Smith here. Hume is clear in insisting that this method is legitimate only in the apprehension of phenomena that can be known by experience. Smith, however, explicitly extends its application to the study of "invisible" phenomena, which by definition go beyond sensory experience; put differently, Smith applies to philosophical inquiry the methods that Hume took care to restrict to common life. Smith's translation of Hume's methods to this new sphere has been noted previously,[20] but what has not been noted is the fact that Smith's translation is not simply an innocent extension of Hume's theory, but rather constitutes a fundamental violation of the *Dialogues*' central claim that the

---

19 See *Treatise*, I.iv.2.34. I.iv.2 is often suggested as the link between Smith and Hume on this point; see Raphael, "'The True Old Humean Philosophy'", 27–29, 34–37; *Essays on Philosophical Subjects*, 41 n. 4 and 42 n. 6; Christopher Berry, "Smith and Science", 118; and Griswold, "Imagination: Morals, Science, and Arts", esp. 23, 26; cf. Skinner, who, in examining the same passage, notes its debts to I.i.4 ("Science and the Role of Imagination", 167 and 184 n. 11).

20 Skinner, "Science and the Role of the Imagination", 171; Raphael, "'True Old Humean Philosophy'", 28.

same operations of imagination that are needed to generate natural or necessary belief in common life become the illegitimate sources of the errors of "fancy" in philosophical inquiry. The radical nature of Smith's appropriation of Hume's epistemology, and particularly his view of the synthetic role for the imagination, thus lies in his application of this form of inquiry to a study of the very class of objects to which Hume says it must not be applied. Thus while Smith has been importantly read as a Humean "nondogmatic" skeptic,[21] his understanding here of the imagination seems to break with Hume's intentions even as it applies Hume's concepts.[22]

Smith's account of astronomy's history provides a useful illustration of the ways in which he modifies Hume's positions. Astronomical speculation begins as a species of wonder prompted by a very unique type of experience, the experience of apprehension of celestial bodies. Such experience is unique owing to the proximity of the inquirer to the phenomena under study. The celestial bodies, that is, are experienced at a distance rather than directly. Experience then, in this instance, is sufficient to demonstrate to an inquirer the existence of the phenomena, but at the same time, experience cannot reveal anything of their natures. Philo is not unaware of this problem, but his own attempt to demonstrate that his theory is not fatal to natural philosophy and to astronomy especially circumvents this challenge by claiming that as a result of Galileo's astronomical studies, "men plainly saw that these bodies became proper objects of experience, and that the similarity of their nature enabled us to extend the same arguments and phenomena from one to the other" (*Dialogues*, 22; cf. 8–10). Philo's claim rests on the fact that Galileo succeeded in his proof that the heavenly bodies operate on the same principles as earthly bodies. But this avoids the central issue, which concerns not the possibility of experiments that prove the similarity of the conjecture, but rather the possibility of conjecture itself. For even if Galileo succeeded in demonstrating their similarity via experience and experiment, such experience could not have provided grounds for the initial conjecture of the similarity between heavenly and earthly bodies that the demonstrations proved. Philo's defense thus fails to address the main problem, namely the rehabilitation of imaginative conjecture. In the case of the celestial bodies, experience is sufficient to convince us of their existence, but imagination

---

21 See especially Griswold, *Adam Smith and the Virtues of Enlightenment* (esp. 165–166, 171); and Griswold, "Imagination: Morals, Science, and Arts", esp. 22, 53–54.

22 See also Schliesser, "Wonder in Scientific Revolutions", 709–710, who suggests that Smith breaks from Humean common sense in welcoming "strangeness" in order to "perhaps spur on the development of new theories". See also Schliesser's emphasis on Smith's shift from Hume's emphasis on a "fundamental skepticism about possible knowledge of nature" to approach inexplicable perplexity as a "*research problem*"; see Schliesser, "Adam Smith's Benevolent and Self-Interested Conception of Philosophy", 330.

is the necessary departure point for subsequent study of their natures.

But this of course opens Smith up to a distinctively Humean challenge. If indeed science can account for new phenomena only by conjecture, what is there to prevent such astronomical conjectures from being less arbitrary than the theological conjectures Philo examined? Smith has a response to this problem, and in giving this response he presents an interestingly mitigated version of Hume's mitigated skepticism. Again, the challenge that he has inherited from Hume is this: if we limit ourselves to experience, we impede scientific progress, yet if we extend conjectures beyond experience, we open ourselves up to the charge of arbitrariness. Smith's response to this challenge is that a particular form of non-arbitrary conjecture exists, a form of conjecture that extends beyond experience yet is itself founded on experience. Smith describes this type of conjecture in his account of the history of astronomical revolutions. When confronted with unfamiliar phenomena, he claims, revolutionary theorists "naturally explained things to themselves by principles that were familiar to themselves" ("Astronomy", II.12). The full force of this claim is only evident when compared to Philo's position. Against Philo's claim that one cannot analogize from like to like, Smith counters that on the grounds of resemblance, analogies between like and like can and in fact must be made for the sake of bridging the gap that would otherwise impede philosophical progress. Hence his admiration of those "who therefore explained to themselves the phenomena, in that which was strange to them, by those in that which was familiar; and with whom, upon that account, the analogy, which in other writers gives occasion to a few ingenious similitudes, became the great hinge upon which every thing turned" ("Astronomy", II.12). This claim comes on the heels of a review of some of the more dubious attempts at philosophical analogy, but its central aim is to demonstrate the necessity of conjecture in scientific discovery. Smith thus counters Philo's suggestion that all conjecture is arbitrary with the argument that conjectures grounded in analogies from experience ought to be distinguished from genuinely arbitrary conjectures. Smith of course agrees that some sorts of conjecture are arbitrary.[23] Nevertheless, some of the most provocative claims in Smith's other essays on "the principles which lead and direct philosophical enquiries" endorse imaginative conjecture:

> To introduce order and coherence into the mind's conception of this seeming chaos of dissimilar and disjointed appearances, it was necessary to deduce all their qualities, operations, and laws of succession, from those of some particular things, with which it was perfectly acquainted and familiar, and

---

23 See *Wealth of Nations* V.i.f.24 and "Astronomy", III.2–3; cf. Hume, *The Natural History of Religion*, 32–37. For a helpful development of these similarities, see Spencer J. Pack, "Theological (And Hence Economic) Implications", esp. 295–300.

> along which its imagination could glide smoothly and easily, and without interruption. ["Ancient Physics", 2]

These and other similar statements in the "History of Astronomy" have frequently been regarded as evidence of Smith's belief that the perception of natural order is strictly an artificial imposition of the mind on the chaos that truly describes the disorganization of matter in the world.[24] While such an interpretation is not wholly without warrant (though a separate essay is needed to determine its ultimate legitimacy), it does not capture the much more radical claim at stake here. For what Smith is most concerned to demonstrate here is not simply the difference between mental order and material disorder, but the need to extend conjecture from the familiar to the unfamiliar via analogy—that is, precisely the leap Philo forbids.

Smith defends such a leap for two reasons, each of which departs from Hume's position. The first is that such conjectures, even if rough-and-ready leaps of faith, are justified by their potential utility. Like Hume, Smith decried "that species of metaphysics which confounds every thing and explains nothing" ("Of the External Senses", 140). Yet Philo's skepticism may well induce similar frustrations. Philo's conclusion is clearly that the triumph of the skeptic is strictly critical; rather than reach any positive conclusion of his own, his aim is to expose the errors of others. In contrast, Smith continually emphasizes the productive capacity of philosophy, as evident in his two most direct definitions of it. The first comes at the start of the *Wealth of Nations*, in which "philosophers, or men of speculation", are famously defined as the group of men "whose trade it is, not to do any thing, but to observe every thing; and who, upon that account, are often capable of combining together the powers of the most distant and dissimilar objects" (*Wealth of Nations*, I.i.9). Read against Philo's account of the skeptic's triumph, the emphasis on synthesis ("combining together") and productivity ("powers") is striking. These same notes are sounded in the definition of philosophy that is given in the "History of Astronomy". Here again the task of the philosopher is combinatory, and indeed again combinatory of that which is familiar in common life but whose connecting principles require methods of discovery that extend well beyond common life. And in this sense, Smith subverts again a central Humean distinction. For Philo, we remember, the vulgar are those who explain everything with vague references to "nature" (*Dialogues*, 46). For Smith, the non-philosophical similarly offer simplistic explanations of natural and social orders that rest on dimly perceived conceptions of "nature". This simple explanation—that "it is their nature" to be so ordered—Smith, like Hume, thinks unsatisfactory ("Astronomy", II.11). But where Hume responds that the proper philosophical response to such a

---

24 See especially Griswold, *Smith and the Virtues of Enlightenment*, 336–344; and restatements in "Imagination", esp. 40, 50, 54, 56 n. 27.

claim is to expose the fallacies in the non-philosophical supposition of natural order, Smith's claim is that a genuinely philosophical response will not merely expose the fallacies, but will engage in constructive inquiry that better explains positions that non-philosophers lack means to express or defend. Hence Smith's second definition of philosophy as "the science of the connecting principles of nature", by which, as he repeatedly makes clear, he means the science of uncovering the same invisible connections between discrete phenomena of which the vulgar speak but cannot describe with precision ("Astronomy", II.12). This is explicitly the task of philosophers "who often look for a chain of invisible objects to join together two events that occur in an order familiar to all the world" ("Astronomy", II.11). Herein then lies Smith's most radical departure from Hume on this front. The vulgar, Smith and Hume agree, speak of natural order, but lacking genuine knowledge can be shown to be speaking nonsense. Confronted by such, the Humean skeptic seeks to expose what is nonsensical in vulgar opinion. But the Smithean philosopher takes an opposite approach; so far from exposing what is fallacious in the vulgar opinion, he dedicates himself to uncovering the principles of connection that elude the vulgar.

Smith develops this account of philosophy as the science of investigating invisible principles again in the following paragraph. But in this second statement he also suggests a second defense of philosophy from Hume's critique:

> Philosophy, by representing the invisible chains which bind together all these disjointed objects, endeavors to introduce order into this chaos of jarring and discordant appearances, to allay this tumult of the imagination, and to restore it, when it surveys the great revolutions of the universe, to that tone of tranquility and composure, which is both most agreeable in itself, and most suitable to its nature. ["Astronomy", II.12]

Here Smith goes beyond the claims made above. Above he has said that philosophy is useful insofar as it promotes scientific progress by revealing the chains of connection that the vulgar posit but cannot prove. But here he points to a second utility of philosophy, which is now conceived as being useful to the inquirer as well as to science, insofar as it promotes tranquility. Smith is insistent that this is the actual effect of philosophical discovery on the mind: "upon the clear discovery of a connecting chain of intermediate events", the anxiety prompted by wonder "vanishes altogether", as "what obstructed the movement of the imagination is then removed" ("Astronomy", II.9). But this therapeutic capacity of philosophy is so pronounced that Smith is hesitant to subsume such a benefit under the rubric of utility. Hence his strong statement that natural philosophers "pursue this study for its own sake, as an original pleasure or good in itself, without regarding its tendency to provide them the means of many other pleasures" ("Astronomy", III.3). Smith has, for a very long time, been seen as inimical to the intrinsic pleasures of the philosophical life, but claims such as these seem to belie this view.[25] And in so doing, not only does Smith align himself with the defenders of the intrinsic superiority of speculation to other human activities, but he also sets forth his sharpest challenge to Hume. Hume's famous claim in *Treatise* I.iv.7 is that retreat to common life is necessary to absolve the mind of the anxieties philosophy induces. This position is replicated in Philo's conciliatory move in *Dialogues* XII, which has been interpreted as a similar or parallel retreat from inquiry to backgammon, or philosophy to friendship—or in Richard Dees's apt phrase, an effort to place "morality above metaphysics".[26] But for Smith the case is exactly opposite. Where Hume sees common life as the necessary antidote to the anxieties induced by philosophy, Smith insists that common life, and its inadequacies at enabling us to resolve perplexities, itself induces anxiety, which philosophy alone can, even if only temporarily, satisfy.

SELECT BIBLIOGRAPHY

Alvey, James E. "The Hidden Theology of Adam Smith: A Belated Reply to Hill". *European Journal of the History of Economic Thought* 11 (2004): 623.

———. "The Role of Teleology in Adam Smith's *Wealth of Nations*: A Belated Reply to Kleer". http://econ.massey.ac.nz/publications/discuss/dp04-06.pdf (accessed November 2005).

———. "The Secret, Natural Theological Foundation of Adam Smith's Work". *Journal of Markets and Morality* 7 (2004): 335–361.

Berry, Christopher. "Smith and Science". In *The Cambridge Companion to Adam Smith*, edited by Knud Haakonssen. Cambridge: Cambridge University Press, 2006, 112–135.

Campbell, T. D., and I. S. Ross. "The Theory and Practice of the Wise and Virtuous Man: Reflections on Adam Smith's Response to Hume's Deathbed Wish". *Studies in Eighteenth-Century Culture* 11 (1982): 65–75.

Cropsey, Joseph. *Polity and Economy*. South Bend: St. Augustine's Press, 2001.

---

25 See Joseph Cropsey, *Polity and Economy*, 8; cf. Schliesser, "Wonder in the Face of Scientific Revolutions", 727.

26 See Richard Dees, "Morality Above Metaphysics"; and Schmidt, *David Hume*, 356–357.

Dees, Richard. "Morality Above Metaphysics: Philo and the Duties of Friendship in *Dialogues* XII". *Hume Studies* 28 (2002): 131–147.

Evensky, Jerry. *Adam Smith's Moral Philosophy*. Cambridge: Cambridge University Press, 2005.

Gaskin, J. C. A. "Hume on Religion". In *The Cambridge Companion to Hume*, edited by David Fate Norton. Cambridge: Cambridge University Press, 1993, 313–344.

———. *Hume's Philosophy of Religion*, 2nd ed. New York: Macmillan, 1998.

Griswold, Charles L., Jr. *Adam Smith and the Virtues of Enlightenment*. Cambridge: Cambridge University Press, 1999.

———. "Imagination: Morals, Science, and Arts". In *The Cambridge Companion to Adam Smith*, edited by Knud Haakonssen. Cambridge: Cambridge University Press, 2006, 22–56.

Hanley, Ryan. "Skepticism and Naturalism in Adam Smith". In *The Philosophy of Adam Smith*, edited by Vivienne Brown and Samuel Fleischacker. London: Routledge, 2010, 198–212.

Hill, Lisa. "The Hidden Theology of Adam Smith". *European Journal of the History of Economic Thought* 8 (2001): 1–29.

Hume, David. *Dialogues Concerning Natural Religion*. Edited by Richard H. Popkin. Indianapolis: Hackett, 1980.

———. *An Enquiry Concerning Human Understanding*. Edited by Tom L. Beauchamp. Oxford: Clarendon Press, 2000.

———. *The Natural History of Religion*. Edited by H. E. Root. Stanford: Stanford University Press, 1956.

———. *A Treatise of Human Nature*. 1739–1740. Edited by David Fate Norton and Mary J. Norton. Oxford: Oxford University Press, 2000.

Kemp Smith, Norman. "Introduction" to Hume, *Dialogues*. Indianapolis: Bobbs-Merrill, 1947.

Livingston, Donald. *Philosophical Melancholy and Delirium: Hume's Pathology of Philosophy*. Chicago: University of Chicago Press, 1998.

Mossner, Ernest C. "Hume and the Legacy of the *Dialogues*". In *David Hume: Bicentenary Papers*, edited by G. P. Morice. Edinburgh: Edinburgh University Press, 1977, 1–22.

Norton, David Fate. "Of the Academical or Sceptical Philosophy". In *Reading Hume on Human Understanding*, edited by Peter Millican. Oxford: Clarendon Press, 2002, 371–392.

Pack, Spencer J. "Theological (And Hence Economic) Implications of Adam Smith's 'Principles Which Lead and Direct Philosophical Enquiries'". *History of Political Economy* 27 (1995): 289–307.

Pack, Spencer J., and Eric Schliesser. "Smith's Humean Criticism of Hume's Account of Justice". *Journal of the History of Philosophy* 44 (2006): 47–63.

Penelhum, Terence. "Hume's Skepticism and the *Dialogues*". In *McGill Hume Studies*, edited by David Fate Norton, Nicholas Capaldi, and Wade Robison. San Diego, Austin Hill Press, 1979, 253–278.

Rae, John. *Life of Adam Smith*. London: Macmillan, 1895.

Raphael, D. D. "'The True Old Humean Philosophy' and Its Influence on Adam Smith". In *David Hume: Bicentenary Papers*, edited by G. P. Morice. Edinburgh: Edinburgh University Press, 1977, 23–38.

Ross, Ian S. *The Life of Adam Smith*. Oxford: Clarendon Press, 1995.

Schliesser, Eric. "Adam Smith's Benevolent and Self-Interested Conception of Philosophy". In *New Voices on Adam Smith*, edited by Leonidas Montes and Eric Schliesser. London: Routledge, 2006, 328–357.

———. "The Obituary of a Vain Philosopher: Adam Smith's Reflections on Hume's Life". *Hume Studies* 29, no. 2 (2003): 327–362.

———. "Wonder in the Face of Scientific Revolutions: Adam Smith on Newton's 'Proof' of Copernicanism". *British Journal for the History of Philosophy* 13 (2005): 697–732.

Schmidt, Claudia. *David Hume: Reason in History*. University Park, PA: Penn State University Press, 2003.

Skinner, Andrew S. "Adam Smith: Science and the Role of the Imagination". In *Hume and the Enlightenment*, edited by William B. Todd. Edinburgh: University of Edinburgh Press, 1974, 164–188.

Smith, Adam. *Correspondence of Adam Smith*. Edited by E. G. Mossner and I. S. Ross. Indianapolis: Liberty Fund, 1987.

——. *An Inquiry into the Nature and Causes of the Wealth of Nations*. Edited by R. H. Campbell, A. S. Skinner, and W. B. Todd. Indianapolis: Liberty Fund, 1981.

——. *Lectures on Jurisprudence*. Edited by R. L. Meek, D. D. Raphael, and P. G. Stein. Indianapolis: Liberty Fund, 1982.

——. *Lectures on Rhetoric and Belles Lettres*. Edited by J. C. Bryce. Indianapolis: Liberty Fund, 1985.

——. "Of the External Senses". In *Essays on Philosophical Subjects*, edited by W. P. D. Wightman. Indianapolis: Liberty Fund, 1982.

——. "The Principles Which Lead and Direct Philosophical Enquiries; Illustrated by the History of Astronomy". In *Essays on Philosophical Subjects*, edited by W. P. D. Wightman. Indianapolis: Liberty Fund, 1982.

——. "The Principles Which Lead and Direct Philosophical Enquiries; Illustrated by the History of Ancient Physics". In *Essays on Philosophical Subjects*, edited by W. P. D. Wightman. Indianapolis: Liberty Fund, 1982.

Streminger, Gerhard. "Hume's Theory of Imagination". *Hume Studies* 6 (1980): 91–118.

Tweyman, Stanley. *Scepticism and Belief in Hume's Dialogues Concerning Natural Religion*. Dordrecht: Martinus Nijhoff, 1986.

Waterman, A. M. C. "Economics as Theology: Adam Smith's *Wealth of Nations*". *Southern Economic Journal* 68 (2002): 907–921.

HUME'S DEATH AND SMITH'S PHILOSOPHY

Chad Flanders

INTRODUCTION

When Smith's "Letter to Strahan" was published, it predictably drew fire for its blatant comparison of Hume to Socrates. Hume, Smith said, "approached the ideal of a perfectly wise and virtuous man, as perhaps the nature of human frailty will permit". The letter to Strahan bears the weight of the comparison to Plato's masterwork, the *Phaedo*: it is a finely wrought piece. Unsurprisingly, Smith's letter has been mostly analyzed in terms of its praise for Hume, its literary content, and historical context, but not so much for its philosophy.[1] Indeed, it is hard to see much philosophical content in it, apart from, perhaps, a recommendation of Hume's philosophy to be inferred from its praise for Hume the man.[2] The letter seems, at best, a fitting tribute to a dear friend of Smith's, but has little real intellectual or philosophical content.

But the idea that the letter is not worth studying as a philosophical document in its own right does not stand up to a close scrutiny. In his letter to Strahan, Smith was not merely paying tribute to his deceased friend, but engaging in a meditation on the worth of public opinion and the possibility of a legitimate sense of vanity about one's own accomplishments.[3] What has been less discussed, however, is the role Hume's death played in the development of Smith's own philosophy. In this essay, I broach the possibility that Hume's death did not leave Smith's philosophy unchanged and that ironically, as a result of the public reaction to Hume's death (and also the public reaction to Smith's letter in praise of Hume), Smith was led to put an even greater distance between his own philosophy and that of Hume's. In his later revisions of *The Theory of Moral Sentiments* (*TMS*), Smith emphasizes more and more the separation of the viewpoint of the impartial spectator from ordinary public opinion, and also becomes more convinced of the necessity of believing in a life after this one, both positions that put him somewhat at odds with his mentor and friend Hume.

My claim in this essay, then, is that we can read with profit the later

---

1 The one exception to this, to my knowledge, is Eric Schliesser's excellent "Obituary of a Vain Philosopher". (Bibliographic information for all references can be found in the Select Bibliography at the end of this essay.)

2 E.g., "This [Smith's letter], it must be acknowledged, is a very artful, though indirect method of recommending Mr. Hume's philosophy to the favour of the public" (James Fieser, *Early Responses to Hume*, 399).

3 See Schliesser, "Obituary".

revisions of *TMS* in light of Smith's reaction to Hume's death. The essay proceeds to this conclusion in three parts. In the first, I speculate on the nature of writing one's biography and argue that Smith's letter completes the biographical project that Hume began in his autobiographical work, *My Own Life* (*MOL*). In the second and third parts, I speculate on how the death of Hume might have affected Smith's philosophy in unHumean ways, in regards to both the determination of moral rightness and the existence of an afterlife.

Smith's philosophy has its interest precisely because it unfolds as a crucial juncture in the process of secularization and modernization. It is fundamentally shaped by the ideas of Hume, but seems to recognize the limitations of Hume's enlightenment project when it comes to ethics and religion. Insofar as we are still wrestling with that project, Smith's philosophy repays careful study, for it reveals both its virtues[4] and its possible shortfalls.

I. SMITH'S "LETTER TO STRAHAN"

I begin with the context of Smith's letter to Strahan, not merely a private letter, but a deliberately public document, composed with the consent and approval of David Hume. So we must first, upon learning of the nature of the letter, ask, what was Smith's motivation in writing it? Given that it is no mere report of the facts of Hume's death but something that was to be published (and was published) as part of Hume's *My Own Life*, what was Smith trying to achieve? There are several possibilities, not each of them exclusive of one another, as I will show.

One possibility is that Smith simply saw himself as completing Hume's autobiography, adding in the final chapter of a book that was not yet complete. Mozart's *Requiem* remained unfinished at his death; it was left to other composers to complete it. To finish a work that remains unfinished by the master is a tribute to the master, but it may also be considered simply as necessary work. It is not clear that much creativity was required in finishing Hume's biography: all that was necessary was to lay out the facts of his final days. This may have been all that Smith thought he was doing.

But the analogy to Mozart is a weak one, for Hume's autobiography, as it stands, is substantially complete—that is, it is complete as a narrative (Hume did not, for example, die in the middle of composing it). Hume's *Life* does not leave us dangling, at least on first impression. Indeed, Hume himself writes at the head of his final paragraph, "To *conclude historically* with my own character" (*MOL*, xl; emphasis added). Hume himself saw the work (and the work of his life) as drawing to an appropriate close. Hume did not see the need for the work to be finished by another hand, because he had finished it himself. Any addition to it, then, might be seen more as a revision of the work rather than a completion of it. I will return to this point, below.

---

4   Cf. Griswold, *Adam Smith and the Virtues of Enlightenment*.

But perhaps no life can truly be complete until its death is taken into account, hence no one can truly write his own biography. This seems to be what Smith thought. One way of getting at death's importance for Smith is contained in Aristotle's remark, "count no man happy until he is dead".[5] A life considered as a whole must include the fortunes of a man not merely up to a point arbitrarily chosen by the man, but until the very end. And to properly consider this remark in the context of Hume's life, we have to look not only to the fame Hume won (or did not win), but more importantly, to his actions and attitudes before his death, for these take on immense importance in considering the success or failure of Hume's life as a whole. If this is true, then we are faced with the fact that an essential part of Hume's life cannot be recorded in his autobiography, and he will require someone else to finish his autobiography—thus Smith's letter *does* figure as an essential chapter in Hume's life, and his work would remain unfinished without it, because the story of his life would remain unfinished.

Let me pause to emphasize this fact, which is also the immensely practical fact that no one can write the account of his own passing, his own last days, and more particularly, his very act of dying. For in dying that person is no longer there to record his own life, his own reactions, and his own death. Hume cannot be in a position to record how he died, for the end of that dying process is his own death—death is not simply an event in one's life that one can look back on in relief or disgust.[6] This means that only another person, an outside observer, can do this. Smith is there to record what Hume cannot record himself—to write the ending of Hume's life when Hume is unable to do so. And if how one dies is an essential part of assessing one's life, of looking at it as a whole, then we are left with the paradoxical fact that a complete life can in the end not be written by the one living it, but only by another.[7] It is thus impossible that an autobiography can be complete in *this* sense.[8] Despite Hume's best efforts, he *can't* give his own "funeral oration". Paradoxically, a complete autobiography has to be a two person affair. Hume recognizes this, if indirectly, when he writes, "I am, *or rather was* (for that is the style I must now use in speaking of myself)" (*MOL*, xl; emphasis added). One cannot literally write from the perspective of one's death.

We need to establish some context for why Smith felt his writing the closing chapter of Hume's life was essential, and not just for the sake of aesthetic completeness, but to make the life properly a life, in the sense of a completed whole. For the familiar fact is that how Hume faced his death was of enormous

---

5   Cf. Aristotle, *Nichomachean Ethics*, Book I.
6   See Wittgenstein, *Tractatus Logico-Philosophicus*, 6.4311.
7   That person, ideally, would be a friend, in the sense of Aristotle's friend as "another self".
8   Unless, of course, it is written in heaven. This is a literary device used, e.g., in the recent novel by Alice Sebold, *The Lovely Bones*.

interest to the critical elite of Hume's day, especially the religious elite.[9] Hume was a reputed atheist, and if he showed fear in the face of death, this would not merely reflect poorly on Hume, but would reflect poorly more generally on the project of living a life without God and without the promise of an afterlife. To this extent, it *was* necessary to give a report of Hume's final days, if only to prove the religious enthusiasts mistaken about Hume's character. In fact, Hume lived his final days in tranquility and without hope of the Christian heaven to come. But as just intimated, more rode on Hume's death than merely his character: it was the very possibility of living a skeptical life with integrity. More was at stake than simply Hume's good name. It was a whole project.[10]

Smith's letter reveals that living an atheistic life was not merely possible, it was even desirable. Hume faced death with happiness and without fear. Thus Smith will write that Hume both in his life and in his death "approached the ideal of a perfectly wise and virtuous man, as perhaps the nature of human frailty will permit" ("Letter to Strahan" [*LTS*], xlix). It is only once we have taken Hume's death into account that we can see that his life displayed the meaning that was inherent in it. Fear of death, in Hume's case, would throw into doubt the meaning of Hume's life. It would also cast into doubt the possibility of leading a life without God. In Hume's case, it is not that he had a fortune that might be wiped out on the eve of his death, thus making his life an unhappy one; it is that he had made a claim about a kind of life that could be possible to live, one that would be tested up to the very moment of his death. If we ended merely with Hume's *Life*, we would have a cliffhanger. We would be left asking: how does it end?

Seen in this light, Smith's account of Hume's death is not a generous but ultimately superfluous tribute to Hume tacked onto the end of an aesthetically complete account of Hume's life. It is a defense against those who might speculate that Hume's project was an impossible one, to be sure, but at the same time, in fact, a completion of Hume's life, to show that Hume's life had

---

9   As the *Monthly Review* put it, "When men of such PARTS and such PRINCIPLES, as those which distinguished the character and writings of Mr. Hume, come to face the immediate terrors of death, the world is always curious to learn in what manner they support the trying conflict: whether the near approach of that awful change of situation which they are about to experience, (in an hour wherein one would think, the boldest mortal would not dare either to DISSEMBLE or to TRIFLE) has produced any change in their *minds*; whether they continue fixed, and stead to their past professions or, whether '*new light*' is let into 'the soul's dark cottage,' as the poet expresses it, 'through the chinks' of its ruins,—opening wider, at the moment when the batter'd fabric is tottering to its dissolution" (Fieser, 264–265).

10 Some people's projects may not be of this nature; of them, it may be possible to write their biographies before they are actually dead, for in some sense, they would have died already. Hume's project was not of this sort.

a shape and a purpose that was revealed perhaps most perfectly in his death. And, as discussed above, it was only an outsider who could do this, preferably a close friend, because Hume could not defend himself in this way, he could not be there to write the ending of his own life. So, in the end, Smith's letter is an integral part of the autobiography; as Smith himself felt, he would not and could not write something separate from it, but rather "*add* a few lines to [Hume's] account of [his] own life".[11]

II. SMITH'S OWN THEORY: REVISIONS

I have just argued that Smith's own letter to Strahan completes Hume's autobiography, which is something that, given the nature of the task, Hume could not do himself. Moreover, I have shown how Hume's dying well was essential to a particular type of project, viz., the project of living a meaningful life without God or the hope of a life after death. Smith's praise of Hume in living (and dying) this life is nearly unconditional: it is praise mixed with wonder not only that such a life was possible, but that Smith had the honor of being so close to the one who lived it.

Smith revealingly ends his letter to Strahan with the observation that people will disagree about Hume's philosophy, "every one approving, or condemning them, according as they happen to coincide or disagree with his own". But, Smith adds concerning Hume's character, "there can scarcely be a difference of opinion" (*LTS*, xlviii). Yet Smith must have known he was being naïve in supposing that all would agree on the greatness of Hume's character. He was perhaps being too trustful (or too hopeful) about how perceptive most public spectators would be. Indeed, as the publication of Smith's letter showed, there would be fierce disagreement about what Hume's character really was.

That disagreement about Hume's character took as its perhaps predictable target Smith's letter to Strahan. Smith wrote about the reception of that letter: "A single, and as I thought, a very harmless Sheet of paper which I happened to write concerning the death of our late friend, Mr. Hume, brought upon me ten times more abuse than the very violent attack I had made upon the whole commercial system of Great Britain."[12] Far from enhancing Hume's fame, Smith had compromised his own. By linking himself to Hume's notorious reputation, Smith had not succeeded in lifting Hume up, but in bringing himself down. Of course, Smith's remark that his letter was merely a harmless sheet

---

11 Smith to Hume, August 22, 1776. In an ironic counterpoint to a story that ends with a deathbed conversion, Hume's story ends with a *non*-conversion, and it is this non-conversion that gives Hume's life meaning, which, in its own way, redeems it. That is why it is essential to record it, in the same fashion as it would be essential to record, in a Christian narrative, the deathbed conversion of the sinner. I am indebted to Danny Priel for this point.

12 Quoted in Mossner, *The Life of David Hume*, 605.

of paper can be read as disingenuous. Smith was coming to the defense of a controversial figure, and he knew it. Nothing could be written about Hume, and in defense of Hume, that would not be grist for some controversy or other. But one might be surprised at the extent of the negative reaction Smith endured. Not only his assessment of Hume's character, but *even his assessment of the facts* would be called into question. One could hardly imagine a more jarring result, and more damning evidence that people are likely to judge everything (even simple facts) "variously, every one approving, or condemning them, according as they happen to coincide or disagree with his own" opinion.[13]

In this section and the next, I will look at how such an event can be viewed, not merely in Smith's assessment of Hume and the worth of literary fame, but in the context of his philosophy as a whole. Smith's ideas about ethics, it might be said, seem decisively shaped by a concern with what other people think.[14] One need only consider Smith's master idea, the impartial spectator, to see this. What is ethical is what would be approved by a person, standing impartially and judging the situation. Smith, in his own way, recognizes the importance of approval by the public, he in is own way is after the approval of spectators. My suggestion in this section is that this understanding of what approval consists in, whose approval matters, and how much it matters, changes in Smith, and (I speculate) changes in part due to the reaction to Hume's life and his death.

I do not want to tie changes in Smith's philosophy too closely to any particular event, and it is clear that the ideas I am about to present were already implicit in Smith prior to the death of Hume. But it stands to reason. Hume after all was Smith's close friend, and we should not assume that a person's philosophy changes only in response to his friend's ideas and not by his friend's life and experiences. What I am going to argue is that for Smith, the idea of an impartial spectator becomes increasingly *less* tied to the emotions and attitudes of people as they are, and more tied to people as they might be. The number of people who can qualify as impartial spectators becomes smaller and smaller to the point of being merely hypothetical. Those actually qualified to judge are few and far between, and the response to Hume confirms this.

Let us begin not with Smith's philosophy as a whole, but by considering

---

13 Evidence was adduced from Hume's "housekeeper" who testified that Hume, when alone, was extremely agitated and could not sleep. His calmness in the face of death was, in other words, a ruse, and Smith was Hume's dupe (Fieser, 322–324). Some were even willing to question Hume's tranquility *a priori*: "Those who allow themselves to understand human nature as it really is, cannot help suspecting that all this specious tranquility must have been affected" (Fieser, 406).

14 See, e.g., David Marshall, who writes that *TMS* "explores the role of sympathy in a world where people face each other as spectators and spectacles" ("Adam Smith and the Theatricality of Moral Sentiments", 592).

the important, but still relatively neglected, section of *TMS* on our "irregularity of sentiments". For it is here that we can sense perhaps most clearly that Smith knew the limits of public sentiment as a reliable judge. The problem with our sentiments, Smith says, is that they are misled by the consequences of events. We see someone who has accomplished a great thing, and we assume that he has intended to do that great thing; it is likewise with those who cause great harm to befall another person. We assume that this was what was intended by the person all along. But these can be mistaken assumptions. The person who did a good deed might not have intended it; the person who has caused harm may have mistakenly caused harm. Our judgments might be wrongly influenced, then, by a person's good or bad *luck*. And this is a mistake, Smith says. We should be judging by one's intentions.

So Smith thinks that our sentiments are irregular, at least in this one domain of feeling. But we can consider this irregularity also in light of Smith's theory of moral sentiments as a whole. For Smith, in this short chapter, recognizes that our sentiments, even the sentiments of the best among us, can be *systematically* misguided. We seem to be built in a way that causes us to misjudge people, and to misjudge them badly. Now, Smith thinks that such factually mistaken sentiments can be justified in the end. What the exact nature of this justification is, I cannot consider now.[15] More important is the recognition that people are not just wrong *some* of the time, but that they can be wrong *all* of the time. This seems to present a prima facie problem for someone who wants to ground morals in the reactions of spectators.

What is interesting for my purposes is one of the remedies Smith suggests to this systematic misperception, the misperception based on the "irregularity of our sentiments" regarding people's true intentions. The remedy comes in a passage at the end of the chapter on our irregular sentiments, and it addresses the plight of the individual who has been wrongly judged. It is hard not to read this passage without thinking that Smith had Hume's circumstances distinctly in mind. The problem the passage considers is what consolation we might have if we intend to do good for mankind, but our good intentions are not recognized for what they are. In this case, Smith says, we do not have reason to despair, because there is something we can turn to. The person who has been slighted, or ignored, or misunderstood can strive "to regard himself, not in the light in which he at present appears, but in that in which he ought to appear, in which he would have appeared had his generous designs been crowned with success, and in which he would still appear, not withstanding their miscarriage".[16] Can we not view this passage in the light of Hume's *Treatise of Human Nature*,

---

15 See Flanders, "'This Irregularity of Sentiments'".

16 *TMS*, 108. The consolation here, we should note, is not unlike what Smith refers to as "religious consolation". I consider religious consolation in the next part of my paper.

the book that failed to win the success Hume so desired, and instead miscarried, in falling "stillborn from the press"?

I introduce the discussion of luck to focus on one place where Smith is faced with a problem: the attitudes of spectators matter, but they are not always right, so what do we do with them? The answer Smith offers is to refine and clarify whose opinion really matters. In this case, it is the "more candid and humane part of mankind" who are the real test of something's worth, and not the majority of men whose sentiments are, Smith admits, "irregular". But the problem, as Smith recognizes in successive drafts of TMS, is that mankind's irregular sentiments are not just confined to one part of moral life—judging intentions in light of consequences—but are pervasive in moral life. We are therefore not just talking about the fact that sometimes people get things wrong, but that most people are likely to be at some risk of getting things wrong all the time. So there is a general problem with trying to ground a moral philosophy in the reactions of others when there is good reason to believe those reactions will be mistaken if not all of the time, then most of the time.

It is in this light that we should read the tortured revisions Smith makes to TMS in the sixth edition. Very roughly, we can identify three phases in the evolution of TMS: first, where the impartial moral spectator is closely aligned to what people actually think, so that the wise man is anxious to conform to people's actual judgments;[17] the second where the impartial spectator is a "demigod" who appears as the judge of mankind, but is yet an independent standard from god himself, and who is anyway called on only occasionally to intervene to correct the judgments of mankind;[18] and finally a third stage where the judgment of a man is sound only insofar as it corresponds to the judgment of God. What we see in this progression is increasingly a "detachment from life", to use Hume's phrase in My Own Life, that is, a detachment from relying on human judgment, even human judgment that is abstracted in measure from the immediate reactions of mankind. In the end the only tribunal that matters, because it is the only tribunal that is not pervasively marred by error, is God's tribunal. For only God's tribunal looks consistently and truly to a man's praise- or blame-worthiness. And man's judgment, according to this third view of the impartial spectator, is good only insofar as it acts in accord with divine judgment. It is no longer the case that the principles of praise and blame are tethered to anything like actual praise and blame, but instead, "the jurisdictions of those two tribunals [that is, of human and divine] are founded upon principles which, though in some respects resembling and akin, are, however, in reality different and distinct" (TMS, 130). This last line was written in the sixth edition of the

---

17 See, e.g., Campbell, who sees Smith's impartial spectator as representing "the average, or normal or ordinary man" (*Adam Smith's Science of Morals*, 134).

18 This change was prompted by Gilbert Elliot's comments on the first edition of *TMS*. See Smith's "Letter to Gilbert Elliot", October 1759.

book, the last edition Smith revised, and the only edition published after Hume's death.

It would take me too far afield to prove this conjecture in any great detail, although I think it can be proven. What seems clear from that discussion is that in the years succeeding Hume's death, as Raphael writes, "Smith had become even more skeptical of popular opinion".[19] The idea that man's judgments, and even man's reflective judgments, could be the sound basis for ethics comes under greater and greater pressure from Smith until it is all but abandoned. It is not hard to imagine that this was done, in part, by a reaction to the treatment of Hume after Hume's death and even to the treatment of Smith. Consider again Smith's statement about the reaction to his letter. Not only is Smith abused for what he had written about Hume, but perhaps more significantly, people are concerned about the wrong thing: Smith had attacked the whole economic system of Britain, but this did not create so much a furor as his "harmless" letter about Hume. Smith had come to distrust human opinion, and his response was to place more and more the basis of ethics in something outside of the human, in God. The impartial spectator, to put the point polemically, turns out to be God.[20]

III. ADAM SMITH AND THE LIMITS OF ENLIGHTENMENT

But Smith's philosophy has a further wrinkle, and one that puts him even more directly at odds with Hume. For it is clear that Smith believed in an afterlife and Hume did not. Moreover, the belief in an afterlife can be tied to Smith's disillusionment with the public. One deserves fame, but one will never get it in this life; thus, it is proper to hope for fame in the afterlife. Smith certainly believed that faith in the afterlife afforded this consolation: the just would be rewarded in heaven. Ironically, it was the death of an atheist that perhaps confirmed Smith in his devout hope that there is a place where men might receive the rewards that the public was too stingy to give them in this life. The unjust reaction to Hume reaffirms Smith in his commitment to religion.[21]

In calling Hume the wisest and most just, Smith was making an obvious comparison to Socrates: Socrates, too, was the wisest and most just. But in making this comparison Smith surely must have been aware that Hume's composure in the face of death was even more remarkable. The *Phaedo*, at least

---

19 Raphael, "Introduction", to *TMS*, 16.
20 Man's judgments are correct, then, insofar as they correspond to God's. It thus follows that if my conjecture about the trajectory of Smith's thought is correct, Smith came less and less to see the impartial spectator as *constitutive* of true judgments. But cf. Griswold, *Adam Smith and the Virtues of Enlightenment*, 145.
21 I find little support for the claim that Smith was a closet atheist. For a good summary of how religion pervaded Smith's thought, see Schneewind, *The Invention of Autonomy*.

as conventionally read, shows Socrates as having a belief in the immortality of the soul, whether a well-reasoned belief or not.[22] Hume, however, did not believe in the afterlife, as his posthumously published essay demonstrates quite clearly. Hume, then, faces his death with only the satisfaction of a life well lived behind him, and no hope of futurity. By facing *this* prospect with calm and equanimity, Smith was able to portray Hume as a hero dying quietly in his own bed.[23]

Smith, by contrast, as Jerry Evensky notes, "enjoyed the comfort of faith".[24] We can see this solely in a negative light, especially given Hume's experience. Friends are finite: they cannot make sure that one's legacy endures forever. Still less are the many to be trusted with appreciating Hume's genius and keeping it alive. Better to trust in an afterlife to guarantee that one will never die rather than to trust that one's fame will carry one past the grave. And indeed, Smith repeatedly refers to the consolations that religion gives us. We can then see Smith's belief in an afterlife as just this: a comfort for the weak. Hume was stronger. It is easy to give this cynical interpretation of Smith; the interpretation is, in its own way, very Humean. We might believe it were it not for Smith's close friendship with Hume.

For it also seems clear that Smith is driven to God out of his philosophical commitments (it is present there from the first editions of *TMS*) and he believes that our motives for believing in an afterlife are not just based on our lower motives, such as a desire for self-preservation or selfish reward. Nor, as Hume alleged, was belief in an afterlife to be understood as deriving outside of our nature and natural sentiments, as an artificial product of the gospels.[25] Smith interestingly sees the afterlife as justified by our nobler sentiments, our sentiments that the world be just, and people be treated as they deserve, if not immediately, then ultimately. We can see this by examining in detail a passage that Smith inserted in the final edition of *TMS*, one almost entirely concerned with the afterlife. Surely Smith knew of Hume's disbelief in the afterlife (*TMS*, 120–134). One can therefore read this extended passage as Smith's final dialogue with Hume.

Smith begins with several striking examples of the problem I have just discussed in the last part: many times men will not be recognized for what they have done, and are falsely the object of blame. He acknowledges the distress that

---

22 Socrates professes dissatisfaction with all of the proffered arguments, but nonetheless *that* he believed in the immortality of the soul seems to be taken as a given.

23 Cf. *TMS*, 238.

24 Evensky, *Adam Smith's Moral Philosophy*, 108. I am much indebted to Evensky's brief but extremely insightful account of Hume and Smith on the afterlife.

25 In his essay, "Of the Immortality of the Soul", Hume writes, "[I]n reality, it is the gospel and the gospel alone, that has brought life and immortality to light" (*Essays*, 590).

this can cause, the disappointment, the frustration of feeling that men will not see you for what you are, and how this is "capable of mortifying so severely men of the soundest and best judgment". Smith writes, apropos of these examples, that the "humble philosophy that confines its views to this life, can afford, perhaps, but little consolation". The earth, to employ a phrase of Montaigne's is an imperfect garden, and we cannot hope that it will have in itself the resources to give us comfort for the wrongs that have been done to us. Religion, on the other hand, Smith says, can give us the comfort that we seek: it can give us a vision of another world, a better world, where the virtuous may find themselves at home, "a world of more candour, humanity, and justice, than the present [and] where virtue" will finally be rewarded (*TMS*, 120).

What concludes the chapter is nothing short of an amalgamation of Hume and religious thought. Or to put it another way: it is Smith's way of splitting the difference between Hume and Christianity. Following fast upon the idea that God's judgment is the one that is the most authoritative, Smith says that we are led by our noblest sentiments to believe that justice will be done in the next world, where God will be the judge, if it is not done in this one. The thought of an afterlife is the thought of the noble and moral man, and not the thought of the one who is fearful of punishment or who lives in another world and not our own. The belief in an afterlife is a belief that is founded (*contra* Hume) at the "roots of human nature".[26] Moreover, the virtuous man, Smith writes, who has the "misfortune to doubt" of an afterlife, "cannot possibly avoid wishing most earnestly and anxiously to believe it" (*TMS*, 132).

The argument here is one that we have come to associate with Kant.[27] A belief in the afterlife is not something we can know, but it is a worthy object of hope—a hope that those who were dutiful in this life may eventually find happiness. The argument seems to have its origin in Smith, although with Smith we have an obviously sentimentalist gloss on it: we are led to believe in immortality not necessarily as an idea of reason (though we can see the reason behind it) but by our noble sentiments of justice. But Smith here takes sentiments seriously, and works from them to an understanding of life after death: he is working from Humean premises to a decidedly non-Humean result.

But if the belief in the afterlife is non-Humean, what follows and what ends the chapter is pure Hume. For once we have established that there is an afterlife and that there the virtuous will be rewarded, we have still left to us the task of defining *who* the virtuous are. And this the Christians have gotten almost

---

26 In his essay on the soul, Hume denies that our passions which lead us to posit an afterlife are "original" (598).

27 Strictly speaking, Kant says we may rationally hope for *God's existence*, not an afterlife, because we should hope that happiness and virtue will be joined. For a recent exposition of Kant's argument, see William Wainwright, *Religion and Morality*, 18.

entirely backwards. Those who will be rewarded in the afterlife are those who have worked and suffered in ordinary life, not those who have given themselves over to mortification of the flesh, isolated in cells. In pretending that *they* will be rewarded in the afterlife, they allege something that is "surely contrary to all our moral sentiments". Rather, it is those such as the "statesmen and lawgivers, all the poets and philosophers" who shall be rewarded in the life to come, for they have "contributed to the subsistence, to the convenience, or to the ornament of human life" (*TMS*, 134). Hume himself wondered, "Shall we therefore erect an elysium for poets and heroes, like that of the ancient mythology?"[28] And here Hume has his answer from Smith: Yes. At least, this is something for which we might reasonably hope. So what we have is the picture of an afterlife, an immortal life, a non-Humean conclusion, which is tied to the idea that the most appropriate inhabitant of such other world would be none other than David Hume!

I began this last section by noting the oft-noticed comparison of Smith's final judgment on Hume with the judgment of Plato on Socrates. But now we may perhaps see another Platonic similarity. It has been argued that the *Republic* is in a sense a response to the death of Socrates: Plato was creating a republic in which what happened to Socrates would not be repeated.[29] Philosophers would be kings rather than being ruled by the many. Smith takes this same idea but puts it into a metaphysical key. The revisions in *TMS* are likewise a response to the death of the master. In Smith's afterlife, Hume will get the recognition he deserves, but was never fully granted in this life.

What this leads to is the odd result that while the death of Hume seems to have driven many changes in Smith's philosophy, Hume's life itself remains somewhat inexplicable in its own terms. Smith writes that a belief in an afterlife "alone can support" the lofty ideas man has of his own dignity and allow man to "maintain his cheerfulness" in his own life (*TMS*, 132). Hume had none of these things, but died cheerfully. He had no wish to believe in another life, a belief to which Smith says the virtuous man is almost inexorably drawn. No wonder Smith was in awe of him. In this light, perhaps, a different description of Socrates is more apt: "of this strange being you will never be able to find any likeness, however remote, either among men who now are or who ever have been".[30]

---

28 "Of the Immortality of the Soul", 594.
29 See, e.g., Myles Burnyeat, "The Impiety of Socrates".
30 Plato, *Symposium* (trans. Jowett).

CONCLUSION

My essay began with Smith's praise of Hume in a letter written after Hume's death. I argued that Smith's letter was not merely some extra praise heaped upon Hume, but was instead a crucial part of Hume's autobiography: we needed to know the ending of Hume's life in order to properly judge whether Hume had succeeded in living a life without God with integrity. I ended with Smith's version of an afterlife, which crucially includes a place for those who, like Hume, have not been recognized with the fame they deserved in this life but who yet stand as benefactors to humankind. Smith seemed to think that such a belief was not merely based on fear of death, but one we are led to by our noblest sentiments. As the developments in Smith's philosophy after Hume's death show, we should not confuse Smith's respect for Hume as a person with an agreement with Hume's philosophy or even with a desire to live life the way Hume did. It may ironically have been the reception that greeted Smith's praise of Hume that led Smith to move his philosophy in unHumean directions. I hasten to add that I have shown that Smith had passable arguments for changing his philosophy, or at least for deepening its metaphysical commitments. But I also think that we should not ignore the great impetus that the death of Hume might have played in Smith's own philosophical development. Hume's greatest impact on Smith might have been greater in his death than in his life.[31]

SELECT BIBLIOGRAPHY

Burnyeat, Myles. "The Impiety of Socrates". *Ancient Philosophy* 17 (1997): 1–12.

Campbell, Tom. *Adam Smith's Science of Morals*. London: Allen and Unwin, 1971.

Evensky, Jerry, *Adam Smith's Moral Philosophy*. Cambridge: Cambridge University Press, 2005.

Fieser, James. *Early Responses to Hume's Moral, Literary, and Political Writings*. Bristol: Thoemmes Press, 1999.

Flanders, Chad. "'This Irregularity of Sentiments': Adam Smith on Moral Luck". In *New Voices on Adam Smith*, edited by Leonidas Montes and Eric Schliesser. Abingdon: Routledge, 2006, 193–218.

---

31 I am grateful to Eric Schliesser for extremely helpful correspondence and lengthy comments on an earlier draft. Danny Priel and Justin Tiwald helped me to clarify my argument at crucial points.

Griswold, Charles L., Jr. *Adam Smith and the Virtues of Enlightenment.* Cambridge: Cambridge University Press, 1999.

Hume, David. "My Own Life". In *Essays: Moral, Political and Literary*, revised edition, edited by Eugene F. Miller. Indianapolis: Liberty Fund, 1985.

———. "Of the Immortality of the Soul". In *Essays: Moral, Political and Literary*, revised edition, edited by Eugene F. Miller. Indianapolis: Liberty Fund, 1985.

———. *A Treatise of Human Nature*, 2nd ed. With an analytical index by L. A. Selby-Bigge. With text revised and notes by P. H. Nidditch. Oxford: Oxford University Press, 1978.

Marshall, David. "Adam Smith and the Theatricality of Moral Sentiments". *Critical Inquiry* 10 (1984): 592–613.

Mossner, Ernest C. *The Life of David Hume*, 2nd ed. Oxford: Oxford University Press, 1980.

Raphael, D. D. "Introduction" to Adam Smith, *The Theory of Moral Sentiments*, edited by D. D. Raphael and A. L. Macfie. Indianapolis: Liberty Fund, 1982, 1–52.

Schliesser, Eric. "Obituary of a Vain Philosopher: Adam Smith's Reflections on Hume's Life". *Hume Studies* 29, no.2 (2003): 327–362.

Schneewind, J. B. *The Invention of Autonomy.* Cambridge: Cambridge University Press, 1998.

Sebold, Alice. *The Lovely Bones.* New York: Little Brown, 2002.

Smith, Adam. "Letter to David Hume". In *The Correspondence of Adam Smith*, edited by Ernest Campbell Mosner and Ian Simpson Ross. Indianapolis: Liberty Fund, 1987.

———. "Letter to Gilbert Elliot". In *The Correspondence of Adam Smith*, edited by Ernest Campbell Mosner and Ian Simpson Ross. Indianapolis: Liberty Fund, 1987.

———. "Letter to Strahan". In David Hume, *Essays: Moral, Political and Literary*, revised edition, edited by Eugene F. Miller. Indianapolis: Liberty Fund, 1985.

———. *The Theory of Moral Sentiments*. Edited by D. D. Raphael and A. L. Macfie. Indianapolis: Liberty Fund, 1982.

Wainwright, William. *Religion and Morality*. Aldershot: Ashgate Publishing, 2005.

Wittgenstein, Ludwig. *Tractatus Logico-Philosophicus*. London: Harcourt, Brace & Company, 1922.

"A DELICATE AND AN ACCURATE PENCIL":
ADAM SMITH, DESCRIPTION, AND PHILOSOPHY AS MORAL PEDAGOGY

Colin Heydt

I. INTRODUCTION

In the mid-18th century, Scottish aristocrats, intellectuals, and members of the professional classes were focused on removing remnants of their nation's cultural, intellectual, moral, and economic backwardness. These elites thought of themselves, as Phillipson puts it, "as agents of improvement who would modernise their province by means of energetic, intelligent and public-spirited leadership and draw it from a state of rudeness to one of cosmopolitan refinement" ("Towards a Definition of the Scottish Enlightenment", 127).[1]

One question raised by the Scottish elite's emphasis on improvement is what role they took moral philosophy in particular to play. It is not a question that has gone unnoticed by commentators. Recent years have seen a variety of authors examining Scottish moral philosophy through the lens of "practical ethics".[2] Phillipson, Sher, Haakonssen, and Griswold, among others, have emphasized the ways in which Scots like Smith, Reid, Ferguson, and Stewart should be interpreted as practical ethicists striving to improve their students, parishioners, and readers.[3]

This paper picks up on this strand of interpretation in the Scottish Enlightenment and analyzes Smith's *The Theory of Moral Sentiments* (*TMS*) in order to understand how the work functions as moral pedagogy.

The idea that some kinds of philosophical prose have the capacity to bring about ethical improvement is at the heart of Adam Smith's *The Theory of Moral Sentiments*, though Smith draws a distinction between the help we can expect from works in jurisprudence and that which we can expect from works in

---

1   Bibliographic information for all references can be found in the Select Bibliography at the end of this essay.

2   Dugald Stewart claims that the "practical doctrines of morality comprehend all those rules of conduct which profess to point out the proper ends of human pursuit and the most effectual means of attaining them; to which we may add all those literary compositions, whatever be their particular form, which have for their aim to fortify and animate our good dispositions, by delineations of the beauty, of the dignity, or of the utility of Virtue" (in Adam Smith, *Essays on Philosophical Subjects*, 278).

3   A sample of these works includes Phillipson, "Adam Smith as Civic Moralist"; Sher, "Professors of Virtue"; Haakonssen, "Introduction" to Thomas Reid, *Practical Ethics*; and Griswold, *Adam Smith and the Virtues of Enlightenment*.

ethics.[4] In jurisprudence, an author can provide precise and accurate rules that tell us exactly what we must do in order to be just in particular circumstances. In ethics, on the contrary, all we can hope for are "loose, vague, and indeterminate" rules for how to be, for example, benevolent or generous (*TMS*, VII.iv.1).

The "ancient moralists" provide the best example of writing in ethics, Smith claims, because they have "contented themselves with describing in a general manner the different vices and virtues, and with pointing out the deformity and misery of the one disposition as well as the propriety and happiness of the other" (*TMS*, VII.iv.3). Their texts "present us with agreeable and lively pictures of manners" that have the capacity to improve the reader by motivating us to be virtuous and by helping "both to correct and to ascertain our natural sentiments with regard to the propriety of conduct". In other words, the texts of ancient moralists both "inflame our natural love of virtue, and increase our abhorrence of vice" and foster more discerning "moral sentiments" that improve the propriety of our conduct (*TMS*, VII.iv.6).

Since *The Theory of Moral Sentiments* is itself a work in ethics rather than jurisprudence, it is not surprising that Smith would follow the lead of the ancient moralists, whose descriptions of virtues and vices he applauds. In order to begin identifying and analyzing the therapeutic features of *TMS*, therefore, this essay scrutinizes Smith's descriptions of a particular virtue and vice with an eye to what the text tries to communicate *to*, and elicit *from*, the reader.

II. RESERVATIONS

Though there is a general enthusiasm for speaking of the Scots as practical moralists, there are a number of reasons why we should be cautious in taking *TMS* as supporting that narrative. The first reason for caution is that Smith wrote a treatise. With some important exceptions, 18th-century treatises tended to have much less to do with moral improvement than works in other genres. Orations, historical works, epic poems, tragedies, comedies, miscellanies, familiar essays, letters, philosophical dialogues, prose satires, sermons, courtesy books, pamphlets, political songs, folktales, and political lectures normally have a greater claim to serving moral and political purposes than does the treatise.[5] Of course, many of these genres would have been entirely unsuited to Smith. He was neither a minister nor a dramatist. He enjoyed poetry but did not write it.

---

4 Stewart characterizes *TMS* as "those speculations of his earlier years, in which he aimed more professedly at the advancement of human improvement and happiness" (in Smith, *Essays on Philosophical Subjects*, 314).

5 This is especially true when one remembers the mid-18th century as one of the high points of didactic fiction. Some sources for this list of major 18th-century literary genres are Howell, *Eighteenth-Century British Logic and Rhetoric*, 535; Prince, *Philosophical Dialogue in the British Enlightenment*, 24–25; and Duff, "Antididacticism as a Contested Principle in Romantic Aesthetics", 264.

Nevertheless, if Smith was particularly focused on writing works that served as vehicles for moral improvement, a number of genres seem to have been better suited to that goal, namely the essay, the dialogue, and the history (ones his friend Hume had employed).

Second, if we examine some of the philosophical writings of the ancients that Smith lauds, we see that they are more explicitly directed to improving the reader, in part because they are committed, in a way Smith is not, to a substantive moral ideal—the sage. These ancient essays, handbooks, discourses, dialogues, and meditations provide, as Pierre Hadot puts it, "spiritual exercises" that promote self-realization and improvement. All spiritual exercises, whether of the Stoic, Epicurean, or Platonic variety, "are, fundamentally, a return to the self, in which the self is liberated from the state of alienation into which it has been plunged by worries, passions, and desires" (Hadot, *Philosophy as a Way of Life*, 103). The spiritual exercises of the Stoic, for example, focus on delineating the true boundaries of the self—what is "up to us". This requires work on the three basic kinds of activity of the soul: judgment, desire, and impulse or inclination to action (dealt with by logic, physics, and ethics respectively) (Hadot, *Philosophy*, 193). Since each of these faculties of the soul depends on us in ways that perception and nutrition do not, we can discipline them. The exercises that someone like Epictetus provides are meant to assist us in disciplining ourselves— in engaging in self-formation on the model of the Stoic sage. The exercises that build habits of desiring and judging are joined with a variety of sayings, advice, and exhortations, all directed at promoting progress towards the human ideal.

Smith's differences with the ancients can be illuminated by Haakonssen's observation that, for Smith, "[b]ecause of the individuality and, not least, the uncertainty of man's life, it is impossible to formulate a universal idea of the highest good or, more generally, the good life. As a consequence, the virtues that promote the goods of life can be characterized only in very general terms and, across cultural and historical divides, this may amount to little more than family resemblance" (Haakonssen, "Introduction", viii–ix).[6] In this respect, Smith shares enough with Montaigne to see differences as often more characteristic of nature than similarities. So though Smith speaks well of ancient writings, their mode of making philosophy practical is not one he repeats.

Another reason for skepticism about the moral, rather than intellectual, value of Smith's text comes from one of his contemporaries. William Thom, a minister in Glasgow, accused Smith and his predecessors in the Chair of Moral

---

6   In a related vein, Phillipson observes ("Adam Smith as Civic Moralist", 181) that "Hume's revolutionary insight [which Smith drew upon] was an injunction to serious moralists to shift their attention from the study of ends to the study of means; to the principles which explain how we acquire moral sentiments and ideas of virtue and to the lessons which a virtuously minded agent could hope to draw from a study of his own moral history and that of mankind in general".

Philosophy of being not nearly practical enough. In 1761, while Smith taught at the university, Thom questioned the value of teaching students theories concerning the foundation of morality: "Might not the time be better spent in teaching them morality, in explaining the nature of the particular virtues? Would not this be more adapted to the capacity of the scholars [students], and incomparably more useful to them through the whole of life?" If the aim of an education should be "to make the youth good men and useful subjects; to prepare them to acquit themselves well in the particular business they are to live by, and to make a manly and decent figure in the companies they may be in", why waste time on abstruse debates concerning morality's foundations? Thom argued that a commercial people needs—along with training in practical mathematics, history, geography, and history of commerce—instruction in "practical morality". Professors should describe "the particular virtues". After all, "[t]o know what virtue is, is useful to men in every station of life; but who is the better for having heard or understood a great many subtle disputes about its origin?" ("Letter to J__ M__, Esq.", 267–268; 274–275).[7]

The textual analysis of *TMS* that follows will reveal the kinds of moral pretensions one can safely assign to Smith's main work in moral philosophy, even as we keep these cautions in mind.

III. SMITH AND THE DEPICTION OF VIRTUE AND VICE

Smith, who lectured on literary style and who paid very careful attention to literary technique, stands as an especially self-aware writer.[8] Appreciating how *TMS* might function therapeutically demands that we attend to those features of the text that structure how the reader experiences it—particularly what she learns from it and how she reacts to it.[9] At the beginning, then, it is essential to distance ourselves from the familiar philosophical style Smith employs in order to recognize the choices Smith makes (and those he rejects) in writing the text.

This section analyzes Smith's descriptions of one virtue and one vice, namely those of prudence and ambition. These are character traits particularly

---

7 For more on Thom, see Donovan, "Evangelical Humanism in Glasgow".

8 Winch notes, for example, that Smith's essay on astronomy and his lectures on rhetoric and belles-lettres, "show that Smith held sophisticated theories [...] about [...] the didactic and rhetorical conventions which govern scientific, historical, and other forms of discourse" ("Adam Smith's 'Enduring Particular Result'", 254).

9 The literature on reader-response theory is voluminous. For a somewhat dated, but still helpful, survey of the basic positions in the field, see Tompkins (ed.), *Reader Response Criticism*. It should also be noted that features of the text are not the only things that structure the reader's experiences. Features of the physical books themselves (e.g., format [folio, quarto, octavo], presentation of the author, binding, etc.) also contribute to how the work is read. See Sher, *The Enlightenment and the Book*, chap. 1.

central to modern commercial society and, more importantly, are examples drawn from two different sections of *TMS*, namely the analysis of moral judgment (Parts I–V) and the analysis of virtue (Part VI). As we shall see, the descriptions of prudence (Part VI) and ambition (Part IV) differ in ways that ultimately indicate differences in the practical purposes served by these two sections of *TMS*.

Prudence

Prudence, a virtue of the selfish passions, and one of Smith's four cardinal virtues along with justice, benevolence, and self-command, is of special importance for market societies.[10] It is the virtue of commercial relations, and it promotes clean, efficient interactions without the social and emotional entanglements accompanying benevolence and gratitude. Its proper business is the "care of the health, of the fortune, of the rank and reputation of the individual" (*TMS*, VI.i.5).

Smith's depiction of the prudent man is dominated by characterizations of the prudent man's conduct along with the general principles that help to account for that conduct. The prudent man is "always sincere" though "not always frank and open". He is "cautious in his actions" rather than enterprising, and "reserved in his speech". He cultivates "sedate, but steady and faithful attachment to a few well-tried and well-chosen companions; in the choice of whom he is not guided by the giddy admiration of shining accomplishments, but by the sober esteem of modesty, discretion, and good conduct" (*TMS*, VI.i.8–9).

The prudent man depends for his success on the reality of his own abilities rather than the appearance of them. He

> always studies seriously and earnestly to understand whatever he professes to understand, and not merely to persuade other people that he understands it; and though his talents may not always be very brilliant, they are always perfectly genuine. He neither endeavours to impose upon you by the cunning devices of an artful impostor, nor by the arrogant airs of an assuming pedant, nor by the confident assertions of a superficial and imprudent pretender. He is not ostentatious even of the abilities which he really possesses. [*TMS*, VI.i.7]

The description of the prudent man goes for two and a half more pages,

---

10 See Donald Winch's statement that "it was Smith's view that the scope for prudence and wisdom increased rather than diminished with the development of society into its more complex forms" ("Adam Smith's 'Enduring Particular Result'", 260).

but these excerpts satisfactorily represent the nature and tone of the description. We learn what things prudent people generally do, the principles that organize their conduct, and what social relationships they pursue.

Smith's writing attempts to strike a balance between concreteness and abstraction. Smith relies on the tradition of the character sketch running from Theophrastus to Hall, Overbury, Earle, and La Bruyere, in order to substitute a discussion of the *prudent man* for *prudence* in general, thereby ensuring that the description retains an element of the concrete.[11] He wants, in other words, to depict a *typified individual* with the quality of prudence rather than the *quality itself*. Smith's literary and philosophical strategy comes out more clearly when it is contrasted with one (Reid's) that uses more abstract language and one (Addison's) that uses more concrete language.

Use of the relatively concrete device of "the prudent man" contrasts Smith's description to the depiction of prudence found in Thomas Reid's lectures on practical ethics and jurisprudence given at the University of Glasgow in the late 1760s. In his notes for these lectures, Reid discusses prudence when treating three of the four cardinal virtues (under the description of duties to ourselves). Though the notes can be rather schematic, leaving us to imagine what Reid's actual lecture was like, the text sets prudence within an ordered array or taxonomy of different virtues and vices. He defines prudence for his young students as "the choice of the proper means for the attainment of our Ends" (*Practical Ethics*, 130).[12] He goes on, in the tradition of natural law pedagogy (and of Aristotle in the *Nicomachean Ethics*), to list those traits from which prudence should be distinguished, including cunning, craft, and dissimulation on the one hand and simplicity and folly on the other. In Reid's description, the basic goal is to get the student to comprehend the nature of prudence itself abstracted from its embodiment in particular instances. Reid's text offers a map of the moral world, oriented by the landmarks that are duties and virtues.

Although Smith's description strives for a level of concreteness, it also maintains some abstractness, which is brought out when we compare Smith's prudent man with an excerpt from Addison's character sketch of the

---

11 For a very good history of the character sketch tradition, see Smeed, *The Theophrastian "Character"*.

12 In discussing Reid, Haakonssen notes that, whereas the theory of morals "is the part of pneumatology that explains how the mind is an active power" (i.e., how morals is possible for beings like us), practical ethics, or morals "is not in the same way explanatory; it is, rather, a taxonomic discipline that systematically arranges the principles of our duty and thus provides a map of the network of typical offices that constitute the moral world" ("Introduction", 58). A practical system of morals is meant, as Reid puts it in his *Essays on the Active Powers of Man*, to be like a system of botany or mineralogy and "to facilitate apprehension and memory" (Essay V, Chapter 2).

newsmonger published in *The Tatler* 155 (April 6, 1710):

> Upon my Enquiry into his Life and Conversation, I found him to be the greatest Newsmonger in our Quarter; that he rose before Day to read the *Post-Man*; and that he would take Two or Three Turns to the other End of the Town before his Neighbours were up, to see if there were any *Dutch* Mails come in. He had a Wife and several Children; but was much more inquisitive to know what passed in *Poland* than in his own Family, and was in greater Pain and Anxiety of Mind for King *Augustus*'s Welfare than that of his nearest Relations.

Differences between Addison's and Smith's descriptions indicate differences in the kinds of moral work the texts can do. First, while the prudent man never engages in specific acts or utterances, the newsmonger discusses Poland, reads the *Post-Man*, and worries about King Augustus. By vividly rendering particular actions, Addison's satire triggers the reader's moral imagination and judgment more readily ("What?! The newsmonger ignores his child's health while concerning himself with a foreign king's?"), and the concreteness allows Addison to deploy the literary technique of having the narrator and newsmonger interact. This turns the reader into a confederate who shares in the narrator's contempt for the newsmonger. The greater abstractness of Smith's text, on the contrary, restricts the capacity of the reader's moral imagination to put itself in the other's situation and render judgments concerning his conduct.

Second, Addison's sketch is written "for the particular Benefit of those worthy Citizens who live more in a Coffee-house than in their Shops, and whose Thoughts are so taken up with the Affairs of the Allies, that they forget their Customers" (*Tatler* 155). This reveals a didactic purpose more rooted in time and place—War of the Spanish Succession-era Britain—than we get from Smith's treatise. Instead, the abstractness of Smith's description indicates that the type of person Smith depicts is not specific to one culture or time, which is a result Smith presumably desired. It makes his analysis less subject to a charge of parochialism.

Thus we see that the choice Smith makes concerning how concretely or abstractly to pitch his description of the prudent man provides interesting clues about what moral work the text might do. Smith is not as interested as Reid is in providing a map or taxonomy for the reader, and he avoids the requisite abstraction. But his text also avoids the level of concreteness one finds in Addison's, thereby indicating that Smith's text both interferes with the reader making moral judgments about the prudent man and situates the reader within a less limited horizon of time and place than does Addison's description of the newsmonger.

If the text assiduously avoids descriptions of prudence with the specificity that elicits moral judgment and the generality suitable to prudence treated in abstraction, what moral work might it do? Most importantly, the text seems well situated to develop the reader's discernment. That is, it seems designed to improve the reader's capacity to correctly identify the prudent man in particular instances, by pointing out the marks (e.g., conduct, principles of action, social relationships) that distinguish the prudent man from those character types with whom he is easily confused (e.g., lucky people, cunning people, misers, controlling people, average people without notable prudence, etc.). This conjecture about Smith's text gains support from his claim that the analogous works of ancient philosophers draw, with "a delicate and an accurate pencil", the sentiment of the heart, which constitutes the essence of virtue, and that this picture "though it will always be in many respects incomplete, may, however, have such a resemblance as to make us know the original when we meet with it, and even distinguish it from other sentiments to which it has a considerable resemblance" (*TMS*, VII.iv.4). Thus, Smith's description of prudence, like its ancient counterparts, enables us to know a virtue and the associated sentiment well enough to be able to differentiate them from those that resemble them.

Refined discernment more readily enables the reader to avoid mistakes—mistakes in identifying people as what they truly are. Whether it is mistaking the flatterer for the friend or the cunning man for the prudent one, these misidentifications can have real consequences (moral, economic, social) for the people involved.[13] Among other things, such mistakes make us unable to explain conduct properly, and they hinder our capacity to anticipate how others will act. Mistakes are also very easy to make since we must infer character traits from actions.[14] The traits themselves are not observable, and someone who is good at identifying their presence is someone who is particularly gifted at sorting out the most salient signs of character traits from ones that are not particularly reliable. Smith guides the reader's observations of moral phenomena, thereby refining the reader's discernment of particular phenomena he might face. It is like learning to identify birds while in the presence of an expert who tells one what to look for—what aspects of behavior, coloration, form, etc., are those that

---

13 It seems reasonable to imagine that in a cosmopolitan, commercial society, the problem of identifying others is exacerbated by division of labor and greater contact with strangers. The complexity of interactions increases and the chance of getting things wrong goes up when compared with life in agrarian or hunter-gatherer communities.

14 Of course, as we see in contemporary literature about the ethical implications of social psychological literature, we may overattribute conduct to character in lieu of attributing it more properly to features of situation. This complicates our identifications of character further. See, for example, Doris, *Lack of Character*.

distinguish among species like the (apparently difficult-to-distinguish) black-capped and Carolina chickadees.

Ambition

Smith introduces the story of the ambitious man in Part IV in the context of discovering "the secret motive of the most serious and important pursuits of both private and public life" (*TMS*, IV.i.7). This secret motive explains much of our commercial activity. It is our propensity to be influenced in sentiment and conduct by an object's *aptness* for fulfilling its end, rather than simply by its sheer utility. This explains why we are willing to spend a great deal of money on a watch that loses only one minute in a fortnight, even though the watch that loses two minutes a day will serve the purpose of getting us to our appointments on time just as well. We are attracted to the finer watch, not because it is more useful (i.e., gets us where we need to be on time), but because its design better realizes its end—telling time. The expensive watch's beautiful design, in other words, attracts us independently of the watch's ultimate utility. The description of the ambitious man acts as an illustration of the power of this secret motive.

Unlike the depiction of the prudent man, the description of the ambitious man is very inward looking and more concrete. At the beginning, we discover what the ambitious man is displeased by, what he sees, imagines, feels, thinks, and is enchanted by. We also learn about the dispositions that lead to and help constitute his ambition:

> The poor man's son, whom heaven in its anger has visited with ambition, when he begins to look around him, admires the condition of the rich. He finds the cottage of his father too small for his accommodation, and fancies he should be lodged more at his ease in a palace. He is displeased with being obliged to walk a-foot, or to endure the fatigue of riding on horseback. He sees his superiors carried about in machines, and imagines that in one of these he could travel with less inconveniency. He feels himself naturally indolent, and willing to serve himself with his own hands as little as possible; and judges, that a numerous retinue of servants would save him from a great deal of trouble. [*TMS*, IV.i.8]

The description then goes on to talk about the ambitious man's behavior over a course of time (unlike in the case of prudence) in order to show the broad arc of the poor man's life. We learn about his constant labor, his sacrifices, and the realization "in the last dregs of life" that he has spent himself for "mere trinkets of frivolous utility" (*TMS*, IV.i.8). So rather than reveal the features that identify and define ambition, the account focuses more on the development of ambition. It is narrative rather than static.

This description is also more Addisonian than that of prudence. We learn what the poor man's judgment is of his father's cottage, and how he feels when walking and seeing the carriages of the rich. The added detail provides traction for our moral imagination, better enabling us to acquire a full enough picture of the ambitious man's situation to make us confident in rendering judgments about it and his conduct. These details and the narrative components of the description of the ambitious man elicit moral judgments from the reader much more readily than the static and more general depiction of the prudent man. Rather than simply providing *information* about what features of the trait enable us to identify its presence, the account of the ambitious man engages the reader in *activity*, namely, the activity of making moral judgments.

The manner in which the story of the ambitious man is told helps to produce these judgments. The reader is given insight into the ambitious man's situation that the ambitious man lacks, putting the reader in a position of interpretive superiority vis-à-vis the person who is being judged. We are told that the ambitious man thinks that if he attained the servants, home, and carriage that he desires, "he would sit still contentedly, and be quiet, enjoying himself in the thought of the happiness and tranquility of his situation" (*TMS*, IV.i.8). The narrator quickly informs the reader that the "distant idea of this felicity [...] appears in his fancy like the life of some superior rank of beings, and in order to arrive at it, he devotes himself for ever to the pursuit of wealth and greatness. To obtain the conveniencies which these afford, he submits in the first year, nay in the first month of his application, to more fatigue of body and more uneasiness of mind than he could have suffered through the whole of his life from the want of them" (*TMS*, IV.i.8). Thus we are told by the narrator that the ambitious man's choices are dictated by his false beliefs concerning repose, contentment, and what produces them. Further, we discover that the ambitious man's sacrifice of the "real tranquility that is at all times in his power" for the idea of "a certain artificial and elegant repose" leads, when he is old and ill, to regret. By showing the consequences over time of the ambitious man's faulty initial dispositions, the narrative structure promotes moral judgment in the reader.

The reader employs judgments in order to distance herself from the character portrayed. Who could want to be like the ambitious man, given the way the narrator has presented him? Knowing that the poor man's son fails to understand the reality of his own situation, readers are brought to feel pity (if they think they are potentially subject to the same problem) or contempt (if they perceive themselves as free from this failing of the understanding).

In addition to engaging the reader's moral sentiments, the story of the ambitious man offers morally useful information. Principally the text offers *causal* information, that is, an understanding of why we can be attracted to things such as carriages, namely that we find the beauty of their design (rather than their utility) compelling. Their beauty, and our awareness that other spectators perceive them as beautiful, leads us to covet them. This type of causal account—explaining why we judge or conduct ourselves in particular ways—is prominent in the first five parts of *TMS*. And this causal information improves our capacity for self-cultivation (and the cultivation of others), because when we reveal the causes that bring about the important events in human life, we know "by what manner and method we may produce similar good effects or avoid Similar bad ones" (*Lectures on Rhetoric and Belles Lettres*, ii.17).

Finally, the story of the ambitious man shows the consequences of ambition, namely, how it can lead to regret.[15] Providing the reader with information about the likely consequences of ambition makes this something akin to a parable. An earlier text in *TMS* offers a possible moral: "The great source of both the misery and disorders of human life, seems to arise from over-rating the difference between one permanent situation and another. Avarice over-rates the difference between poverty and riches: ambition, that between a private and a public station: vain-glory, that between obscurity and extensive reputation" (*TMS*, III.iii.31). The poor man's son acts as an object lesson, which presumably serves to "increase our abhorrence of vice" (*TMS*, VII.iv.6) by teaching us the wages of this particular sin.

IV. MORAL WORK AND *THE THEORY OF MORAL SENTIMENTS*

We have examined descriptions of one virtue and one vice with the goals of determining what kinds of moral work the descriptions provoke and how the text—through form, style, rhetoric, and content—tries to do that. Though one should be careful not to take this as an exhaustive account of the practical purposes served by Smith's descriptions, the analyses of his descriptions of prudence and ambition begin to show us the manner in which Smith's writing is (and is not) meant to improve the reader.

Hume, in a well-known letter to Hutcheson concerning Book III of the *Treatise*, responds to Hutcheson's complaint that he seems to lack "Warmth in the Cause of Virtue". He argues that his interest in explaining moral life rules out being too strong an advocate for virtue: "There are different ways of examining the Mind as well as the Body. One may consider it either as an Anatomist or as a Painter; either to discover its most secret Springs & Principles or to describe the Grace & Beauty of its Actions. [...]. An Anatomist [...] can give very good Advice to a Painter or Statuary: And in like manner, I am perswaded, that a Metaphysician may be very helpful to a Moralist; tho' I cannot easily conceive these two Characters united in the same Work" (*The Letters of David Hume*, 23–33). Hume, among other things, thus delineates two basic roles for the moral

---

15 The moral utility of literature was sometimes justified on similar grounds. For example, a 1763 discourse delivered to the Edinburgh Belles Lettres Society defends Romances as being morally useful because they reveal the consequences of actions. See Bator, "The University of Edinburgh Belles Lettres Society", 297.

philosopher. The painter/moralist inspires love of virtue through portraying its beauty. The anatomist/metaphysician explains the secret springs and principles that organize our moral life.

This division continues to be a very popular way for scholars to talk about the different roles for moral philosophers in the Scottish Enlightenment. A recent review shows the extent of the debate on the nature of anatomy and painting and on their respective places in Hume's writing.[16] P. B. Wood, to take one of many potential examples, uses Hume's distinction as a guide to talking about the relations of morals and metaphysics in Aberdeen specifically, and Scotland more generally.[17] He questions the emphasis placed on moral didacticism or "painting" by Phillipson and Sher, and reveals a tradition, stemming especially from Turnbull, where natural philosophy and metaphysics ground practical moralizing. But analyzing causal relations (metaphysics) and making the moral life appear attractive (moralizing) are two of a larger number of possible treatments of moral phenomena.

The analysis of Smith's descriptions of prudence and ambition suggests that Hume's identification of two roles for the moral philosopher should be taken as a helpful but incomplete starting point. In Smith, along with the metaphysician and the moralist, we find the diagnostician, who examines the mind and conduct with an eye to improving our capacity to identify particular moral phenomena (e.g., the presence of prudence). So that if we identify the metaphysician/anatomist with causal analysis and the moralist/painter with motivating descriptions, the diagnostician would provide the reader with identifying features of objects of moral concern, like virtues, vices, situations, and types of actions, such that we could pick them out in the complex swirl of ordinary life. These three different roles for the moral philosopher (moralist, metaphysician, diagnostician) reflect three different ways that texts try to impact moral practice.

The diagnostic role is what we find fulfilled in the description of prudence and what can be found elsewhere in Part VI of *TMS*. As discussed, there is little attempt made in the portrait of prudence to *motivate* or to *explain* prudence. Rather, the text provides the reader with the identifying features of prudence, so that the reader will be able to recognize prudence when she sees it and not mistake something else for it. Readers receive direction for organizing their attention and for discerning the essential from the inessential.

The moralist wants to affect the will. The moralist's text affects the will (i.e., affections, passions, desires) most often by evoking moral judgments in the reader. The concrete situations and characters that we find in narratives provide the imagination with requisite objects and contexts for judgment. Absent narrative and characters to judge, as in Smith's treatment of prudence, the text's

---

16 Abramson, "Happy to Unite, or Not?"
17 Wood, "Science and the Pursuit of Virtue in the Aberdeen Enlightenment".

capacity to motivate the reader remains limited. And given the ordinary goals and stylistic restrictions found in traditional genres of expository, philosophical writing, even where we find the occasional narrative or anecdote—as in Smith's discussion of the ambitious man—it is not surprising that historical narratives and literary texts are often far superior for motivating readers.[18]

The metaphysician, alternatively, by providing us with knowledge of causes, offers us greater control over our conduct and the development of our characters.[19] The metaphysician's is the dominant mode in Parts I through V of *TMS*. It is there, amidst his efforts to further the "science of man", that we find Smith searching for the "secret springs and principles" that explain our moral judgments and some of our aesthetic ones.[20] The focus of the description of the ambitious man, for example, is on a causal account—both how one becomes ambitious and how ambition leads to regret.

As we've seen in the brief mention of Reid, these three modes are not the only ones the moral philosopher can take on. There is also the systematizer or taxonomist who, in his natural law incarnation, offers an ordered array of duties to God, ourselves, and others that show us the landscape of our moral world—there is no causal analysis here, no attempt to guide our identification of individuals, and no direct attempt to motivate the reader. This clarity about the general map of our moral world and the associated moral knowledge yields ethical benefits, according to Reid, by making it more difficult to describe what we are doing in self-serving ways. It also provides students with a sense that the moral world is coherent, that it has a rational, even providential, structure.[21]

---

18 One genre that is available to philosophers and that has a particularly good record at motivating students is the philosophy lecture. In this genre, the professor can model an attractive picture of moral life for students. This helps to explain the great popularity of Scottish professors Hutcheson, Ferguson, Stewart, and Beattie, among others. This hints at a very large field of oral genres with practical effects (including Socratic conversation and psychotherapy, among others) beyond the scope of this paper.

19 One is reminded here of Bacon's advocacy for a "Georgics of the Mind" through which we learn how to culture the mind rather than merely to describe the nature of the good, and his criticism of moralists that only do the latter. See Bacon's *The Advancement of Learning*, book II.

20 It is relevant here that an alternative title to *TMS* for its fourth edition was "An Essay towards an Analysis of the Principles by which Men naturally judge concerning the Conduct and Character, first of their Neighbours, and afterwards of themselves". See Ross, "Adam Smith's 'Happiest' Years as a Glasgow Professor", 82.

21 Ross notes that Smith consistently wanted to give "coherence to the intellectual world he explored for the benefit of his students" whether that meant providing them with systems of rhetoric, ethics, jurisprudence, or economics (Ross, "Adam

This study provides rudimentary categories that parse the morally relevant work philosophical texts do (especially those written in expository form). This work includes providing the reader with three different kinds of morally important information (causal, diagnostic, taxonomic) and promoting one kind of activity (moral judgment). Of course, texts other than *TMS*—particularly those in other philosophical genres and written in different styles—often provide different kinds of knowledge (e.g., genealogical) and do different kinds of work (e.g., self-critique).

As an historical investigation, the textual analysis found here, by revealing what kinds of therapeutic potential texts do and do not possess, allows greater precision in determining how 18th-century moral philosophy could have contributed to realizing the Enlightenment value of improvement. More specific to Smith, it enables us to get clearer about how the structure and content of *TMS* may or may not function therapeutically. We can fathom the different ways in which Smith can be thought of as a practical ethicist and the manner in which different parts of the *TMS* contain therapeutic potential. Though Smith rejects sermonizing in moral philosophy and avoids presenting substantive moral ideals of the kind we find among many ancient thinkers, he nevertheless offers, at the least, beneficial causal and "diagnostic" knowledge along with some light moral inspiration.[22]

An antecedent philosophical interest that leads to the "practical moralists" of the Scottish Enlightenment is the question whether philosophy has anything to offer someone who desires to be better than she is. If we improve

---

Smith's 'Happiest' Years", 81–82). It is interesting to consider the ways in which these different systems do and do not depend on principles (e.g., sympathy, division of labor) that allow for better causal explanation of relevant phenomena (e.g., moral judgment, a nation's wealth).

22 Careful consideration of Smith's descriptions assists us in evaluating readings of the nature of Smith's moral philosophy. For example, Schneewind, in *The Invention of Autonomy*, asks what Smith's moral theory does to "guide our sentiments, and thereby direct our actions" (394). He answers that because Smith's ethics cannot provide us with well-defined moral rules, it "is essentially a matter of rhetoric", which serves to "refine [our sentiments] and exhort the young". But Schneewind seems to be ignoring morally efficacious cognitive work other than articulation of rules, namely the kind of work one finds in the descriptions of prudence and ambition discussed here. These descriptions transform our experience of moral phenomena and lead us to render potentially different judgments in the face of these phenomena. If moral philosophy changes how we describe our moral world, through, for example, altering our identifications of the character traits of others or through changing our understanding of what consequences follow from the desires that support ambition, then it offers a guide for our sentiments and conduct that arises from better description rather than from prescription.

by reading texts of moral philosophy, then how, exactly, are we made better? One cannot answer this question, however, without paying more attention than we do now to how such texts function. In particular, one needs to know not only what kinds of moral information the texts communicate, but also how that information is communicated and what types of responses the texts strive to elicit from readers, because philosophy impacts us, if it does, not only by changing our beliefs, but through promoting certain kinds of activity in us (e.g., moral judgment or self-critique). Texts act upon us, in other words, both by what they *say* and by what they *do*. Examining texts with these issues in mind requires considering their form, style, and rhetoric, along with their propositional content. The analysis presented here offers models for how to scrutinize philosophical texts from a practical point of view and categories that help distinguish among the practical purposes philosophical texts can serve.[23]

SELECT BIBLIOGRAPHY

Abramson, Kate. "Happy to Unite, or Not?" *Philosophy Compass*, vol. 1, no. 3 (2006): 290–302.

Addison, Joseph. *The Tatler* 155 (April 6, 1710).

Bacon, Francis. *The Advancement of Learning*. Edited by W. Wright. Oxford: Clarendon Press, 1869.

Bator, Paul. "The University of Edinburgh Belles Lettres Society (1759–1764) and the Rhetoric of the Novel". *Rhetoric Review*, vol. 14, no. 2 (Spring 1996): 280–298.

Doris, John. *Lack of Character*. Cambridge: Cambridge University Press, 2002.

Donovan, Robert. "Evangelical Humanism in Glasgow: The American War Sermons of William Thom". In *The Glasgow Enlightenment*, edited by Sher and Hook. East Linton, Scotland: Tuckwell Press, 1995, 227–243.

---

23 Earlier versions of this paper were presented at a conference on Adam Smith's *The Theory of Moral Sentiments* held at R.I.T. in May 2006 and at the PNWC Seminar on Early Modern Philosophy held at Lewis and Clark College in March 2007. I am grateful for the useful feedback received at both. In addition, I would like to thank Ryan Hanley, Rebecca Kukla, Hugh LaFollette, Eric Schliesser, and the editor of the *History of Philosophy Quarterly* for invaluable suggestions and criticisms.

Duff, David. "Antididacticism as a Contested Principle in Romantic Aesthetics". *Eighteenth-Century Life* 25 (Spring 2001): 252–270.

Griswold, Charles Jr. *Adam Smith and the Virtues of Enlightenment.* Cambridge: Cambridge University Press, 1999.

Haakonssen, Knud. "Introduction" to Thomas Reid, *Practical Ethics.* Princeton, N.J.: Princeton University Press, 1990.

Hadot, Pierre. *Philosophy as a Way of Life.* Translated by Michael Chase. Oxford: Blackwell Press, 1995.

Howell, Wilbur Samuel. *Eighteenth-Century British Logic and Rhetoric.* Princeton, N.J.: Princeton University Press, 1971.

Hume, David. *The Letters of David Hume,* vol. 1. Edited by J. Y. T. Grieg. Oxford: Oxford University Press, 1932, 32–33.

Phillipson, Nicholas. "Adam Smith as Civic Moralist". In *Wealth and Virtue: The Shaping of Political Economy in the Scottish Enlightenment,* edited by I. Hont and M. Ignatieff. Cambridge: Cambridge University Press, 1983, 179–202.

———. "Towards a Definition of the Scottish Enlightenment". In *City and Society in the 18th Century,* edited by Paul Fritz and David Williams. Toronto: Hakkert, 1973, 125–147.

Prince, Michael. *Philosophical Dialogue in the British Enlightenment.* Cambridge: Cambridge University Press, 1996.

Reid, Thomas. *Essays on the Active Powers of Man.* Edinburgh: John Bell, 1788.

———. *Practical Ethics.* Edited by Knud Haakonssen. Princeton, N.J.: Princeton University Press, 1990.

Ross, Ian Simpson. "Adam Smith's 'Happiest' Years as a Glasgow Professor". In *The Glasgow Enlightenment,* edited by Sher and Hook. East Linton: Tuckwell Press, 1994, 73–94.

Schneewind, J. B. *The Invention of Autonomy.* Cambridge: Cambridge University Press, 1998.

Sher, Richard B. *The Enlightenment and the Book.* Chicago: University of Chicago Press, 2006.

———. "Professors of Virtue: The Social History of the Edinburgh Moral Philosophy Chair in the Eighteenth Century". In *Studies in the Philosophy of the Scottish Enlightenment*, edited by M. A. Stewart. Oxford: Clarendon Press, 1990, 87–126.

Smeed, J. W. *The Theophrastian "Character".* Oxford: Clarendon Press, 1985.

Smith, Adam. *Essays on Philosophical Subjects.* Edited by J. C. Bryce and W. P. D. Wightman. Indianapolis: Liberty Fund, 1982.

———. *Lectures on Rhetoric and Belles Lettres.* Edited by J. C. Bryce. Indianapolis: Liberty Fund, 1985.

———. *The Theory of Moral Sentiments.* Edited by D.D. Raphael and A.L. Macfie. Indianapolis: Liberty Fund, 1982.

Thom, William. "Letter to J_ M_, Esq. on the Defects of an University Education". In *The Works of the Rev. William Thom [...] Consisting of Sermons, Tracts, Letters, etc.* Glasgow: James Dymock, 1799.

Tompkins, Jane, ed. *Reader Response Criticism.* Baltimore: Johns Hopkins University Press, 1980.

Winch, Donald. "Adam Smith's 'Enduring Particular Result': A Political and Cosmopolitan Perspective". In *Wealth and Virtue: The Shaping of Political Economy in the Scottish Enlightenment*, edited by I. Hont and M. Ignatieff. Cambridge: Cambridge University Press, 1983, 253–270.

Wood, P. B. "Science and the Pursuit of Virtue in the Aberdeen Enlightenment". In *Studies in the Philosophy of the Scottish Enlightenment*, edited by M. A. Stewart. Oxford: Clarendon Press, 1990, 127–149.

INDEX

A

Action: acceptability of, 104; communicative, 62; from duty alone, 103*n16*; meritorious, 101; morally wrong, 104; proper, 101; punishable, 101, 106

Actions: judgment based on motives and consequences, 105, 106

Activity: imaginative, 119*n8*

Activity, commercial: deceptive nature of sense of fairness in, 5; distribution in, 88; in early Scotland, 20, 21; evaluating from moral perspective, 75; injustice in as form of theft, 73, 74; manipulation and coercion in, 5, 73, 74; manipulation of while giving appearance of fairness, 92; political aspects of, 72, 73, 74; as political realm with manipulation and coercion, 90; power relations in, 92; pursuit of self-interest through, 71; social contexts of, 5, 6

Adam, James, 22

Adam, Robert, 22, 25

Adam Smith Problem, 3, 4, 35, 36, 45–69, 71; solution to, 63–69

Addison, Joseph, 11, 17, 23, 27, 216, 217

Admiration, 77, 77*n13*

Aesthetics: early writings on, 22; evolution of, 16; lack of in lower classes, 17, 26

Afterlife, 203–206

Agency: availability of, 14; moral life and, 14

Alienation, 4, 58, 61, 213; between agent and spectator, 52; caused by social division of labor, 55; caused by technical division of labor, 55; forms of, 55

Ambition, 219–221

Anger, 152–154; toward causes of hurt, 161

Approbation: from appropriate conduct, 3; consequences of desire for, 37; factual, 140; incentivization of morally questionable actions and, 42; just and proper objects of, 140; loss of, 41; from material possessions, 3, 4, 35, 36, 37–40; mechanism for gaining, 37–40; moral, 3, 36, 37, 38, 39, 39*n5*, 40; positive consequences of, 38, 39; relation to fellow-feeling, 124; relation to sympathy, 126; self, 142; social, 40; sources of, 102; theoretical descriptions of, 4; trading moral for material, 40; wealth, 3; willingness to take risks for, 40; worthiness for, 171

Approval. *See* Approbation

Aristotle, 111, 197

Ashcraft, Richard, 74

Atheism, 198, 203*n21*

Authenticity, 64

B

Beattie, James, 20, 22, 26, 27

Beauty: criteria of, 26

Beliefs, 7; imagination and, 117

229

Benevolence, 124*n17*; built on principle of commonness, 65; butcher, brewer, baker and, 166, 167, 168; justice and, 65; possibility of, 65
Bissonette, Vincent, 8, 137–150
Bittermann, Henry, 71, 89
Blackburn, Simon, 95, 125
Blame, 141
Blaug, Mark, 74*n10*
Brandt, Roger, 99
Buckle, Stephen, 72, 72*n5*, 78*n14*
Buffier, Claude, 26
Burke, Edmund, 18
Burney, Charles, 29, 31
Butcher, brewer, baker, 165–172; agreements with customers, 167, 168, 169; benevolence and, 166, 167; obligations of, 166, 167, 168; providing for others and, 167; self-interest of, 45; trust and, 166; understanding of exchange and, 166
Butler, Joseph, 128*n25*, 129, 151, 151*n1*, 153, 157, 160, 161

C

Calvinism, 20
Campbell, George, 22
Campbell, T.D., 78*n15*, 102, 115, 116
Capital, 56; accumulation of, 84; owners of, 84
Capitalism: general truth of, 2; labor struggles in, 6; moral critique of, 71–72
Causality: Hume on, 141–143; naturalistic, 8, 144; rooted in imagination, habit, experience, 144; specificities and inconsistencies of, 141
Cause and effect, 176, 179
Chambers, Ephraim, 15
Chambers, William, 23
Cleanthes, 175–182
Cohen, Edward, 76
Commerce: ethicolegal regulations of, 5; morally neutral or corrupt, 82; securing moral foundation through, 74
Commercial: exchange relations, 53, 54, 57; society, 4, 5, 41, 42, 46, 53–57
Communication: detachment of arts from, 24; need for sympathetic social relations for, 66, 67; sympathy as means of, 57; theoretical problems in, 15
Compassion, 115, 116, 117, 120*n10*, 127; as fear for self, 129
Conjecture: analogy and, 188; arbitrary, 179; beyond experience, 179; imaginative, 178, 186; justified by potential utility, 188; necessity of in scientific discovery, 187; non-arbitrary, 187; possibility of, 186
Conscience, 49, 101; ability to listen to, 53; formation of, 50; guilty, 143; of integrity, 160; naturalized, 143; properly-working, 144*n10*; use of, 140
Consciousness: secret, 146
Context: in arts, 14; in commercial activity, 5, 6; differences in, 19, 20; domination by texts, 17; importance of, 14; importance of spectator identification, 24; morality and, 3; sympathy in determination of, 32; of time of writing of *The Theory of Moral Sentiments*, 19–23; understanding the past and, 14; in which works are made, 18; of writing, 16

Conversation: art of, 32; context and, 32; as sacred, 32
Cosmogony, 177
Critique of Judgment (Kant), 23
Custom, 108*n*23, 110

D

D'Alembert, Jean, 15, 16
Darwall, Stephen, 78, 95, 96, 115
Death: in assessment of life, 10; autobiography and, 197; fear of, 198, 198*n*9
De Brosses, Charles, 30
Deontology, 7, 106; role of sentimentalism in, 106*n*21
Descartes, René, 47
Dialogues Concerning Natural Religion (Hume), 10, 173, 174, 175–182
Dickey, Laurence, 35, 38
Dogmatism: skeptical, 175; theological, 175
Dubos, Abbé Jean-Baptiste, 17, 22

E

Economy: political, 5, 75, 82
Education: fragmentation of, 14; rhetoric as core of, 14; time for, 61; universal, 61
Eggleston, Ben, 109*n*25
Eliot, George, 131
Elliot, Gilbert, 125*n*20
Elliott, John, 83*n*22
Emotion: vicarious, 120
Empathy, 96, 97; defining, 97*n*4; as deliberate act, 97*n*4; need for sensitivity to, 95; paradigm cases of, 97*n*4
Empiricism, 18
Emulation, 140*n*6
Epicurus, 123*n*16
Essays (Hume), 14
Essence: social relations in production, 53, 55–57
Ethics: defense of, 105–106; of growth, 87–90; judgment of impartial spectator and, 64; non-utilitarian, 5, 64; normative, 6, 96; practical, 211; striving for, 146; virtue, 95; of virtue, 95
Evensky, Jerry, 42, 204
Evil, 137, 144, 149
Exchange: butcher, brewer, baker and, 166, 167; importance of cooperation in, 167; obligations and, 167; role in division of labor, 167
Experience: adjustment of rules and, 104; appreciating others', 97, 116; causality and, 144; common, 183; of emotion, 99; of leisure, 16, 17; objective and subjective conditions of in space and time, 49–53; objective judgments in, 18; of other cultures, 26; rule formation and, 103; sensory features of, 19, 20; speculation beyond, 10, 183; understanding phenomena beyond, 10

F

Fancy, 182
Feeling(s). *See also* Fellow-feeling: bodily, 7, 122; community, 116*n*3; endorsement of, 127; fellow, 7, 37, 51, 78, 97, 115, 116, 117; of the heart, 164; "invisible", 119; of joy, 122, 123*n*15; judgment and, 23; negative response to, 127; of others, 118–121; role in moral life, 95; sharing, 78, 117, 127; sympathy and, 7
Fellow-feeling, 97, 115, 116, 117,

121–123; non-inclusive, 122; recognition of, 126
Ferguson, Adam, 22
Firth, Roderick, 99, 99*n*9
Fitzgibbons, Athol, 74*n*10
Flanagan, Owen, 105
Flanders, Chad, 10, 195–207
Fleischacker, Samuel, 82*n*21
Fontenelle, Bernard, 17
Free enterprise system: invisible hand in, 2, 2*n*2, 73, 165, 166; in *The Wealth of Nations*, 1, 2
Froese, Paul, 2*n*2

G

Gerard, Alexander, 22, 23, 25
Gerrek, Monica, 6, 7, 95–111
Girard, Abbé, 16
Göçmen, Doğan, 4, 45–69
God: existence of, 174, 175; as impartial spectator, 11; judgment of, 202
Goldman, Alvin, 95, 97*n*4, 98, 102
Gordley, James, 72, 72*n*4, 82
Gordon, Robert, 96*n*2, 130*n*29, 131
Gratitude, 9, 100, 101, 102, 162
Gregory, John, 17, 22, 31
Grief: alleviation of, 123*n*15
Griswold, Charles, 115, 118, 127, 211
Growth: ethics of, 87–90; infinite, 88

H

Haakonssen, Knud, 72*n*5, 78*n*14, 80, 80*n*19, 211, 213
Habit: changing fashion and, 23
Hadot, Pierre, 213
Hanley, Ryan Patrick, 10, 173–190
Happiness: means of, 1, 2; mutual, 57; nature of, 180; of others, 45, 52; pleasure in others', 151; in *The Theory of Moral Sentiments*, 1, 2; unwarranted, 125

Hare, R.M., 99
Harrington, James, 67, 68
Heath, Eugene, 125
Herzog, Don, 80*n*17
Heydt, Colin, 11, 211–225
History: knowledge of past outcomes but not intentions, 19
History of Astronomy (Smith), 77, 174, 182
History of England (Hume), 19
Hobbes, Thomas, 127, 129
Hochstrasser, T.J., 72*n*5
Hoffman, Martin, 119
Hollis, Martin, 166, 167
Hont, Istvan, 73, 88
Humanism, 14
Human nature: concern for happiness of others and, 45
Hume, David, 1, 18, 72, 126, 163; account of justice, 151; acquisition of learned skills and, 24; anti-speculative philosophy of, 138; assault on theology and philosphy by, 10; challenge to Smith's account of ethics, 65; comparison of *Treatise* with Smith's moral theory, 115; critique of metaphysics, 175; *Dialogues Concerning Natural Religion*, 10, 173, 174, 175–182; disagreements with Smith, 183–190; discussions with Ramsay, 23; discussions with Smith over sympathy, 124, 124*n*18, 124*n*19; *Essays*, 14; feels benevolence is impossible, 65; founder of discussion society, 22; *History of England*, 19; idea of virtuous life and, 71; ideas of taste, 146*n*12; incorporation of skepticism by Smith, 144–145; on justice,

162; on matters of taste, 24; on morality based on sympathetic social relations, 65; moral skepticism of, 64–67; *My Own Life*, 196, 202; naturalistic view of causality, 8; nonbelief in afterlife, 203–206; on non-utilitarian ethical society, 64, 65; "Of the Standard of Taste", 22; philosophizing as cause for anxiety by, 10; position on utility, 15; public attack on religion by, 173, 174; public reaction to death of, 11; public utility and, 9; reaction of Smith to death of, 195–207; reference to principle of comparison, 117*n4*; refusal of Smith to publish *Dialogues* of, 10, 11; rejection of dogmatism by, 175; rejection of imaginary change of character in sympathy, 129*n27*; relations with Smith, 2, 173; on resentment, 157; "sensible knave" of, 9, 159–165; stress on feeling and action by, 95; theory of sympathy, 95; *A Treatise of Human Nature*, 115, 117*n4*, 141, 201, 202; views on objectivity of critical judgments, 22; writings on causality, 141–143

Hutcheson, Francis, 22, 71, 72, 120

I

Ignatieff, Michael, 73, 88
Image: reflected, 50; self, 50
Imagination: abuses of, 182; beliefs and, 117; causal, 139–145; changing places with sufferer in, 116; cognitive states and, 117; conjecture and, 178; connections through, 141–143; constitution of others and, 50; illusions of, 120; labor required for, 24; liability in philosophy, 180; necessity in common life, 180; placing self in situation of others and, 51; restrained by judgment, 179; role in causal apprehension, 185; role in sympathy, 121*n11*; skepticism and, 173–190; sympathetic, 8, 145–148, 149; sympathy as act of, 96, 97, 97*n4*, 117; synthetic role for, 186; unable to be foundation for inference, 178

Imitation, 28
Impartiality, 162
Improvisation: in language and speaking, 15; in musical performance, 27, 32; presupposition of preparation for, 27; propriety in, 27; thought and, 15

Indignation, 162
Individual(s): in commercial society, 53–57; economic isolation of, 54; effects of division of labor on, 55; as equals among equals, 4; power positions of, 4; as representatives of different social classes, 4; social, 4

Infanticide, 79*n16*, 106–111
Innocence, 144; guilty persons and, 143; lack of belief in, 144, 145; resentment and, 152; sympathetic imagination and, 147–148; in *The Theory of Moral Sentiments*, 137–150

Inquiry: constructive, 189; fragmentation of, 13; historical, 80; imaginative, 176, 177, 180; legitimacy of, 176, 177; objective judgments in, 18; philosophical, 10,

174, 175, 181, 186; pursuit beyond experience, 178, 180; speculative, 175

J

Johnson, Samuel, 14, 115
Jones, Peter, 2, 3, 13–32
Judgment: aesthetic element in, 13; balance in use of sentiment and reason in, 106; comparative, 23, 24; critical, 24, 25; dependence on that of others, 139; divine, 202; embedded in social life, 25; feeling and, 23; of God, 202, 203; justifiable, 13; of merit, 99, 99n10, 100, 102; moral propriety of, 3; of motives/consequences in actions, 7; natural, 77; objectivity and, 18; of one's own behavior, 101; of propriety, 99, 99n10, 100, 102; rules of justice and, 73; social construction in, 77; standards in, 23; of taste, 18; theory and, 17
Judgment, moral, 6, 7, 9, 76–81, 78, 80, 81–87; on economic exchanges, 82; impartial spectator and, 98–104; standards of, 80–87; sympathy and sentiment in, 96–104; on use of labor time, 82
Jurisprudence, 5; critical, 80; ethics of growth and, 87–90; medieval, 72; natural, 75–81; political economy and, 82; tension between components of, 74; theory of, 72
Justice, 65; acquired, 160; branches of, 160; built on separation of *mine* and *thine*, 65; cultivation of, 76; domestic, 87; moral judgments and, 73; motives to, 158; natural, 160; necessity of for existence of society, 157n5; provision for the poor and, 73; public utility and, 9, 157–159; regulation of, 71; restricted to property, 163; role of others in development of, 155

K

Kames, Lord, 22, 23, 117
Kant, Immanuel, 22, 25, 31, 106, 107, 205n27; *Critique of Judgment*, 23

L

Labor, 81*tab*; appropriation of value of, 57; demand for, 88; division of, 53, 55, 61–62; exploitation of, 85; liberal rewards for, 88; as measure of exchangeable value of commodities, 82, 83; natural price of, 83n25; real value based on, 6, 75; recompense of, 85; social class and, 56; struggles with capital, 6; time, 82; wage, 85
La Bruyère, Jean de, 22
Lacan, Jacques, 47
Landlords, 56, 57
Language and speech: abstract, 216; changing meanings in, 16; eighteenth century, 2; encouragement of, 17; importance of to chattering class, 17; improvisation and, 15; natural, 119n7; relations to the world, 15, 16; of uneducated, 13
Law: ancient, 79; criminal, 162; feudal, 87; natural, 88; previously serving interests of society, but no longer, 80; of primogeniture, 79; shift

in European systems of, 73; usefulness of existing, 80
Law, natural, 89; free market and, 71–90; regulation of markets and, 73; social contract in, 72, 73; of succession, 79
Learning: central to socialization, 25
Lectures in Jurisprudence (Smith), 59, 73, 79
Legislation: essential condition of social transformation, 80; moral judgment and, 81–87; relationship to wealth creation, 82; standards of moral judgment and, 80
Legislators: adjustment of social norms by, 78; generation of societal regulations by, 73, 74; motivation for, 78; natural jurisprudence and, 75–81; role in creating conditions making scientific study of society possible, 76–81; "science" of, 73
Lethargy, 182
"Letter to Strahan" (Smith), 195, 197–199; as philosophical document, 195
Levy, David, 40
Liberalism, 88
Locke, John, 14, 74, 83

M

Macfie, A.L., 35, 36
Mandeville, Bernard, 71, 127; description of commercial exchange relations, 65, 66; morality based on sympathetic social relations, 65; moral skepticism of, 64–67; on non-utilitarian ethical society, 64, 65
Market(s): asymmetries of power and, 73; competitive, 76; economic, 72, 90; exchanges, 87; free, 1, 2, 2*n*2; prices, 82, 86, 87, 88; regulation of, 73; value, 81*tab*
Marx, Karl, 71, 80
Meaning: of great music, 28; interpretation and, 24; in process and product, 24
Mercantilism, 42
Midgley, Mary, 95
Milton, John, 115*n*2
Mirroring: mutual, 4, 49–53, 50–51; of others, 48, 49; self-image and, 4; theory, 47–49
Misery, 154–157
Montaigne, Michel de, 205, 213
Montes, Leonidas, 74*n*10
Moral: actions, 3; agents, 7; behavior, 37, 38, 40; conduct, 36; corruption, 103; education, 9; evaluation, 79; ideal, 105; improvement, 213; judgment, 6, 76, 78, 80, 81–87; justification, 80*n*17; life, 14; norms, 169; obligations, 164; pedagogy, 211–225; philosophy, 14, 71; responsibility, 152; risk, 38; rules, 103, 104; rules of conduct, 37; sentiment, 1, 6, 13, 115–132, 162, 201; spectatorship, 90; theory, 2, 105; tradeoffs, 42; work, 221–225
Morality: condemnation of some actions and, 106; context and, 3; differing systems of, 58; feeling and action in, 95; importance of rules of, 158; of infanticide, 106–110; need for sympathetic social relations for, 66, 67; practical doctrines of, 211*n*2, 214; purpose of systems of, 64; regulation of, 72; resentment in accounts of, 8, 9;

role of resentment in, 151–172
More, Thomas, 67, 68
Music, 26, 27; contributions by, 32; detachment from everyday life, 30; gap in skills possessed by performers and audiences, 30; improvisation in, 32; instrumental, 27, 28; lost, 28, 29; meaning of, 28; in oral culture, 30; rapid obsolescence of, 31; sensual pleasure in, 28; universal performance in, 27; vocal, 27, 28, 29, 30
My Own Life (Hume), 196, 202

N

Nature: rational understanding of, 140
Nihilism, 58
Norton, D.F., 127

O

Objectivity, 18
Observer, ideal: differences from impartial spectator, 99; lack of emotional response by, 99, 99*n*9; omniscience of, 99*n*9
"Of the Nature of that Imitation" (Smith), 27, 28
"Of the Standard of Taste" (Hume), 22
Oncken, August, 35
Otteson, James, 121

P

Pack, Spencer, 72*n*5
Paganelli, Maria Pia, 3, 4, 35–43
Pain, 122*n*14
Partiality/impartiality, 7
Passion: dignity of, 156; original, 125, 127; sympathetic, 50, 51, 125; unshared, 147; unsocial, 151–152

Peil, Jan, 84*n*26
Perception, 117*n*5
Perrault, Charles, 22
Perrault, Claude, 17, 22, 25
Phaedo (Plato), 195
Phillipson, Nicolas, 211
Philo, 175–182, 187, 188
Philosophy: anti-speculative form of, 138; in common life, 183; defining, 188, 189; economic activities and, 73; holistic approach to, 13; "humble", 8, 137–150; importance of fancy to, 182; mental, 14; mental tranquility and, 10; moral, 14, 71, 78; as moral pedagogy, 211–225; natural, 178; productive capacity of, 188; provision of foundations for legal systems through, 72; true, 179; utility of, 189; wonder and, 183
Pitson, Tony, 7, 115–132
Plato, 11, 111, 195
Platonism, 14
Pleasure: bodily, 123*n*16; of not suffering, 117*n*4; in others' happiness, 45, 46, 151; relation to desire and motivation, 123*n*16; sympathy as source of, 122*n*14, 123–127
Pope, Alexander, 23, 138
Positivism, 64
Poverty, 85, 86
Power: access to means of controlling, 80; balance of, 80; relations, 80, 83
Praise: anticipation of, 142; deserved, 140; imagined, 142; love of, 141; unjust, 145; virtue and, 143; worthiness, 8, 140*n*7, 141, 144
Prasch, Robert, 88*n*34
Price(s): actual, 6; central, 87;

distribution of property and, 6; formation of, 74; as ideological construction, 75; market, 5, 6, 75, 82, 86, 87, 88; natural, 5, 6, 75, 83, 84, 84*n26*, 86, 87, 88; nominal, 86, 87

Principle of Minimal Psychological Realism, 105

"The Principles Which Lead and Direct Philosophical Enquiries" (Smith), 10

Pritchard, Michael, 8, 151–172

Production: monopolization of means of, 56; ownership of, 57; social relations and, 5, 55–57

Profit, 4, 6, 9, 56, 81*tab*

Prudence, 215–219; blinded by glitter of wealth, 41; as virtue of commercial relations, 11

R

Ramsay, Allan, 18, 22, 23, 26

Raphael, D.D., 35, 36

Raynor, David, 125

Realism: common-sense, 53

Reason, 117*n5*; development of, 161; from effect to cause, 179; inert character of, 30; limited capacity of, 180; loss of, 120*n10*; restricted to experience, 177; sufficient for knowledge of divine, 175

Reciprocity: utilitarian concept of, 66

Reid, Thomas, 8, 9, 11, 22, 117, 119*n7*, 127, 151, 151*n2*, 160, 161, 162, 163, 164, 211, 216

Relativism, 7, 104, 105, 139

Religion: comfort in, 8, 145, 149; consolation and, 201*n16*; failure of sympathy and, 149; natural, 173; as palliative to suffering, 137, 138, 139; for situations where philosophy is useless, 138*n4*

Remorse, 102*n14*

Rent, 4, 6, 56, 81*tab*

Repentance, 103*n15*

Resentment, 100, 106; anger as form of, 9, 152–154; children and, 152–154; consequences of, 164; as defensive response, 8, 9; deliberate, 9, 157, 161; excessive, 155; as expression of justice, 9; fear of, 154; humbling of, 155; indignation as, 156, 162; innocence and, 152; morality and, 151–172; as morally suspect, 152; natural, 162; need for support from others and, 154–157; nobility of, 157; objects of, 162; pre-moral, 153; private injury and, 9; production of, 161; prone to excess, 9; proper sense of, 9; role in accounts of morality, 8, 9; role of reflection in, 157; as safeguard of justice, 152; sentiment of, 89; siding with the target of, 154, 155; sudden, 153, 157, 161, 162; sympathy and, 156; taming, 8, 9, 151–172; as unsocial passion, 8; utility of, 9; violation of rules and, 9

Revenue, 55; forms of, 4, 5; sources of, 56

Rhetoric: as core of education, 14

Richardson, Jonathan, 17

Rights: overriding, 88; perfect/imperfect, 6, 73, 87, 89; property, 84, 88; to safety, 160; violations of, 9, 161

Robertson, S., 127

Robertson, William, 22

Robison, Wade, 1–11

Rollin, Charles, 14

Ron, Amit, 5, 71–90
Rosenberg, Nathan, 41
Rousseau, Jean-Jacques, 27, 71, 117n4

S

Schliesser, Eric, 72n5, 76, 174n8, 195n1
Science: determination of standards of moral evaluation and, 81; ideological construction and, 81–87
Scotland: discussion societies in, 21, 32; early commercial activity in, 20, 21; eighteenth century life in, 2, 3; influence of climate on character in, 20; lack of leisure for arts in, 21, 26; primitive conditions in, 20, 21; Smith's public speaking in, 14
Self: approbation, 142; becoming self-critical by means of others, 48, 49; in commercial society, 53–60; constitution of, 47–53; distance from, 51; as genesis of impartial spectator within, 49; in mirror of others, 48, 51–53; observance of own behavior, 52; seeing as others would, 53
Self-deception, 158
Self-interest, 166; constraint in pursuit of, 171; turning to public advantage, 76; utilitarian, 45, 46
Selfishness: sympathy and, 127–131
Self-love, 57, 58, 128, 169, 170; coincident with virtue, 128n25
Sensible knave, 9, 159–165; consideration of infidelity by, 163; duplicitous, 160; impartial spectator and, 165; moral constraints on, 169; public support for rules by, 160; rule-breaking and, 9, 158; self-interest of, 160
Sentimentalism, 6, 95–111; as basis of reason-based moral theories, 105; infanticide and, 106–111; treatment of animals and, 111
Sentiments: of approbation, 124, 124n19, 125; intellectual, 183; irregular, 201, 202; judgment of moral acts and, 105; making moral decisions and, 7; misguided, 201; moral, 1, 6, 13, 115–132, 162, 201; moral theory and, 95–111; of others, 118; public, 201; of resentment, 89; role in making moral judgments, 6; of sufferer, 26; sympathetic, 50, 51
Shaftesbury, Lord, 17
Shakespeare, William, 115n2
Simulation, 130, 131
Skepticism: critical, 182; dogmatic, 175; fundamental, 186n22; as ground-clearing exercise, 181; imagination and, 173–190; insupportable, 182; limited to experience, 175; mitigated, 181, 182; as negative enterprise, 181; of popular opinion, 203
Slote, Michael, 95, 96, 97n4, 98, 106n21
Smith, Adam: account of sympathy by, 7, 115–132; acquisition of learned skills and, 24; advocacy for legal reforms, 75; anthropological view of, 46, 47; belief in afterlife, 203–206; claim of pleasure of mutual sympathy, 126; claims concerning human nature, 45–69; commercial society and, 53–63; common-sense realism of, 53; concept of benevolence

and justice, 65; concern over meaningless or wordless music, 31; conditional justification for possibility of utopia, 67–69; contribution to Ramsay-Hume debate, 25, 26; defense of controversial figure, 199–203; "A Delicate and an accurate Pencil", 11, 213; depiction of virtue and vice, 214–221; description of commercial exchange relations, 65, 66; descriptions of prudence and vice, 11; disagreements with Hume, 183–190; distances philosophy from that of Hume, 11; distrust of human opinion by, 11, 203; essay on music, 26, 27; examination of prices by, 74; failure to honor Hume's will, 10, 11, 20, 173, 174; fellow-feelings and, 7, 37, 78; founder of discussion society, 22; *History of Astronomy*, 77, 174, 182; on human nature, 47–49; "humble philosophy" of, 8, 137–150; incorporation of Hume's skepticism by, 144–145; interest in modern natural law, 71–90; interest in political dimensions of economic activity, 72; on issue of infanticide, 107; on judging what is good, 18; on justice, 157–159; *Lectures in Jurisprudence*, 59, 73, 79; "Letter to Strahan", 195, 197–199; limits of Enlightenment and, 203–206; on matters of taste, 24; mirror theoretical approach to constitution of self, 47–53; moral interest in economics, 5, 75–81; moral philosophy of, 64–67; natural system of perfect liberty of, 87; non-utilitarian concept of reciprocity, 66; "Of the Nature of that Imitation", 27, 28; philosophizing as remedy for anxiety by, 10; "The Principles Which Lead and Direct Philosophical Enquiries", 10; proposes universal education, 61; reaction to Hume's death, 195–207; recommendation of religion by, 138, 138$n4$; rejection of dogmatism by, 175; relations with Hume, 2, 173; "science of the legislator", 74, 75–81; sensory life of, 20; sentimentalism of, 95, 96; on taste and criticism, 13–32; theory of communicative action of, 62, 63; theory of jurisprudence, 89; *The Theory of Moral Sentiments*, 8, 19–23, 35–43, 46–53, 107, 108, 115–132, 137–150, 211–225; theory of sympathy, 95, 115–132; understanding of jurisprudence, 71–90; use of impartial spectator, 78, 79, 79$n16$; utopia of sympathetic society of, 4, 60–69; view of legislation against historical experience and social practice, 77, 778; *The Wealth of Nations*, 35, 79, 88

Smollett, Tobias, 21
Snow, N.E., 116$n3$, 120$n9$
Social: behavior, 24; change, 80; class, 4, 54, 56, 57, 61–62; cohesion, 25; contract, 88, 106, 107; custom, 105; distance, 37$n3$; individuality, 4, 5, 46–53, 57, 58; inequality, 54; needs, 50;

practices, 77, 78; prosperity, 40; psychology, 14; relations, 4, 5, 54, 57, 80; status, 40; systems, 6, 77, 78; values, 84*n26*, 89

Society: balance of power in, 80; closed, 62, 63; divisions of, 63; exclusion from, 63; fragmented by social class, 62; harmony of, 62, 145*n11*, 146, 147; historical development of, 56; individuality, 60; machine-like operation of, 77, 78; market, 55; mirror theory and, 48, 49; mutual advantage and, 5; non-utilitarian, 57; primitive, 79, 83; reforms of, 5; stages in development of, 56, 57; sympathetic, 5, 46, 60–69; understood against historical predecessor, 80

Society, commercial, 4, 5, 41, 42, 46, 53–60; accumulation of wealth in, 87; destruction of communitarian structures of feudal society by, 59; differentiation of trades in, 55; distribution of time in, 61, 62; division of labor in, 61–62; dynamism of, 59, 60; economic isolation of individuals in, 55; economic separation in, 54; historical development of, 55; impartial spectator and, 72; individuals in, 53–57; justification of, 59; lack of sympathetic relations in, 57; legal foundations for, 81–87; measuring value in, 87; natural price in, 84; need for leisure to enjoy education in, 61, 62; power of exchange in, 53, 54; provision of guides for cultivation of justice through, 76; situation of individuals in, 57; social class structure of, 61–62; social inequality in, 54; social relations in, 57; undermining of respect in, 63; virtuous life in, 71; wealth in, 59

Socrates, 11, 203, 204, 204*n22*

Solomon, Robert, 95

Sorrow: derived from sorrow of others, 47; propensity to identify with, 122; from sorrow of others, 127

Sovereign: duties of, 87

Speaking. *See* Language and speech

Spectator: attentive, 116; identification of with other person, 129*n28*, 145; ignorant, 16

Spectator, impartial: absence of, 71; ambivalence of sympathy and, 148; as analytic device, 90; capability for sympathetic accuracy, 99; commercial society and, 72; communal standards and, 78; as conscience, 101; defining conditions for mutual understanding by, 25; differences from ideal observer, 99; differences in those from differing cultures, 104*n18*; evaluation of conditions shaping supply and demand and, 86; explains interaction between social and legal changes, 79; few who qualify, 200; God as, 11; importance to success of sentimentalist ethic, 98; internal, 101; as judge of mankind, 202; as judge of propriety of an act, 98; as judge of soundness of rules, 104;

judges motive of agent and consequences of action, 99, 100; mechanism behind, 140; moral judgment and, 98–104; moral rules as substitute for, 6, 7; ordinary individuals as, 6; of our own conduct, 154; partiality to oneself and, 155; representing viewpoint of ordinary persons, 99; satisfying demands of, 171; seeing self from point of view of, 9; sentiments of, 165; separation from ordinary public opinion, 11; sympathy and, 6, 78, 79, 96, 104; understanding system of law and, 79

Speculation: philosophical, 10; utility of, 10

Stewart, Dugald, 211$n2$, 212$n4$

Stock: accumulation of, 56; capital and, 56; subsistence and, 56

Subjectivism, 139

Subsistence, 61

Suffering, 117$n4$; unjust, 137

Sugden, Robert, 126

Suits, David, 1–11

Sulzer, J.G., 31

Supply and demand, 6, 81tab; determination of value and, 87; fairness of wages and, 89; manipulation of, 86; variations in, 87

Surprise, 77

Sympathy, 96–98; account in *The Theory of Moral Sentiments*, 115–132; as act of imagination, 96, 97, 97$n4$; affective dimension of, 7; affect match and, 97, 100, 101, 104; ambivalence of, 148; arising from situation of passion, 50; of audiences, 14; centrality to moral psychology of Smith, 115–132; commercial exchange relations and, 57; complete, 126; complications of, 116; defining, 6, 97, 115$n2$; in determination of contexts, 32; direct, 99$n10$; distinction between perfect/imperfect rights and, 73; as economic basis for *The Wealth of Nations*, 115; as emotional transfusion, 120; epistemological dimension of, 7; evaluation of propriety of others feelings and, 78; failure of, 149; as fellow-feeling, 7, 115, 116, 118–123, 128; founding on imaginary change of situation, 120–121; imagination and, 117; impartial spectators and, 6, 78, 79; indirect, 99$n10$; intentionality of, 27, 97; as means of communication, 57; as mode of moral judgment, 78; "motor mimicry" and, 119; mutual, 57, 58, 62, 63–69, 123$n15$, 126, 129; naturalness of, 7; non-egocentric form of, 131; as original principle of human nature, 119$n7$; pleasure of, 126, 127; preconditions for, 66, 67; relation to approval, 126; role in moral life, 6, 95; role of imagination in, 121$n11$; scope of process of, 7; selfishness and, 127–131; sharing sadness and, 120$n9$; simulation and, 130; situational and contextual mode, 78; as social need, 50; spontaneity of, 119, 119$n8$, 146; stages of, 7; for those resembling ourselves, 66, 67; two-stage process of, 116, 119; uncertain, 149;

universal, 146n12

T

Taste: after-admiration resulting from familiarity and, 23; award for, 21, 22; concepts of, 17, 18; custom and fashion in, 25; debates on judgments of, 23; Hume on, 146n12; labor required for, 24; as metaphor, 18, 24; reference to custom in, 23; universal, 146n12

Theory: of character, 50; of cognition, knowledge, judgment, and decision, 49; of communicative action, 62, 63; of the constitution of the self, 49–53; contract, 6; economic, 5; to explain and predict economic behavior, 76; ideal observer, 99; and judgment, 17; of jurisprudence, 72; mirror, 47–49; moral, 2, 95–111, 105; of moral sentiment, 6, 115–132, 201; natural law, 88; normative moral, 6; of self, 47–49; selfish, 127, 129; social contract, 7, 106, 107; of social individuality, 60

The Theory of Moral Sentiments (Smith), 14; account of sympathy in, 115–132; approbation generated by material possession, 36; as complement to *The Wealth of Nations*, 60–69; consistency in different editions of, 35–43; consistency with *The Wealth of Nations*, 3; contextual dimensions of time of writing, 19–23; contrast in different editions of, 4; differences in various editions of, 39; discussion of infanticide in, 107, 108; evolution of, 202; innocence in, 8, 137–150; means of happiness and, 1, 2; mechanism for gaining approbation and, 36, 37–40; mirror passage in, 47; as moral pedagogy, 211–225; notion of sympathy in, 115; public reception of, 1; relation to *The Wealth of Nations*, 35–43; revisions in, 199–203; on selfishness, 151–152; taming resentment in, 152; as "theory" book, 36, 42; theory of jurisprudence in, 89; theory of social individuality in, 46–53

Thom, William, 213, 214

Thought: dynamics of, 13; improvisation and, 15; shallow, 2; substituted for by talk, 17

A Treatise of Human Nature (Hume), 115, 117n4, 141, 201, 202

Tribe, Keith, 71

Trust, 169; butcher, brewer, baker and, 166; exploitation of, 166; importance of, 2; in open society, 62, 63

Truth: achievement of, 183; of capitalism, 2

Turnbull, George, 13, 25

U

Utilitarianism, 7, 105, 106, 107, 109n25

Utility, 58; in commercial society, 64; frivolous, 1; justice and, 9, 157–159, 162; of philosophical speculation, 10; pleasure and, 17; principles of, 5; public, 9, 157–159, 162, 164; of resentment, 9

Utopia: as criticism of commercial society, 64–67; defining, 64; ideal, 64; justification for possibility of, 67–69; obstacles to, 67; preconditions for possibility of, 67; realist, 5, 64; in sympathetic society, 60–69; types of, 67, 68

V

Value: of labor, 57; labor time, 82; market, 81*tab*; maximization of, 170; measurement by natural prices, 85; measurement of, 6, 87; moral evaluation based on natural prices, 83, 84; natural, 81*tab*; real, 5, 6, 81*tab*, 83, 84, 88; social, 84*n26*, 89

Viner, Jacob, 35

Virtue: coincident with self-love, 128*n25*; depiction of, 214–221; ethics of, 95; praise and, 143; prudence, 215–219

W

Wages, 4, 6, 56; determination of, 85

Watts, Isaac, 14

Wealth: accumulation of, 87; behaviors/consequences under different levels of, 42; commercial, 41, 42; creation of, 82; dismissal of moral conduct in achievement of, 36, 37; distribution among social classes, 56; legitimacy of inequality of, 84; monopolies and, 42; reckless behavior and, 41; relationship to legislation, 82; visible accumulation of, 37, 38

The Wealth of Nations (Smith), 35, 79; account of self in commercial society, 53–60; approaching, 53; approbation generated by material possession, 36; commercial exchange relations in, 4; commercial society in, 5; as complement to *The Theory of Moral Sentiments*, 60–69; concerns with issue of justice in, 88; consequences of acting in world of politics, revenue, and arms, 40–42; consistency with *The Theory of Moral Sentiments*, 3, 35–43; constraints in gaining approbation in, 36; free enterprise system and, 1; generation of social prosperity and, 40; importance of private interest in, 165–172; inheritance law in, 79; natural price in, 84; nature and causes of, 75; as "practice" book, 36, 42; probability of success/failure claims in, 39; provision for the poor in, 73; public reception of, 1; rules for exchange of goods in, 82; "science of the legislator" in, 75–81; situation of individual in commercial society in, 53–60; spending on durable goods and, 40; system of natural liberty in, 35; unanswered moral questions in, 2

Winch, Donald, 215*n10*

Wonder, 77, 183; as motive for speculation, 10

Writing: arbitrary nature of, 15; audiences for, 16; identification of contexts in, 16; improvisation and, 15; original intentions of, 16; slow obsolescence of, 31; tyranny of, 18

Y
Young, Jeffrey, 74*n10*

CONTRIBUTORS

Vincent Bissonette (Ph.D., CUNY) teaches English at Allendale Columbia School in Rochester, NY. He has published on the poetry of Dryden, Coleridge, and Tennyson.

Chad Flanders is an Assistant Professor of Law at Saint Louis University School of Law. Prior to joining Saint Louis University, he clerked for the Alaska Supreme Court and the 10th Circuit Court of Appeals.

Monica L. Gerrek, Ph.D., is a Research Associate in the Department of Bioethics at Case Western Reserve University serving as the Director of Ethics Education at MetroHealth Medical Center. She is also a Lecturer at Cleveland State University. Her current interests are in empathy, its role in moral theory, and its place in the healthcare professional-patient relationship.

Doğan Göçmen is Associate Professor in Philosophy at Dokuz Eylül University (Izmir/Turkey). His research interests lay in the philosophy of the Enlightenment and Karl Marx. Currently, he works on Hegel's reception of Kant and on Aristotle and the Moderns. He published the first monograph on "The Adam Smith Problem" and various papers on Scottish Enlightenment and Adam Smith.

Ryan Patrick Hanley is Associate Professor of Political Science at Marquette University. He is the author of *Adam Smith and the Character of Virtue* (Cambridge, 2009), editor of the Penguin Classics edition of Adam Smith's *Theory of Moral Sentiments* (Penguin, 2010), editor of the *Princeton Guide to Adam Smith* (Princeton, forthcoming), and current President of the International Adam Smith Society.

Colin Heydt is an Associate Professor of Philosophy at the University of South Florida. He works predominantly on the history of ethics and political philosophy, with a focus on 17th–19th century British thought.

Peter Jones is Emeritus Professor of Philosophy at the University of Edinburgh, where he was also Director of the Institute for Advanced Studies in the Humanities. His 12th book is *Ove Arup: Master Builder of the Twentieth Century* (Yale, 2006).

Maria Pia Paganelli teaches economics at Trinity University. Her PhD is from George Mason University. She works on Adam Smith, David Hume, 18th century monetary theories, and also explores the links between the Scottish Enlightenment and the results from behavioral economics.

Tony Pitson is Honorary Research Fellow in the Department of Philosophy of the University of Stirling. He is the author of numerous articles on philosophers of the Scottish Enlightenment, and his book *Hume's Philosophy of the Self* was published in 2002. His current interests lie in the attempt to apply the realist interpretation of Hume to his account of the self and also in the role of the passions in Hume's moral psychology.

Michael S. Pritchard is Willard A. Brown Professor of Philosophy and Co-Director of the Center for the Study of Ethics in Society at Western Michigan University. His books include: *Communication Ethics* (with James A. Jaksa); *On Becoming Responsible*; *Reasonable Children*; *Professional Integrity*; and *Engineering Ethics: Concepts and Cases*, 4th ed. (with C.E. Harris and Michael J. Rabins). He is co-editor (with Elaine Englehardt) of *Teaching Ethics*, the official journal of the Society for Teaching Ethics Across the Curriculum.

Wade L. Robison is the Ezra A. Hale Professor of Applied Ethics at the Rochester Institute of Technology. He has published extensively in philosophy of law, David Hume, and practical and professional ethics. His book *Decisions in Doubt: The Environment and Public Policy* (University Press of New England, 1994) won the Nelson A. Rockefeller Prize in Social Science and Public Policy.

Amit Ron is an Assistant Professor of Political Science at Arizona State University's School of Social and Behavioral Sciences. He is interested in political theory and particularly in the history of political economy and in democratic theory.

David B. Suits is Professor of Philosophy at Rochester Institute of Technology. Among his research interests are Epicureanism, anarchism, and the philosophy of mind.

COLOPHON

DESIGN	Bruce Meader
PRODUCTION	Lisa Mauro
TYPEFACE	Adobe Minion Pro
PRINTING	Lightning Source USA

green press
INITIATIVE

RIT Press is committed to preserving ancient forests and natural resources. We elected to print this title on 30% post consumer recycled paper, processed chlorine free. As a result, for this printing, we have saved:

2 Trees (40' tall and 6-8" diameter)
1 Million BTUs of Total Energy
227 Pounds of Greenhouse Gases
1,024 Gallons of Wastewater
64 Pounds of Solid Waste

RIT Press made this paper choice because our printer, Thomson-Shore, Inc., is a member of Green Press Initiative, a nonprofit program dedicated to supporting authors, publishers, and suppliers in their efforts to reduce their use of fiber obtained from endangered forests.

For more information, visit www.greenpressinitiative.org

Environmental impact estimates were made using the Environmental Defense Paper Calculator. For more information visit: www.papercalculator.org.